THE Wonder Devotional book™

Daily Adventures with God

Child Evangelism Fellowship® Inc.

General Editor and Project Coordinator: Lynda E. Pongracz

Text Editor: Cynthia Channell

Development Team: Lisa J. Deam, Rev. Jerry W. Hanson, Deborah Koenig, Lynda E. Pongracz, Terrie Taylor, Elaine Weller.

Writers: Dr. Martha J. Wright (*God the Father*), Sharron R. Oyer (*God the Son*), Lisa J. Deam (*God the Holy Spirit*), Beverly Blades (*Victory*), Brenda J. Hanson (*God's Word and Me*), Emily C. Ramsdell (*Witnessing*), Lora Oates (*Worshiping God*), Sally A. Middleton (*Obeying God*), Timothy J. Fisler (*Living for God*), Lynda E. Pongracz (*Trusting God*), Jean C. Torjussen (*Taking a Stand*), Annette Haines (*What I Believe*).

Theological Consultants: Rev. Arthur Cobb, M. Joe Cox, Rev. Dair Hileman, Dr. Timothy D. Martin, Jim Neigh, Rev. John Romano, Rev. D. Bruce Seymour, Rev. Brian Thom, Dr. Mark Yelderman.

Editorial Committee: Patricia R. Johann, Cheryl L. Oetting, Lynda E. Pongracz, Dr. Martha J. Wright.

Layout/ Design: Marvin R. White, III

Cover: Larry Smith and Associates
Cover Illustration: Keith R. Neely

Special thanks to Child Evangelism Fellowship President Reese Kauffman, Marshall J. Pennell, Stephen Bates, Dr. A.A. Baker and the CEF worldwide family for their input, prayers and support.

Library of Congress Cataloging-in-Publication Data (pending)

The Wonder Devotional Book: Daily Adventures with God

ISBN 1-5597-6119-9 (sbk)
ISBN 1-5597-6120-2 (pbk)
Printed in the United States of America

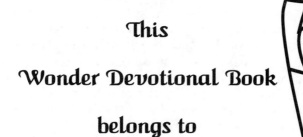

This

Wonder Devotional Book

belongs to

_____

May God use this book

to help you grow

to be more like Him

in your Christian life.

Are You Ready for an ADVENTURE?

Getting to know God is a great adventure! Did you know that God wants you to spend time with Him each day? He does! We call that special time with God a "quiet time." It's a time to quietly sit and read and think about God and to talk to Him in prayer.

The Wonder Devotional Book has been written to help you in your quiet time. Each devotional will help you to learn more about God, about yourself and about the world around you. The best part is that there's a new devotional adventure every day of the year!

Choose a special time each day for your quiet time–maybe when you first wake up in the morning or just before you go to bed at night. Be sure you have this book, a pen or pencil and your Bible if you have one.

Are you ready to start on your adventure?
Here's a road map to help you!

Your first stop– DEVOTIONAL STATION!

Here's what to do each day . . . starting with devotional #1!

Talk to God. Ask Him to help you to understand the things you will be reading during your quiet time.

Read the Bible memory verse. It's at the top of the page. If you have a Bible, try to find the verse for yourself. See how quickly you can memorize this verse!

Read the devotional. Each one will answer an important question such as: Who is God? Does God always answer prayer? Why should I obey God when others don't? Take your time reading the devotional and think about what it says.

Write your answer. Read the question following the devotional and write your answer. Writing helps you remember what you've learned!

Talk to God again. There's a prayer starter at the end of each devotional, but you can make up your own prayer. You can pray about other things, too. Thank God for all He does for you. Talk to God about problems or ask Him to help you or someone you love. God is looking forward to hearing from you!

But that's not all! There are more exciting places to visit on your adventure!

MEMORY ZONE

Special pages scattered throughout *The Wonder Devotional Book* list some great Bible verses for you to read. See how many of these verses you can memorize. Let a friend or family member test you to see if you can say all the verses on a page.

ACTIVITY CENTER

At the end of the first month of devotionals in *The Wonder Devotional Book*, you'll find a fun Mailbox Club activity page. Answer the questions and fill in the missing words. Also, there's a special place to write something you'd like your Mailbox Club friend to pray about for you.

When you finish, carefully tear the page out of your book. Put it in an envelope, add postage stamp amd mail it to:

The Mailbox Club
P.O. Box 190
Warrenton, MO 63383-0190

Your friend there will mark it, write a personal note and send it back to you. You also will get a new activity page to do at the end of your second month of devotionals.

Wow!

You have a whole year's worth of exciting places to visit in *The Wonder Devotional Book*! Don't wait another day. Turn to devotional #1 and get started on your daily adventures with God!

TABLE OF CONTENTS

Witnessing

Worshiping God

What I Believe

Who Is God?

 The heavens declare the glory of God; the skies proclaim the work of his hands. **Psalm 19:1**

Have you ever wondered who God is? Some people think that God is an old man who lives in the clouds. Others think that He is someone who causes bad things to happen when we do something wrong. Some people think that the sun and stars are gods because they give us light. Other people say, "There is no God."

The Bible, God's Word, tells us that the one true God is a Spirit. He doesn't have a body like you and me. That's why we can't see Him, but He sees and hears and loves. God is every-where. God is the Creator. He made the world and every-thing in it—the mountains, oceans and animals. God also made you and me. We are His most special creation, and He loves us very much.

Grown-ups and children all need God. All people have something inside telling them there is a God. This book will help you learn about God. You will learn how great and won-derful God is. You will learn how to love Him and live closer to Him even though you cannot see Him. Are you ready for the ex-citing adventure of getting to know God?

 Write down who you think God is.

_____

_____

_____

You can pray:

 Dear God, thank You for being a great God! Thank You for creating me. Help me to learn more about You so that I will love You. In Jesus' name. Amen.

Are There Many Gods?

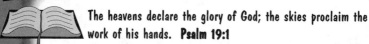
The heavens declare the glory of God; the skies proclaim the work of his hands. **Psalm 19:1**

Some people worship many gods, but the Bible tells us that there is only one true living God. The Bible says that God is three Persons, but He is one God. That is something we cannot understand. The Bible teaches us about God the Father, God the Son and God the Holy Spirit. They are the three Persons.

God the Father lives in Heaven, but He is everywhere. He is holy and without sin. God rules over His creation. He is in control of all things. He loves everyone.

Jesus is God the Son. He died for our sins and rose again. All people can have their sins for-given if they trust in Him as their personal Savior. After Jesus rose from the dead, He went up into Heaven. Now Jesus is with His Father, God.

God the Holy Spirit came to Earth after Jesus returned to Heaven. He helps people to know that they are sinners. He then comes to live in the hearts of those who trust in Jesus. The Holy Spirit also helps us understand God's Word, the Bible.

God the Father, God the Son and God the Holy Spirit—they are the Trinity. They are three in one. All agree completely.

GOD THE FATHER

Can you name the three Persons of the Trinity?

_____

_____

_____

You can pray:

Dear God, thank You for sending Jesus to be our Savior. Thank You for the Holy Spirit who lives in the hearts of those who believe in Jesus. In Jesus' name. Amen.

How Old Is God?

The heavens declare the glory of God; the skies proclaim the work of his hands. **Psalm 19:1**

Maybe you think that because God created the world, He must be at least two million years old! Wrong! God is eternal. There never has been a time that He has not existed. There will never be a time when He will stop existing.

Think of a circle. You cannot tell where the circle begins and ends. It is one continuous ring. A circle can remind you that God is eternal. The Father, the Son and the Holy Spirit always have existed and always will. We have a hard time imagining that.

The Bible says " . . . from everlasting to everlasting you are God" (Psalm 90:2). How long is that? It is forever. If you have believed in Jesus as your Savior, God has given you eternal life. Will it ever end? No! You are God's child forever! God wants to guide your life. Because He is eternal—He always has been and always will be—He can see what has happened, what is happening and what will happen. What a guide to have! How great God is!

Will you trust your Heavenly Father who is eternal? You cannot see what will happen in the future, but God sees and wants to direct your life.

How would you explain to a friend that God is eternal?

_____

_____

_____

You can pray:

Dear God, thank You that You will never leave me because You are eternal. Thank You that I can trust You because You will always be there for me. In Jesus' name. Amen.

How Powerful Is God?

The heavens declare the glory of God; the skies proclaim the work of his hands. **Psalm 19:1**

The 4 1/2 million-pound spaceship Columbia blasted off with a long fiery tail. Two minutes later, it had reached an altitude of 23 miles. It circled the globe at 17,000 miles per hour. Imagine the power that it took to push that huge rocket through space at that speed!

Did you know God is more powerful than that? The Bible says, "The Lord is . . . great in power . . ." (Nahum 1:3). He made the heavens and Earth. God spoke and it was there! He is almighty. He rules over all nations. God's power has no limits. He can make anything happen.

The Bible tells about Abraham and Sarah. God promised them that they would have many children, but no children were born. One day, God sent an angel to Abraham when he and Sarah were almost 100 years old. The angel told him that the following year Sarah would have a son. That was impossible! When Sarah laughed, the angel said, "Is anything too hard for the Lord?" (Genesis 18:14). Sure enough, Sarah had a son! Because God is all-powerful, He could make this impossible thing happen. The next time you have a problem, remember that God is very powerful and wants to help you.

GOD THE FATHER

Can you name some ways that God is powerful?

_____

_____

_____

You can pray:

Dear God, You are the mighty God! Help me to trust You when I have a problem that seems impossible. Help me to remember that You are Ruler over all. In Jesus' name. Amen.

Why Did God Create People?

. . . Just as sin entered the world through one man, and death through sin, and in this way death came to all men, because all sinned. **Romans 5:12**

Have you ever wondered where all the people on Earth came from? God made them all! After God made the beautiful Earth, He made one man. He made that man out of the dust of the Earth and breathed life into him. God called that man Adam. Later, God caused Adam to sleep and took a rib from his side to make the first woman. God gave Adam this woman, Eve, to be his wife. Adam and Eve lived in the beautiful garden that God made.

Soon Adam and Eve had many children. When the children grew up, they had children. Soon there were many people on the Earth. Today there are so many people it is hard to count them all!

God did not create people because He was lonely. He made us so that we could love Him and praise Him. The Bible says, "Great is the Lord, and most worthy of praise . . ." (Psalm 48:1). God wants people to praise Him because He is great and good.

When you see all that God has made, you can say, "How great God is!" You can praise Him when you pray. Tell Him that you love Him and that you need Him. You can never praise God enough.

 Write down three things you can praise God for today.

_____

_____

_____

You can pray:

Dear God, thank You for creating me. I love You and praise You because You are so great. In Jesus' name. Amen.

6

How Did Sin Enter the World?

. . . Just as sin entered the world through one man, and death through sin, and in this way death came to all men, because all sinned. **Romans 5:12**

God made everything in the world beautiful and good. But many things in our world are not beautiful and good anymore. There is sickness, sadness, fighting and killing. Why did things go so wrong?

God placed the very first people, Adam and Eve, in the garden. He told them they were not to eat the fruit from one certain tree or they would die. God's enemy, Satan, tricked Eve into eating the fruit. Adam ate it, too. In choosing to disobey God, they sinned.

God told Adam that they would have to leave the garden. They would have pain and sickness and their bodies would die. Sin separated Adam and Eve from God, who is holy and perfect.

Ever since Adam and Eve sinned, everyone is born sinful and separated from God. The Bible says, "For all have sinned . . ." (Romans 3:23). Sin is thinking, saying or doing things that break God's laws. It is sin in your heart that causes you to do bad things. You cannot get rid of your sin by yourself. You deserve to be punished for your sin. Only God can forgive you so that you will not be separated from Him forever.

What sad things happened when Adam and Eve sinned?

_____

_____

_____

You can pray:

Dear God, thank You that You love me even though I have sinned. Thank You that You forgive me. In Jesus' name. Amen.

What Did God Do about Sin**?**

. . . Just as sin entered the world through one man, and death through sin, and in this way death came to all men, because all sinned. **Romans 5:12**

GOD THE FATHER

The most wonderful story in all the world is the story of what God did so that we could have our sins forgiven.

After Adam and Eve sinned, God promised to send a Savior. You and I know today that the Savior is the Lord Jesus Christ, God's only Son. He was born into this world as a baby. When He became a man, He gave Himself to die on the cross for our sins.

As Jesus died, God placed upon Him the sins of the **whole world.** The Bible says, "God made him who had no sin to be sin for us . . ." (2 Corinthians 5:21). Jesus did not deserve to die. He had no sin of His own. He was perfect, but He took your place on the cross. If Jesus had not given His precious blood to take your punishment, you could never be forgiven of your sins. Jesus died and was buried. Three days later God brought Him back to life. Jesus later returned to Heaven where He is alive today. God kept His promise to pay for sin. He sent His own beloved Son to be the Savior of the world.

Write down why you think Jesus had to die.

_____

_____

_____

You can pray:

Dear God, thank You for sending Your only Son, Jesus, to die on the cross for me. Thank You for Your great love. In Jesus' name. Amen.

How Can I Be Forgiven?

> . . . Just as sin entered the world through one man, and death through sin, and in this way death came to all men, because all sinned. **Romans 5:12**

Now you know Jesus died for your sins. Are you wondering how you can be forgiven? The Bible says that Jesus is the only way to God. "I [Jesus] am the way and the truth and the life. No one comes to the Father [God] except through me" (John 14:6).

Jesus wants to be your Savior. You cannot save yourself from sin. You're not saved from sin's punishment by doing good things. You can't be forgiven by saying prayers, giving money or trying to please God. God says there is only one way, and that is through His Son, Jesus.

The Bible says, " . . . Believe in the Lord Jesus, and you will be saved . . ." (Acts 16:31). To believe means to trust completely in the Lord Jesus. His death on the cross is the only payment for your sins that God will accept. When you choose to trust in the Lord Jesus as your Savior, God says you are forgiven. You are rescued from the punishment of your sins. You will not be separated from God in a place of punishment when you die. You'll live with God forever in Heaven someday.

GOD THE FATHER

What do you need to believe to be forgiven of your sins?

_____

_____

_____

You can pray:

Dear God, I know that I'm a sinner. I believe in Your Son, Jesus, who died to take the punishment for my sins and rose again. I want Jesus to be my Savior. In Jesus' name. Amen.

Is God Really Perfect?

... just as he who called you is holy, so be holy in all you do. **1 Peter 1:15**

GOD THE FATHER

Do you know someone who never does anything wrong or never makes a mistake? Certain people have searched for many years for someone who is perfect. They never found such a person.

The Bible says in 1 John 1:5, ". . . God is light; in him there is no darkness at all." This verse means that God is holy and pure. There is no sin at all in Him. There is not even one little bit of badness in God. He is set apart from sin—set apart from all that is evil or bad. God and sin are opposites like light and darkness. God is holy. The Father is holy; the Son, the Lord Jesus Christ, is holy; the Holy Spirit is holy.

There is someone who is perfect—that is God! Only God is perfect. We have all sinned and sin separates us from God. Because God is holy, He has to punish sin. But He gave His Son to die for sin so that we could be forgiven and made holy. When you believed in Jesus as your Savior, you were forgiven of your sins and made holy before God. Aren't you glad?

 How are we different from God?

_____

_____

_____

You can pray:

Dear God, You are holy and perfect. You alone are good. Thank You that I can come to You as a holy God through the Lord Jesus, who is my Savior. In Jesus' name. Amen.

What Does It Mean That God Is Holy?

... just as he who called you is holy, so be holy in all you do. **1 Peter 1:15**

Isaiah was one of God's great prophets. God also spoke to Isaiah. God told Isaiah to tell people that one day the Savior of the world would come.

One day God spoke to Isaiah in a vision. A vision is like a dream. Isaiah said that he saw God seated on a throne, high and exalted. Above God were angels. The angels called out to each other, "Holy, holy, holy is the Lord Almighty; the whole earth is full of his glory" (Isaiah 6:3). When Isaiah saw the vision, he was afraid. He saw how sinful he was compared to God. The vision helped him to see that God is holy.

What does it mean that God is holy? He is 100% pure. He never sins—He is perfect. God always does what is right. He is completely good. God hates sin.

If we are sinners, how can we pray to God? God wants us to talk to Him. He told Isaiah not to be afraid. He also tells us not to be afraid. When we believe in the Lord Jesus as our Savior, He takes our sin away and makes us clean so that we can talk to God who is holy.

GOD THE FATHER

What do you think it means that God is holy?

_____

_____

_____

You can pray:

Dear God, You are a holy God. Thank You that the Lord Jesus has taken away my sin so that I can pray to You. In Jesus' name. Amen.

Does God Expect Me to Be Holy?

 But just as he who called you is holy, so be holy in all you do. **1 Peter 1:15**

GOD THE FATHER

When the prophet Isaiah saw the vision of God and the angels covering their faces in reverence, he saw how holy God is. If you were Isaiah, what would you be thinking? Maybe you would think about how sinful you really are.

If you have trusted in Jesus as your Savior, God expects you to live a clean life. He expects you to be holy. You have a choice. You can give in to sin or you can choose God's way. God will help you to say "no" to sin. He expects you to obey His Word, the Bible, and do what is right. God expects you to tell the truth and always be kind, loving and patient with others. He wants you to be honest and to behave in a way that pleases Him.

Remember that God lives in you to give you the power to live a clean, holy life and to not sin. When you do sin, however, think about how holy God is. Confess your sin to Him right away. God says if you will confess your sins–that is tell Him about the wrong you have done–He will forgive you (1 John 1:9). Will you choose to be holy?

 In what ways does God want you to be holy?

_____

_____

_____

You can pray:

 Dear God, thank You that You are a holy God. Please give me the power to live a holy life. In Jesus' name. Amen.

Who's in Charge?

But just as he who called you is holy, so be holy in all you do. **1 Peter 1:15**

Has your mother ever said to you, "You're in charge?" When you're put in charge of something, you are like a king reigning over it. You have control and are responsible for seeing that the assignment is carried out.

Have you ever wondered who's in charge of the world? The Bible tells us that God is sovereign. That means He is in charge or in control of all things. He is the highest ruler. No one is over God. God reigns over everything and everybody all the time. Nothing can happen unless God allows it to happen. He is in control of everything day and night–24 hours a day, seven days a week, 52 weeks a year. He never sleeps or goes away on vacation.

How long will God reign? The Bible says, "The Lord will reign for ever and ever" (Exodus 15:18). God was always in control and He always will be in control. What does that mean for you? No matter what happens in your life, you don't have to be afraid or upset because God is in control. He loves you, and He wants you to trust Him completely. God is the greatest. He is sovereign. He is the King of kings.

GOD THE FATHER

What does it mean that God is sovereign?

_____

_____

_____

You can pray:
Dear God, I praise You because You are in control of all things. Help me to trust You each day. In Jesus' name. Amen.

#

What Are God's Rules for Us**?**

But just as he who called you is holy, so be holy in all you do. **1 Peter 1:15**

G O D   T H E   F A T H E R

Long ago God gave His people ten special laws to show them how holy He is and how sinful people are. The laws also tell us how God wants His people to live. We call these laws the Ten Commandments:

•**You shall have no other gods before me.** (Worship God alone.)

•**You shall not make for yourself an idol.** (Don't let anything take God's place in your life.)

•**You shall not misuse the name of the Lord your God.** (Only use God's name with respect.)

•**Remember the Sabbath day by keeping it holy.** (One day a week is to rest and worship God.)

•**Honor your father and your mother.** (Treat your parents with respect.)

•**You shall not murder.** (Protect life; never take life away.)

•**You shall not commit adultery.** (Married people are to be true to each other.)

•**You shall not steal.** (Don't take something that is not your own.)

•**You shall not give false testimony.** (Don't lie; tell the whole truth.)

•**You shall not covet.** (Don't want things that belong to others.)

When God spoke these commandments the people were afraid. But Moses, their leader, explained that God was showing them how great He is in order to keep them from sinning. The Israelites said they would obey God. Will you?

 Why did God give the Ten Commandments?

_____

_____

You can pray:

 Dear God, I want to live for You by keeping Your laws. Help me to do what is right every day. In Jesus' name. Amen.

14 Is God Sovereign over Me?

But just as he who called you is holy, so be holy in all you do. **1 Peter 1:15**

God is sovereign–He is always in control. God does whatever pleases Him. He decides whether we can do what we have planned. He has total control over all people. Nothing that happens in our lives is ever out of God's control.

Have you ever thought that things in your life are out of control? Maybe someone you love has been injured in an accident or died of a terrible disease. Perhaps your family is having a hard time because one or both of your parents have lost their jobs. Maybe someone is being mean to you or treating you unfairly. When you are sick, or when troubles come, you must believe that God loves you and that everything is under His control. He will do what is best for you even though you may not think the situation is good.

The Bible says, "And we know that in all things God works for the good of those who love him" (Romans 8:28). Nothing that happens to you is too small for God not to know about. Nothing is too big for Him to control it. When you can't understand why things happen, just remember that God is in control. You can trust your loving Heavenly Father.

GOD THE FATHER

What should you remember when you are going through difficult situations?

_____

_____

_____

You can pray:

Dear God, thank You that You are in control of my life. Help me to remember that You love me and will do what is best for me. In Jesus' name. Amen.

Does My Life Show That God Is in Charge?

But just as he who called you is holy, so be holy in all you do. **1 Peter 1:15**

God never promised that His children would have a life free from problems and pain. God allows difficult things to happen in our lives as He carries out His plan for us.

It is just as important to trust God as it is to obey Him. When you do not trust God, you are doubting that He is in control and that He is good. God wants you to learn to trust Him every day, all day. He wants you to trust Him in the good times and the difficult ones. Trusting God means believing with all your heart that He is in control and that He is doing what is best for you.

How does your life show that God is in charge? When you are facing a problem, your first response should be to trust God (rely on Him). You can trust Him because you know that God has allowed the problem for a certain reason. Talk to God in prayer and tell Him your problems. As you trust God, He will give you peace, a calmness on the inside. Thank Him for working in your life to make you more like Jesus.

Why is it important for you to trust God?

_____

_____

_____

You can pray:

Dear God, help me to trust You in the good times and the difficult ones. Thank You for Your peace. In Jesus' name. Amen.

16 Why Does God Punish Sinners?

Give thanks to the LORD, for he is good; his love endures forever. **Psalm 118:1**

Have you ever said, "That's not fair?" No one can ever say that of God. God is always fair (or just) in everything He does. The Bible says that God "does no wrong, upright and just is he" (Deuteronomy 32:4). God is our judge, and He judges fairly.

Since Adam and Eve, everyone is born into this world with a "want to" to sin. God is holy; He hates sin. He cannot let people do wrong without punishing them because He is just and fair. The Bible says, "For the wages of sin is death . . ." (Romans 6:23). Wages are what we earn for what we do. What do we earn for sin?

Yes, death. God said that because of sin we deserve to be separated from Him forever. That's the punishment our just God placed on sin. It is called eternal death.

But God sent His only Son, the Lord Jesus Christ, to die on the cross and take the punishment we deserve for sin. People who reject the Lord Jesus will be lost forever in a terrible place called Hell. All who believe in Jesus as their Savior are saved from the punishment they deserve (Acts 16:31).

GOD THE FATHER

How does God punish sinners?

_____

_____

_____

You can pray:

Dear God, You are always fair in everything you do. Thank You that Jesus took the punishment that I deserve for sin so that I can be saved. In Jesus' name. Amen.

How Much Does God Love Me?

 Give thanks to the LORD, for he is good; his love endures forever. **Psalm 118:1**

GOD THE FATHER

You know what love is, don't you? When you love someone, you want to be near him. You want to take care of him and do nice things for him. You're quick to forgive him if he does something wrong.

God's love is so much greater and more wonderful than the love we have for other people. God says in Jeremiah 31:3, "I have loved you with an everlasting love." God's love is so great that it lasts forever! His love for you will never end.

There was never a time that God didn't love you. He loved you even before you were born. He knew exactly when you would be born, what color hair and eyes you would have and who your parents would be. He loves you so much that He wants the best for you.

God has so much love that He sent His perfect, only Son, the Lord Jesus, to die in your place on the cross. Jesus' death on the cross is the greatest picture of God's love. He has promised that if you believe in Jesus as your Savior, He will someday take you to Heaven to live with Him forever. Can you see how much God loves you?

In what ways does God show He loves you?

_____

_____

_____

You can pray:

 Dear God, thank You for Your great love for me. Help me to love You and give You my best. In Jesus' name. Amen.

18 **W**hat Is God's Grace**?**

 Give thanks to the LORD, for he is good; his love endures forever. **Psalm 118:1**

Have you ever received a gift you didn't deserve? The gift was given to you out of love. God is so great that He gives us His grace because of His love for us.

Grace is God showing His love to you even though you don't deserve it. You can't earn God's grace. You do not deserve to be saved from sin and to have eternal life. But God showed His grace by saving you from sin's punishment when you trusted in Jesus as your Savior. God also shows His grace by giving you strength and guidance, and by taking care of you each day.

God, by His grace, gives you strength to handle difficult problems in your life. Isn't God's grace wonderful?

If you know Jesus as your Savior, you can be thankful that God saved you by His grace. The Bible says, "For it is by grace you have been saved, through faith . . ." (Ephesians 2:8). You can also depend on God each day for the grace you need to live for Him. Because God shows His grace to you, you should show His grace to others. Have you ever thanked God for His grace in your life?

GOD THE FATHER

How does God show His grace to you?

_____

_____

_____

You can pray:

 Dear God, thank You for saving me by Your grace. Thank You, too, for the blessings I do not deserve that You give me each day. In Jesus' name. Amen.

What Is God's Mercy?

 Give thanks to the LORD, for he is good; his love endures forever. **Psalm 118:1**

GOD THE FATHER

Have you ever thought about how merciful God is? The Bible says, "The Lord is compassionate [merciful] and gracious . . . he does not treat us as our sins deserve . . ." (Psalm 103:8-10).

Mercy is willingly forgiving someone who has done wrong rather than punishing him. It is showing kindness, especially when it is not deserved. That's what God has done for you. Instead of giving you the punishment you deserve for your sin, God in His mercy forgave you when you believed in Jesus as your Savior.

God shows mercy–kindness and love–to you every day in many ways, even though you don't deserve it. He provides for your needs. He hears and answers your prayers.

Now God expects you to be merciful to others. You can be kind and help those in need. You shouldn't look down on others or judge them. Being merciful may mean being a friend to someone others reject. It means being patient with younger brothers or sisters, even when they bother you.

God promises a special blessing to those who are kind and merciful. They will receive mercy. So if you show mercy, don't be surprised when others are merciful to you.

Why should you show mercy to others?

_____

_____

You can pray:

 Dear God, thank You for showing me Your mercy and grace that I don't deserve. Help me to be merciful to others. In Jesus' name. Amen.

20 Why Do Good Things Happen to Bad People?

Give thanks to the LORD, for he is good; his love endures forever. **Psalm 118:1**

Why do people who don't love God sometimes have so many good things happen to them? Maybe they have a lot of money or fame. Yet, some people who love God have so many struggles. It just doesn't seem fair.

God is sovereign, remember? He is in control of all things, including the lives of those who reject Him. God directs their lives according to His purpose and plan. Proverbs 16:9 says, "In his heart a man plans his course, but the LORD determines his steps." God allows people to make their own choices, yet they eventually do what God planned that they would do.

Sometimes it seems so unfair when we see good things hap- pen to bad people. God allows these things to happen because of His mercy and grace. But God is just. One day, each person will stand before Him. Those who have not believed in God's Son, the Lord Jesus, will be punished for their unbelief. Those who have trusted in Jesus as their Savior will be rewarded. Many who have not had very much in this world, will be rich in Heaven!

Don't be jealous of others who have more than you do. Thank God for what you have and for what He allows in your life– both good and bad. He loves you and is in control of everything that happens.

GOD THE FATHER

 Why do good things happen to bad people?

_____

_____

You can pray:

Dear God, thank You for being so good. Help me to trust what You are doing in my life and in the lives of other people. In Jesus' name. Amen.

Will God Ever Let Me Down?

 Give thanks to the LORD, for he is good; his love endures forever. **Psalm 118:1**

GOD THE FATHER

Has someone ever broken a promise to you? You were really counting on someone and he let you down. Maybe you have wondered who you can really depend on.

The Bible says that there is someone who will never let you down, who will never break His promises to you–that is God! God will always be faithful to His Word and to every promise He has made in it. Since God is perfect, He cannot fail you even one time! The Bible says, "Know therefore that the LORD your God is God; he is the faithful God . . ." (Deuteronomy 7:9). That truth should give you peace and confidence as you live each day.

What if you are unfaithful to God? What if you let Him down? Will He still be faithful to you? Will He let you down? The amazing thing about God is that even though we are unfaithful to Him, He will be continually faithful to us. When things are not going as you would like and you have problems that seem out of control, you can be confident that God will never let you down. Thank Him for standing with you and being faithful each day.

 How do you know God will never let you down?

_____

_____

_____

You can pray:

 Dear God, thank You that You will always be with me and will never let me down. Thank You for being faithful each day. In Jesus' name. Amen.

Can I Really Believe God?

Give thanks to the LORD, for he is good; his love endures forever. **Psalm 118:1**

Has anybody ever lied to you? It is hard to believe people when it seems as if everyone lies from time to time. In many different situations people often ask, "What is the truth?"

God is all truth–He never lies. God sees and knows all things as they really are. The Bible says that "God is not a man, that he should lie . . ." (Numbers 23:19). Because God is holy (without sin), He could not be anything else but true.

Not only God Himself is truth, but His Word, the Bible, is the truth. His Word is totally trustworthy. Psalm ll9:151 says that all the commands of the Lord are true. If you know Jesus as your Savior, you can trust God completely as you obey everything He says in His Word. God's promises are true. He has always kept His promises from the beginning of time. Many years ago God made a promise to a man named Noah never again to destroy the world with a flood (Genesis 9:11-13). When you see a rainbow, you can remember that God is Truth. He kept His promise to Noah, and He will keep His promise to you. You can believe with all your heart in the God of Truth.

GOD THE FATHER

 Why can you believe what God says?

_____

_____

_____

You can pray:

 Dear God, thank You that You are Truth and that I can believe what You say. In Jesus' name. Amen.

Does God Know Everything? 23

GOD THE FATHER

Have you ever met someone who thinks he knows it all? Maybe he can answer all your questions or get an "A" on tests at school. You think he's the smartest person in the world. But, no matter how much your friend knows, he doesn't know anything compared to God. God knows everything.

God has all knowledge–He knows everything in the whole world. Because God is all-wise, He uses all of that information in the best way possible. Since God made and understands all things, He has perfect plans.

He knows what is best for you. In His wisdom, He carries out His plans for you. God knows exactly what He is allowing in your life even though some things may be hard. He is working through those situations for your good and His glory. Each thing that your loving Heavenly Father allows to happen in your life is wise and good.

The Bible says, "How many are your works, O LORD! In wisdom you made them all . . ." (Psalm 104:24). God made everything and He knows everything. He loves you and wants you to trust Him completely. Will you trust Him today?

How does God use His wisdom in your life?

_____

_____

_____

You can pray:

Dear God, You made everything and know everything. I will trust You today, knowing that everything that happens in my life is from You. In Jesus' name. Amen.

What Is the Fear of the Lord?

... let us be thankful, and so worship God acceptably with reverence and awe. **Hebrews 12:28**

Moses, the great leader of the Israelite people, was old and would soon die. One day he told the priests they should read the law to the people aloud every seven years. He said, "Assemble the people–men, women and children . . . so they can listen and learn to fear the LORD your God and follow carefully all the words of this law" (Deuteronomy 31:12). When the law was read, the people would learn more about God and His Word. The children would also hear the law and learn to fear and obey the Lord.

What does it mean to fear the Lord? It means that you become so aware of how holy and powerful God is that you are really afraid of disobeying Him. You do not want to displease God. When you fear God, you understand His greatness and you reverence Him—show Him respect and love. You think about Him with awe and wonder because of His great power. Fearing God also means that you worship Him, serve Him and trust Him.

Do you realize how really great and awesome God is? If you do, you will want to please and obey Him more than anything else.

GOD THE FATHER

How does God want you to fear Him?

_____

_____

_____

You can pray:

Dear God, thank You for being my Heavenly Father and for loving me so much. Help me to please You in all things by obeying You. In Jesus' name. Amen.

How Do I Reverence God? 25

. . . let us be thankful, and so worship God acceptably with reverence and awe. **Hebrews 12:28**

How would you act if you were invited to visit a king? Would you run into his throne room laughing and talking? Would you ignore the king or call him by his first name? You would probably be quiet and respectful. What if you were invited to meet with the King of all kings, God Himself? How would you act? No doubt you would show Him great reverence.

To reverence God means to show loving respect for Him and His Word. You do not show reverence for God when you speak about Him in a careless way or use His name as a swear word. Because God is perfect and pure, it is a serious thing to Him when His children fail to reverence Him. You should not approach God lightly, as if He were not important. He is the most important one in all of the universe.

God is holy and He deserves your reverence. Be careful how you speak about God. Think about how holy God is before you use His name in a wrong way. Your reverence for God shows others that you have a special relationship with Him. Will you show honor and reverence for God today with your life?

Name three ways you can show reverence for God.

_____

_____

_____

You can pray:

Dear God, thank You that You are a great and holy God. Help me to reverence You today and every day. In Jesus' name. Amen.

26 What Does God Do for Me?

. . . let us be thankful, and so worship God acceptably with reverence and awe. **Hebrews 12:28**

All of us have needs– things we must have like food, clothing and shelter. Probably your parents take care of these things for you. But did you know that it is God who has provided so that your needs will be met?

God knows about your basic needs. He also knows you have the need to be loved, accepted and to feel safe and protected. Perhaps those who are supposed to take care of you have not been able to meet your needs. Your family might have to depend on others for help. At times, you may try to meet your own needs. But God wants you to look to Him first to provide for you. He is your Heavenly Father who cares for you more than anyone else could.

There is no need too great or too hard for God to supply. He promises, "And my God will meet all your needs . . ." (Philippians 4:19). God has all of the riches in the world. He never lacks anything, so He is well able to supply any need.

God does not promise to supply everything you want, but your needs will never go unmet. Depend on God. Tell Him about your needs and trust Him to provide for you.

GOD THE FATHER

How does God take care of you?

_____

_____

_____

You can pray:

Dear God, thank You that You have the power to meet all my needs. Help me to trust You. In Jesus' name. Amen.

What Does God Do in the World?

. . . let us be thankful, and so worship God acceptably with reverence and awe. **Hebrews 12:28**

GOD THE FATHER

Have you ever wondered what God does all day? What in the world does God do? First, you know that God created the world and everything in it. The Bible says, " . . . You made the heavens, even the highest heavens, and all their starry host, the Earth and all that is on it, the seas and all that is in them. You give life to everything . . ." (Nehemiah 9:6). God is the owner of all.

Another thing that God does in the world is to rule over His creation. God has complete control over all things. He has control over the universe, the animals, the nations of the Earth and over people. He has control over nature–the sunshine, thunder, lightening, rain and snow. All nature obeys His will. God keeps everything in the world going according to His plan. He always has the good of His creation at heart.

Does it sometimes seem that God is not in control? Maybe it's because there are so many bad things happening in the world. God is taking care of all things. You don't need to worry because God is taking care of this big world and He's taking care of you!

Name two things that God does in the world.

_____

_____

_____

You can pray:

Dear God, thank You that You are in control of the world and everything in it. Help me to trust You and to not worry. In Jesus' name. Amen.

28 Do I Appreciate God?

. . . let us be thankful, and so worship God acceptably with reverence and awe. **Hebrews 12:28**

When someone does something nice for you, you normally say "thank you." You tell that person how much you appreciate what he or she did. Sometimes you may even buy the person a gift.

God has done so many wonderful things for you. He loves and cares for you. How do you tell Him that you appreciate all that He has done? One way is to give God honor. To give honor to God means to give Him a high place in your thinking. You also show honor when you tell others how great He is. The Bible says in Psalm 66:2, "Sing to the glory of his name; offer him glory and praise!" Instead of bragging when someone gives you a compliment, you honor God by saying, "Thank you. It was God who helped me." You are giving the honor to Him for what He does in your life.

God is the one who is worthy of our praise and honor. Will you honor Him today and every day? When God helps you, tell Him how much you appreciate His help. Let others know how great your Heavenly Father is. They will want to know Him, too.

GOD THE FATHER

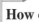 How can you show God that you appreciate Him?

_____

_____

_____

You can pray:

Dear God, I love You and appreciate You. Thank You for all You have done for me. In Jesus' name. Amen.

Does God Know about Things in My Life? 29

. . . let us be thankful, and so worship God acceptably with reverence and awe. **Hebrews 12:28**

GOD THE FATHER

Have you ever tried to explain something to a friend, and he just stared at you? Maybe you think, *Doesn't anybody understand what I think or feel?*

God knows everything in the whole world, and God knows everything about you. The Bible says, "You [Lord] know when I sit and when I rise; you perceive [know] my thoughts . . . you are familiar with all my ways" (Psalm 139:2-3). God knows your thoughts and how you feel at any time of the day. He knows when you get up in the morning and when you go to bed. He sees your tears and hears your laughter. God knows when you're frustrated and when you're sad. He knows the tiniest movement that you make. He also knows every secret sin. Although God knows all about you, He still loves you!

Not one thing in your life goes unnoticed by God. Maybe no one else understands you and your situation, but God understands completely. He knows about your past, your present and your future. Because God knows the future, He can prepare you for it. Isn't it great to know that God knows all about you? Trust Him to do what is best in your life.

Name four things that God knows about you.

_____

_____

_____

You can pray:

Dear God, thank You that You know all about me, and You love me. Help me to trust You to do what is best for me. In Jesus' name. Amen.

Does God Care about Me?

. . . let us be thankful, and so worship God acceptably with reverence and awe. **Hebrews 12:28**

Do you ever feel like no one cares about you? When hard things happen, you might feel like you're all alone. But there is someone who always cares. That someone is God.

If you know the Lord Jesus Christ as your Savior, you can trust God to take care of you. Perhaps when you get home from school you have to be alone while your parents are at work. Maybe you live where there is violence and you worry about being safe. It's natural to feel afraid sometimes–our world can be a very scary place! Do you think God knows about the dangers in your life? Yes, and He cares. What should you do when you feel alone or scared? The Bible says, "Cast [put] all your anxiety [worries] on him [God] because he cares for you" (1 Peter 5:7). No matter what the problem is, God can take care of you.

Because you're His child, God has a plan for your life. He can work out any situation no matter how difficult it may be. When you're in a difficult situation, tell God about it. Think about how powerful He is–He can do anything! Thank Him that He loves and cares for you.

GOD THE FATHER

How do you know God cares for you?

_____

_____

_____

You can pray:

Dear God, thank You that You love and care for me. Help me to trust You in everything that happens. In Jesus' name. Amen.

How Can I Be Aware of God Each Day?

Let us be thankful, and so worship God acceptably with reverence and awe. **Hebrews 12:28**

G O D   T H E   F A T H E R

David was a shepherd boy. He took care of his sheep far from home. He led his sheep to eat green grass and to drink fresh water. At times David played his harp. He loved God and made up songs about Him. David was always thinking about God.

Do you think about God during the day? Do you know that He is with you even though you can't see Him? You should think about Him many times every day. When you see the flowers or hear the birds sing, you can think about how wonderful God is. When you think about God while you're at school or at play, you will want to please Him.

If you are thinking about God while you play, you will not become angry or selfish. If you think about God while you do your school work, you will do a good job. If you think about God a lot, how can you do sinful things? How can you worry or be sad? The Bible says, "You [God] will keep in perfect peace him whose mind [thoughts] is steadfast [focused on God]" (Isaiah 26:3). God wants you to think of Him very often.

Name some specific times when you can think about God.

_____

_____

_____

You can pray:

Dear God, thank You that You are with me. Help me to think about You all the time and remember how great You are. In Jesus' name. Amen.

THE TRINITY

The Lord is one God in three persons.
See if you can fill in the blanks below.

God the F_____

God

God the S_____

God the H_____ S_____

I show my reverence for God by . . . _____

_____

Prayer Request

"Dear Mailbox Club Friend,
            Please pray for . . ."

_____

_____

Name _____ Birthday _____ Age ____ Grade ____
      (Please Print)
Parent/ Guardian _____

Mailing address _____ Apt. # _____

City _____ State _____ Zip _____

Go on to the back of this page.

THINKING IT OVER!

Month One – God the Father

1. What does it mean that God is eternal? _____

_____

2. What is sin? _____

_____

3. How can you be forgiven? _____

_____

4. What does "God is holy" mean? _____

5. List two of God's rules for us: _____

_____

_____

6. How can you know God will keep His promises? _____

_____

If you need help, you can look back in this month's devotionals.
The number in ( ) tells you which devotional to check for each question.
1. (3)   2. (6)   3. (8)   4. (10)   5. (13)   6. (21)

When you're finished with the front and back of this page, carefully tear it out of your book. Put it in an envelope and address
it to: CEF Mailbox Club
          P.O. Box 190
          Warrenton, MO 63383-0190
Put a small piece of tape on the bottom to keep it folded. Add a
stamp and mail your activity page. Your friend at the Mailbox
Club will mark it, write you a personal note, and send it back to
you. You will also get a new activity page to do at the end of
next month's devotionals.

32 What Is Prophecy?

But when the time had fully come, God sent his Son . . .
Galatians 4:4

Can you imagine what it would be like to have God talk to you from Heaven? What would He sound like? What would He say?

Hundreds of years ago God talked to special men called "prophets." These men told others what God said. Sometimes they wrote it down for people to read. The prophets reminded people of God's great love for them. God also used the prophets to warn people to stop doing wrong or they would be punished.

God often told the prophets what was going to happen in the future. Since God knows everything, this was not hard for Him to do. The people knew it was a message from God. Only He could know these things.

Because God spoke through a prophet, the message was called a "prophecy." Many of these special messages can be found in the Bible. These messages were not just for the people then. They're for you and me today! God's most exciting messages were about His Son, Jesus. You'll learn what these were as you keep reading in the next few days.

GOD THE SON

Name something you are glad God already knows about.

_____

_____

_____

You can pray:

Dear God, thank You that You know all things, even before they happen. Help me to read Your Word every day. In Jesus' name. Amen.

Who Were God's Prophets?

But when the time had fully come, God sent his Son . . .
Galatians 4:4

GOD THE SON

Who is the smartest person in the world? God, of course! He even knows what will happen in the future! The Bible says, "Lord, You know all things . . ." (John 21:17). Nothing surprises God! Have you ever wished you knew what was going to happen like God does?

Before the Lord Jesus came to Earth, God gave His chosen prophets special ability to know and write about the future. They told others what was going to happen. Many might have thought these men were very smart, but God's Holy Spirit told these prophets what to say. " . . . but men spoke from God as they were carried along by the Holy Spirit" (2 Peter 1:21). Whatever they said came true!

The first prophet to write a book in the Bible is Isaiah. His book is near the end of the Old Testament.

The prophets spoke to groups of people. They loved God and the people very much. Some people treated them badly when they shared God's messages. Others did not believe them. Many didn't like what they said. But these bold prophets did not quit sharing God's messages with others.

How did the prophets have the boldness to share God's messages?

_____

_____

_____

You can pray:

Dear God, help me to be bold like Your prophets when I tell others about You. Thank You for giving me the courage not to quit. In Jesus' name. Amen.

34 What Did God's Prophets Say about Jesus?

But when the time had fully come, God sent his Son . . .
Galatians 4:4

Do you like to read mysteries? A mystery is a secret that you figure out by using clues.

After God made the first man and woman, He promised to send a Savior to Earth. This special person would take the punishment for the wrong things they had done. The Savior also would be punished for your sins. No one knew who it would be. It was a mystery. But God gave clues to the prophets, His messengers. We find them written in the Old Testament of the Bible.

Here are just a few of many clues the prophets wrote. God's promised Savior would be born in the city of Bethlehem. He would be born in a stable—like a barn. He would be in the family of King David. He would be rejected by the people and killed! The prophets told how He would die and why. They even said He would come back to life! Who is the Promised Savior? You are right, the Lord Jesus Christ!

Some of these clues were written 700 years before Jesus ever came! There was no way the prophets could have known these things before they happened unless God had told them.

GOD THE SON

List three clues you learned about the Promised Savior.

_____

_____

_____

You can pray:

Dear God, I know Jesus is the one You promised to send. Thank You that He took the punishment for my sins. I believe in Jesus, Your Son! In Jesus' name. Amen.

Did God's Prophecies about Jesus Come True? 35

But when the time had fully come, God sent his Son . . .
Galatians 4:4

GOD THE SON

"Could this be the Promised One from God?" many people wondered as they met the Lord Jesus! They had read the clues the prophets had written. They waited and watched. Then, at just the right time in history, Jesus came! "But when the time had fully come, God sent his Son."

One by one each clue the prophets had given about Jesus came true. Of all the cities in the world, He was born in Bethlehem. He was born in a stable. He was from the family of King David! Nazareth would become His hometown. All the prophecies about the Savior's birth had come true.

When He was grown, He did many amazing things that only God could do. But He was rejected by the people and treated very badly. He was nailed to a cross between two thieves. There He took the punishment for the sins of the whole world—including yours. All the prophecies about the Savior's death had come true. On the third day after Jesus died and was buried, He came back to life! Then, He returned to Heaven to be with His Father. The prophets had written all this and more. Jesus is the Promised One!

Why don't some people believe Jesus is God's Promised Savior?

_____

_____

_____

You can pray:

Dear God, thank You for sending the Lord Jesus to Earth at just the right time as You promised. You are a great God! In Jesus' name. Amen.

Is Jesus Really the Savior God Promised?

But when the time had fully come, God sent his Son . . .
Galatians 4:4

"**Follow me. I will help you get to Heaven.** Be good like me and someday you will be with God! I will show you the way." Many people have said this, but they were not telling the truth. Today, millions think men like Buddha or Mohammed will show them God's way. Others think they can find their own way to Heaven.

When Jesus lived on Earth, He said, "I am the way and the truth and the life. No one comes to the Father except through Me" (John 14:6). He was not only telling the truth, He was the truth! Only by believing (trusting) in Jesus, who died for your sins, can you be forgiven and come to God. Then, you can know you have life in Heaven with God forever.

Who did the Father send to Earth to be the Promised Savior? The Bible says, " . . . the Father has sent His Son to be the Savior of the world" (1 John 4:14). Savior means the one who saves us from our sins. Only Jesus was God's perfect Son. Only Jesus was punished for your sins. Only Jesus came back to life. Only Jesus is the Savior God promised.

GOD THE SON

 Copy 1 John 4:14 below and say it to a friend.

_____

_____

_____

You can pray:

 Dear God, I am glad I know the truth about Your Son, Jesus. Keep me from being tricked by others. In Jesus' name. Amen.

What Will Jesus Do in the Future?

But when the time had fully come, God sent his Son . . .
Galatians 4:4

GOD THE SON

When Jesus entered the city of Jerusalem, the people shouted, " . . . Blessed is . . . the King of Israel!" (John 12:13). The prophets had said the Promised Savior would someday rule the world. They thought that time had come, but Jesus hadn't come to Earth for that reason. He came to die for our sins. The people didn't understand this. They were sad and confused when Jesus did not become king right away. Instead, He was put to death on a cross.

However, Jesus came back to life again and lives in Heaven. God's Word says that someday Jesus will come back to rule the world as King. "When the Son of Man [Jesus] comes in his glory, . . . he will sit on the throne . . . All the nations will be gathered before him . . ." (Matthew 25:31-32). Can you imagine what it will be like when Jesus is King? He is going to make a new earth. There will be no death, no tears, and no pain. What a wonderful place it will be!

All of those who have trusted the Lord Jesus as Savior will be with Him forever! Those who haven't will be separated from God in a terrible place of punishment. If you haven't yet trusted in Jesus as your Savior, you can pray the prayer below.

Write the date and place here when you trusted Jesus as your Savior.

_____

_____

_____

You can pray:

Dear God, I know I am a sinner. I believe in Jesus, who died to take the punishment for my sin and rose again. Please forgive my sins. In Jesus' name. Amen.

Why Does God Keep His Promises?

> But when the time had fully come, God sent his Son . . .
> **Galatians 4:4**

Have you ever made a promise you did not keep? "I promise I will be good from now on!" "I promise I will never speak to you again as long as I live!" "I promise I will never ask for another thing if you just get me what I want now!"

Has God ever made a promise He did not keep? No! God always keeps His promises because God is truth. You can believe what He says. Some things He told the prophets have not happened yet, but we know they will someday. The Bible says, "For the word of the Lord is right and true; he is faithful in all he does" (Psalm 33:4). We have already seen hundreds of prophecies come true, just as God promised!

The greatest promise God has made was to send Jesus to Earth. Why did God make that promise? God knew you needed a Savior. You have sinned and need to be forgiven. Why has God kept His promise? Because God is truth—He does not lie (Titus 1:2). Another reason He has kept His promise is because He loves you. You don't deserve His love or kindness, but because of Jesus, you can now be a child of God.

GOD THE SON

 Write a poem to God, thanking Him for His love.

_____

_____

_____

You can pray:

 Dear God, thank You for your love. I don't deserve Your love or kindness. You love me even when I sin. You are wonderful! I love You, too. In Jesus' name. Amen.

Where Did Jesus Come From?

 In the beginning was the Word, and the Word was with God, and the Word was God. **John 1:1**

G
O
D

T
H
E

S
O
N

Before time began on Earth, the Bible says Jesus lived. He did not begin as a baby in Bethlehem. He was in Heaven before coming to Earth. He did not have a beginning, and He will live forever. How could this be? Because Jesus was, and is, God!

Jesus was not an angel who became God. He was not a man who later became like God. He has always been God. In fact, Jesus made the universe. "For by Him [Jesus] all things were created [made]: things in heaven and on earth . . ." (Colossians 1:16).

At just the right time in history, God sent His Son, Jesus, to be born as a baby so He could live on Earth like you and me. "The Word [Jesus] became flesh . . ." (John 1:14). While living on earth, Jesus proved He was God by His words and actions. He healed the sick, brought dead people back to life and calmed storms! He forgave sins and never once sinned!

During Jesus' life on Earth, God the Father spoke about Him from Heaven. God said, "This is my Son, whom I love; with him I am well pleased" (Matthew 3:17). God the Father wanted us to know for certain that Jesus truly is God the Son.

Write down a verse from today's lesson that could help you explain who Jesus is.

_____

_____

_____

You can pray:

 Dear God, I know Jesus is Your Son. Thank You for helping me know and believe the truth. In Jesus' name. Amen.

How Could Jesus Be Both God and Man?

In the beginning was the Word, and the Word was with God, and the Word was God. **John 1:1**

The King of the universe born as a baby? How could this be? That is exactly what happened. Jesus, God the Son, left His wonderful home in Heaven to come to Earth and be born as a baby. The Bible says, "The Word [Jesus] became flesh and made his dwelling [lived] among us . . ." (John 1:14). It was a miracle!

In Heaven, Jesus had all power and authority as God. When He became a human, Jesus willingly gave up His right to those things. He became like you and me. He got hungry, thirsty and tired. He felt pain and sadness. But because Jesus was still God the Son, He never sinned. He was completely God and man—perfect in every way.

Why did Jesus come to Earth as a human? He came to take your punishment for sin. " . . . [Jesus] humbled Himself and became obedient to death—even death on a cross!" (Philippians 2:8). He came to Earth to make a way for you to go to Heaven. Even when He was dying, there was never a moment that He was not God.

You don't have to understand how Jesus could be both God and man. You just need to believe that He was. God can do anything!

GOD THE SON

What are two things Jesus gave up when He came to Earth as a human?

_____

_____

_____

You can pray:

Dear God, even though I can't understand all about You and Your Son, Jesus, I believe what the Bible says. You are the mighty God! In Jesus' name. Amen.

How Was Jesus Born?

 In the beginning was the Word, and the Word was with God, and the Word was God. **John 1:1**

G O D   T H E   S O N

Mary was amazed at what she heard! An angel told her, "You will be with child and give birth to a son, and you are to give him the name Jesus. He will be great and will be called the Son of the Most High" (Luke 1:31-32). Mary didn't know how this could happen. She was a virgin. Without touching her in any physical way, God would place the baby within her. It was a miracle!

God gave Mary a husband named Joseph. He would help Mary take care of the baby Jesus. Joseph knew that God Himself was Jesus' real Father. An angel had visited Joseph, too, with the news. Perhaps he had read what the prophets had said about the coming Savior.

There was no room to stay in Bethlehem. Jesus was born in a stable. The Bible says, " . . . She [Mary] wrapped Him [Jesus] in cloths and placed Him in a manger [a feeding place for animals]" (Luke 2:7). This was all part of God's plan. Everything about His birth had come true, just as the prophets had said. This tiny baby lying in the manger was the Savior of the world!

 Write down the words to your favorite Christmas song about baby Jesus.

_____

_____

_____

You can pray:

 Dear God, thank You for sending Jesus to Earth in such a special way. It may not be Christmas now, but Happy Birthday, Jesus! In Jesus' name. Amen.

as Jesus Like Me?

In the beginning was the Word, and the Word was with God, and the Word was God. **John 1:1**

What was Jesus like as a boy? As the perfect Son of God, Jesus was different from you in many ways. But, there are some ways in which He was like you. He had a human body that got hungry and tired. He could be happy or sad.

Because He had a human body, He "grew in wisdom and stature, and in favor with God and men" (Luke 2:52). These are ways that you should be growing, too!

Jesus grew in "wisdom." When Jesus was twelve years old, He went to the temple (place of worship) where He talked with the religious leaders. They were impressed with His understanding and His answers. This story is in Luke 2:41-52.

Jesus grew in "stature." His body became bigger and His muscles grew stronger.

Jesus grew in "favor with God." Everything He did pleased His Father, God. Jesus knew His Father was watching and helping Him all the time!

Jesus grew in "favor with men." Others admired and respected Him.

Are you growing in these important ways? Are you making wise choices? Are you getting bigger and stronger? Are you pleasing God in all that you do? Do you treat others with respect and kindness?

GOD THE SON

How can you grow to be more like Jesus?

_____

_____

_____

You can pray:

Dear God, help me to grow up to be like Your Son, Jesus. Thank You. In Jesus' name. Amen.

What Did Jesus Do on the Earth?

43

In the beginning was the Word, and the Word was with God, and the Word was God. **John 1:1**

GOD THE SON

"It's a miracle!" Jairus must have joyfully shouted. "My little girl was dead, but Jesus brought her back to life!" News spread quickly throughout the country (Matthew 9:18-26). Blind people could suddenly see (Luke 18:35-43). Crippled people could walk (Luke 5:17-26). Many sick people were being healed (Mark 6:53-56). And that's not all! Jesus walked on water (Mark 6:45-51). He made giant storms go away by simply speaking (Mark 4:35-41). Demons obeyed His commands (Matthew 17:14-18). Twice He fed thousands of people with just a little bit of food (John 6:3-13; Mark 8:1-10).

It seemed there was no limit to Jesus' mighty power! Whatever the problem, He could take care of it. These miracles showed God's power and love. Jesus was proving that He truly was the Son of God, just as the prophets had said!

The Bible says, "Jesus did many other things as well. If every one of them were written down, I suppose that even the whole world would not have room for the books that would be written" (John 21:25). What problem do you have in your life today? Whether it's big or small, Jesus can help! Tell Him about it and trust Him to do what's best for you.

Write down a big problem that Jesus can help you with.

_____

_____

_____

You can pray:

Dear God, Your power proves You can take care of my problems. Please help me to trust You with my problem today. In Jesus' name. Amen.

Why Is Jesus Called the **Word**?

In the beginning was the Word, and the Word was with God, and the Word was God. **John 1:1**

Words can be important! They tell others what you think, feel, or know to be true. Imagine a world without words!

The Bible says that Jesus "was the Word." This means that Jesus was God's message to you. Everything Jesus spoke told us how God thinks and feels. Everything Jesus did showed us what God would do.

Jesus was "the Word" as He taught how God wants you to think and behave. Not only did He say it, He showed you perfectly how to do it!

Jesus also taught about God's plan for you to have eternal life by believing on Him as your Savior. He is called "the Word of life." "That which was from the beginning, which we have heard, which we have seen with our eyes . . . and our hands have touched . . . the Word of life" (1 John 1:1).

When people listened and looked at Jesus, they were listening to and looking at God!

Since Jesus is God's message to you, it is very important that you know Him! What Jesus said and did is found in the books of Matthew, Mark, Luke and John in the Bible. Other books may help you, too, like this devotional book.

GOD THE SON

What have you learned about Jesus that you didn't know before?

_____
_____
_____

You can pray:

Dear God, help me get to know You better every day. In Jesus' name. Amen.

Was Jesus Ever Tempted to Sin?

In the beginning was the Word, and the Word was with God, and the Word was God. **John 1:1**

Have you ever wanted to be perfect? Maybe you have even tried. If someone told you he or she was perfect, I am sure you would watch very carefully for proof!

When Jesus lived on Earth, He proved He was perfect! Satan tempted Him many times to do wrong, but He never did! One day Satan visited Jesus in a wilderness in Judea. "If you are the Son of God," he taunted, "tell these stones to become bread" (Matthew 4:3). He was tempting Jesus not to follow God's plan.

Two other times Satan tempted Jesus to become proud and show His power. Satan even tried to get Jesus to worship him! Jesus knew God's plan for His coming to Earth, and this was not it! He was determined to do only what His Father wanted.

Did Jesus ever give in? No! He could not sin, for He was God's perfect Son. He was exactly who He claimed to be, and He proved it! Jesus spoke the truth to Satan from God's Word. Satan eventually left Him.

Jesus proved many times His power over Satan. That is why the Lord Jesus can help you when you are tempted to do wrong.

What can you do when you are tempted to sin?

_____

_____

_____

You can pray:

Dear God, please help me when I am tempted to disobey You. I will depend on Your power to say "no." In Jesus' name. Amen.

46

What Happened in the Room Upstairs?

For God so loved the world that he gave his one and only Son, that whoever believes in him shall not perish but have eternal life. **John 3:16**

It was the night before Jesus was to be killed. His thirty-three years on Earth were almost over. The special Jewish holiday called the Passover had come. The prophets had said this would be the time of His death. Jesus met with his twelve close followers in an upstairs room for their last meal together (Luke 22:7-23).

The bread and wine Jesus passed to His disciples that night had special meaning. The next day He would die on a cross. The bread and wine were to be reminders of His wounded body and His blood that would flow on the cross as payment for our sins. Judas was there eating with Him.

Before the meal was over, Judas left the room to go and betray Jesus by leading His enemies to Him. (John 13:21-30)

Jesus made some wonderful promises to His followers. Then, they sang one last song together and left. It was a night they would never forget.

Jesus told His followers to continue to remember His death in the same way He had demonstrated in the upstairs room. Today we call this Communion or the Lord's Supper. We are to remember His death in this way until He comes again.

GOD THE SON

How was the night in the upstairs room important for us today?

_____

_____

_____

You can pray:

Dear God, thank You for giving this special way to remember what Jesus did for me. In Jesus' name. Amen.

Why Was Jesus on Trial? 47

For God so loved the world that he gave his one and only Son, that whoever believes in him shall not perish but have eternal life. **John 3:16**

The night in the upstairs room had been special to Jesus and His disciples. But the religious leaders who hated Jesus wanted to have Him killed! Why? Because Jesus had said He was the Son of God. He claimed to be the Messiah–the one God promised to send into the world to save everyone from sin. The leaders refused to believe Him. They arrested Jesus and put Him on trial.

Since Jesus had done nothing wrong, the religious leaders had to get men to tell lies about Him. For hours, Jesus listened to their lies and He was painfully beaten. The religious leaders wanted Jesus put to death, so they took Him to Pilate, the governor. "He has claimed to be the Son of God!" the leaders declared. "For this He must die!" Jesus did not say a word. (John 19:7-9)

Pilate asked Jesus, "Don't you realize I have power either to free you or to crucify you?" Jesus answered, "You would have no power over me if it were not given to you from above" (John 19:11). Jesus knew that being on trial was part of God's plan. The time had come for Him to suffer and die for the sins of the world.

If you had been at Jesus' trial, what would you have told about Jesus?

_____

_____

_____

You can pray:

Dear God, I believe Jesus is Your Son, just as He said. Thank You that He was willing to suffer and die for my sin. In Jesus' name. Amen.

GOD THE SON

Where Were Jesus' Friends?

For God so loved the world that he gave his one and only Son, that whoever believes in him shall not perish but have eternal life. **John 3:16**

Before Jesus was arrested and put on trial, He had talked with one of His disciples named Peter. Jesus told Peter, "'. . . this very night, before the rooster crows, you will disown [deny] me three times.' But Peter declared. 'Even if I have to die with you, I will never disown you!' And all the other disciples said the same" (Matthew 26:34-35). But that night, when Jesus was arrested, his disciples ran away. They were afraid.

Peter followed at a distance. It was a horrible sight! Jesus was accused of things He didn't do. He was whipped, beaten, slapped, punched, mocked and spit upon. One could hardly recognize Him because of the bruises and blood.

Peter sat outside, warming himself by the fire. A servant girl pointed to him and said, "You also were with Jesus..." (Matthew 26:69).

"I don't know what you're talking about," Peter replied (Matthew 26:70). Two other servants said they recognized Peter as one of Jesus' followers, but two more times Peter denied that he knew Jesus. Then the rooster crowed. As Jesus was led out of the trial, He looked at Peter, and Peter remembered Jesus' words. How could he have denied Jesus? Peter went away, crying bitterly.

GOD THE SON

Write about a time when you spoke up for Jesus, even though it was hard.

_____

_____

You can pray:

Dear God, I am sorry for the times I have pretended not to know You. Help me to be brave to speak up for You. In Jesus' name. Amen.

Why Did Jesus Have to Die?

For God so loved the world that he gave his one and only Son, that whoever believes in him shall not perish but have eternal life. **John 3:16**

GOD THE SON

Jesus' arms were stretched out as soldiers nailed him to a wooden cross. The pain was horrible. The Lord Jesus was being crucified.

The mocking crowd said, "Come down from the cross, if you are the Son of God!" (Matthew 27:42). Because Jesus was the Son of God, He would not come down. God the Father placed on His perfect Son the sin of the whole world. "God made him [Jesus] who had no sin to be sin for us . . ." (2 Corinthians 5:21). Jesus willingly bled and died on the cross to take the punishment that God required for sin.

Hours later, darkness came over the whole countryside. Jesus cried out, "My God, My God, why have you forsaken Me?" (Matthew 27:45). The perfect, holy God could not look at His Son, who had taken upon Himself the sin of the world.

Later Jesus said, "Father, into Your hands I commit My spirit!" (Luke 23:46), and Jesus died. Some of the soldiers who had seen all that had happened said, "Surely he was the Son of God!" (Matthew 27:54). When Jesus took the punishment for sin on the cross, He did all that was necessary to be called the Savior.

Finish this sentence: Jesus had to die because . . .

_____

_____

_____

You can pray:
Dear God, thank You for being willing to send Your Son to die in my place. In Jesus' name. Amen.

Who Moved the Stone**?**

50

For God so loved the world that he gave his one and only Son, that whoever believes in him shall not perish but have eternal life. **John 3:16**

A friend named Joseph asked for permission to take Jesus' dead body down from the cross and bury Him. After His body was wrapped in special cloths, they placed Him in a tomb, or cave. A huge stone, requiring several men to move it, was rolled in front of the entrance. The religious leaders asked Pilate to assign armed soldiers to guard the tomb day and night. (Matthew 27:57-65)

Suddenly, on the third day, there was an earthquake! An angel came down from Heaven and rolled the stone from the door! The guards shook with fear and fell down as if they were dead. A few women, who were Jesus' friends came to visit the tomb. They brought spices to put on Jesus' body, but when they arrived, the women were surprised to see a shining angel sitting on top of the stone! The tomb was empty! Jesus was gone! (Matthew 28:1-4)

The angel said, "Do not be afraid, for I know that you are looking for Jesus, who was crucified. He is not here; he has risen, just as he said. . . . go quickly and tell His disciples he has risen from the dead . . ." (Matthew 28:5-7). The women ran to tell the disciples.

GOD THE SON

What would you have said to Jesus the day He came back to life?

_____

_____

_____

You can pray:

Dear God, because Your Son came back to life, I can live forever with You in Heaven! You are an awesome God! In Jesus' name. Amen.

Can I Know for Sure That I Am Forgiven?

For God so loved the world that he gave his one and only Son, that whoever believes in him shall not perish but have eternal life. **John 3:16**

Have you ever wondered if you are really forgiven? One of the last things Jesus said as He hung on the cross was, "It is finished!" He meant that He had done all that is necessary to pay for your sin. God loved you when you didn't deserve it. Jesus died for you so you could be forgiven. If you have trusted Jesus as your Savior, God kept His promise. He has forgiven you, and you have eternal life. One Bible writer says, "I write these things to you who believe in the name of the Son of God so that you may **know** that you have eternal life" (1 John 5:13). Also, the Bible says that when God forgives you, He won't remember your sins anymore (Hebrews 8:12).

Maybe you're thinking, but I don't feel like I'm forgiven! Your forgiveness does not depend on how you feel. It is based on your faith in Jesus and what He has done for you. Put your name in His promise: "For God so loved [your name] that he gave his one and only Son, that if [your name] believes in him [your name] shall not perish but have eternal life" (John 3:16).

 How do you know you are forgiven?

_____

_____

_____

You can pray:
Dear God, thank You for keeping Your promise to me. Thank You for forgiving me and for the gift of eternal life. In Jesus' name. Amen.

What Can I Give to God?

For God so loved the world that he gave his one and only Son, that whoever believes in him shall not perish but have eternal life. **John 3:16**

If you've received the Lord Jesus Christ as your Savior, you're probably just beginning to realize the wonderful gift He is! Jesus is your friend and helper. He is God's free gift to you!

When someone gives you a wonderful gift, you usually want to give that person something in return. Perhaps you are so grateful for God's gift of the Lord Jesus that you would like to give Him something special. But what do you give to God, who owns everything? The gift He wants most is you! One of the Bible writers said, "I urge [plead with] you, brothers, in view of God's mercy, to offer your bodies as living sacrifices, holy and pleasing to God" (Romans 12:1).

A sacrifice is an offering or gift. You can tell God you want to give yourself to Him. Give Him your eyes and ears, your feet and your hands. Give Him your mind and your heart. Give Him every part of you to do what pleases Him. Why should you present your body to God? Because you love Him. He wants you to be holy, set apart, for Him to use in whatever way He chooses. Will you give yourself to God now?

GOD THE SON

Write a thank you note to God for His gift to you.

_____

_____

_____

You can pray:

Dear God, I give myself to You. I will go where You want me to go, do what You want me to do and be what You want me to be. In Jesus' name. Amen.

Did Jesus Really Come Back to Life**?**

. . . Christ died for our sins according to the Scriptures, that He was buried, that He was raised on the third day according to the Scriptures . . . **1 Corinthians 15:3-4**

GOD THE SON

"Jesus, alive from the dead? I'll prove it's not true!" Many people have said this from the first day Jesus came back to life. Some are still saying it today! Maybe you've also wondered if Jesus truly came alive again. He did! And there is much evidence to prove it is true.

Some have tried to prove Jesus didn't really die. They say He just fainted and that His disciples pretended that He died and came alive again. But Jesus' enemies made sure He was dead before His body was taken down from the cross. They also made sure no one could steal His body and pretend He had risen.

After Jesus came back to life, over five hundred people saw Him on at least fifteen different occasions! They touched Him, talked to Him and ate with Him. Many of these witnesses were tortured and killed by Jesus' enemies. If it were not true, they certainly would have said so to save their own lives.

For hundreds of years, millions of people all over the world have testified that Jesus is alive! Even though we can no longer see Him with our eyes, we can see Jesus changing lives and answering our prayers.

How do you know that Jesus is alive?

_____

_____

_____

You can pray:

Dear God, thank You that Jesus is alive, and that He is working in my life today. In Jesus' name. Amen.

What Were Jesus' Last Words**?**

. . . Christ died for our sins according to the Scriptures, that He was buried, that He was raised on the third day according to the Scriptures . . . **1 Corinthians 15:3-4**

If you were not going to see your family and friends for a very long time, what would you say to them? I am sure you would choose your words very carefully. It would be important for them to remember your last instructions.

After Jesus came back to life, He stayed on earth for forty more days (Acts 1:3). Then, it was time for Him to return to Heaven. His family and friends would not see Him for a very long time. What were Jesus' last words to those He loved? "Go into all the world and preach the good news to all creation" (Mark 16:15).

Jesus' instructions are for you and me as well. Tell others everywhere the good news about the Lord Jesus Christ. He died, taking the punishment for your sin. He came back to life three days later. Now anyone can believe in Him and receive His gift of everlasting life.

Do you know someone who needs to hear about Jesus? Plan a time to tell him or her. Do you know others who are sharing the good news about Jesus? Perhaps you could pray or give money to help them.

Who will you share the good news about Jesus with this week?

_____
_____
_____

You can pray:

Dear God, help me to tell others about You. Also, use me to help others share Your good news. In Jesus' name. Amen.

GOD THE SON

How Did Jesus Return to Heaven?

 ... Christ died for our sins according to the Scriptures, that He was buried, that He was raised on the third day according to the Scriptures ... **1 Corinthians 15:3-4**

One day, Jesus had taken His disciples up on a mountain. He had finished giving His last instructions to them. Now it was time for Him to return to Heaven. Suddenly, as the disciples watched in silent amazement, Jesus began rising into the air. As He rose higher and higher, the disciples had to strain their eyes to see Him. Finally, a cloud hid Him from their sight. It was amazing! Jesus' mighty power had taken Him back to His home in Heaven. (Acts 1:9-10)

As the disciples continued to stare into the sky, two angels appeared and spoke to them. "This same Jesus, who has been taken from you into heaven, will come back in the same way you have seen him go into Heaven" (Acts 1:11). One day Jesus will return from Heaven in the clouds!

What did the disciples do next? First, they worshiped the Lord Jesus. Then, they returned to the city with great joy (Luke 24:52). Can you imagine how the disciples felt telling others what they had just seen? What an exciting day it had been. And how exciting to know that, one day, Jesus will return!

What would you have done if you had seen Jesus go up into Heaven?

_____

_____

_____

You can pray:

Dear God, I'm glad You are alive in Heaven! Help me to tell the good news about You to others. In Jesus' name. Amen.

56

What Is Jesus Doing in Heaven?

. . . Christ died for our sins according to the Scriptures, that He was buried, that He was raised on the third day according to the Scriptures . . . **1 Corinthians 15:3-4**

About 2,000 years have passed since the Lord Jesus Christ left the Earth to return to Heaven. What has He been doing all this time? One thing He's been doing is to prepare a beautiful home for His children! Jesus promised, "In my Father's house [Heaven] are many rooms . . . I am going there to prepare a place for you" (John 14:2).

Will this home look like a fine house in Asia, Africa or America? Will it look like a grand castle in Europe or a beautiful island home? We can't begin to imagine! Nothing on Earth will come close to its beauty! A perfect God who loves you very much is making this perfect place!

Not only is the Lord Jesus preparing a place for you, He is preparing you for that place! He wants you to be ready to enjoy all that He is making for you. For this reason, He is also praying for you. "Christ Jesus . . . is at the right hand of God and is also interceding [praying] for us" (Romans 8:34). Isn't it wonderful to know that Jesus is thinking about you right now? He loves you, He prays for you and He looks forward to being with you forever!

GOD THE SON

What do you think your place in Heaven might look like?

_____

_____

_____

You can pray:

Dear God, thank You for preparing a special place just for me. Thank You for praying for me so I will be ready for that special place. In Jesus' name. Amen.

Is Jesus Really Praying for Me?

> . . . Christ died for our sins according to the Scriptures, that He was buried, that He was raised on the third day according to the Scriptures . . . **1 Corinthians 15:3-4**

GOD THE SON

Yes! Jesus is praying for you. One thing He is praying is that you will stand strong against the temptation to sin. Jesus remembers what it was like when Satan tempted Him on Earth. He knows that you still have that "want to" to sin. He prays that you will say "no" to temptation.

The Bible says that Satan stands before God's throne, day and night, accusing us of our sins (Revelation 12:10). Every time we give in to sin, Satan points out our guilt to God. That's when the Lord Jesus speaks to God the Father for us. The Bible says, " . . . we have one who speaks to the Father in our defense–Jesus Christ, the Righteous one" (1 John 2:1). Jesus, the perfect One, is like your lawyer. He tells the judge, God the Father, that you are not guilty because He already paid for your sin by dying on the cross. No accusation from Satan can stand up to Jesus' defense!

When God declares you "not guilty" and He forgives you, it's not because you deserve it. God is being merciful to you because of His Son, Jesus, who has prayed for you. Aren't you glad that the Lord Jesus prays for you every day?

Why do you need Jesus to pray for you?

_____

_____

_____

You can pray:

Dear God, thank You for Jesus, who prays for me. Thank You for Your forgiveness. In Jesus' name. Amen.

58 When Will Jesus Return to Earth?

. . . Christ died for our sins according to the Scriptures, that He was buried, that He was raised on the third day according to the Scriptures . . . **1 Corinthians 15:3-4**

Suddenly, when we least expect it, Jesus will come back to Earth! The prophets foretold that Jesus would come the first time, and He did. The prophets have also told us to look for His coming again. The Bible says, "For the Lord Himself will come down from heaven, with a loud command, with the voice of the archangel and with the trumpet call of God . . ." (1 Thessalonians 4:16). Jesus Himself also promised His return to Earth someday. "And if I go and prepare a place for you, I will come back and take you to be . . . where I am" (John 14:3). He is coming to take His children home to Heaven.

When will it happen? He didn't say. It could happen any day at any time. The Bible does tell us certain events to look for that would be clues to Jesus' return. His coming could take place in your lifetime! If you have not trusted the Lord Jesus as your Savior, this could be frightening news! You will be left to endure much suffering. But you can trust in Him today! If you have already trusted the Lord Jesus Christ as your Savior, you should be excited about seeing Him face to face!

GOD THE SON

If you knew Jesus was coming today, how would you spend your time?

_____

_____

_____

You can pray:

Dear God, thank You that Jesus is coming back again. Help me to be ready for His return. In Jesus' name. Amen.

How Can I Be Ready for Jesus' Return?

. . . Christ died for our sins according to the Scriptures, that He was buried, that He was raised on the third day according to the Scriptures . . . **1 Corinthians 15:3-4**

GOD THE SON

If you have ever taken a trip, you know it is important to prepare. Right now you need to prepare for your trip to Heaven. If you've never trusted Jesus Christ as your Savior, now is the time to do that. The Bible says, " . . . now is the time of God's favor, now is the day of salvation" (2 Corinthians 6:2). Tell God you are sorry for your sin. Thank the Lord Jesus for taking your punishment for sin on the cross. Ask Him to make you His child. Don't wait; you may not get another chance.

If you have already trusted the Lord Jesus as your Savior, now is the time to get to know God better. Now is the time to obey His Word. The Bible says, "And now, dear children, continue in him [stay close to Jesus], so that when he appears we may be confident and unashamed before him at his coming" (1 John 2:28). If you are living close to Jesus Christ, you will not be ashamed to see Him when He appears. As you continue reading the devotionals in this book, you'll learn many more things you can do to prepare for your trip to Heaven.

What can you do today to get ready for your trip to Heaven?

_____

_____

_____

You can pray:

Dear God, thank You that I can be with you in Heaven someday. Help me to prepare now for the day I will see You. In Jesus' name. Amen.

This is the end of the section of "God the Son" devotionals.

It is time to do your next activity page. It came to you in the mail after you sent in the activity sheet following devotional 31 in your book.

Remember to add your prayer request so your mailbox friend can pray for you. When you finish the whole page, fold it on the lines so the Mailbox Club address shows. Put a small piece of tape on the bottom to keep it folded. Add a stamp and mail your activity page.

Your work will be marked and sent back to you, along with a personal note. The activity sheet for the next set of lessons will be sent to you, too.

Enjoy getting to know God better with your next group of devotionals!

GOD
the Holy
Spirit

Who Is the Holy Spirit?

Don't you know that you yourselves are God's temple and that God's Spirit lives in you? 1 Corinthians 3:16

Have you ever received something that came with a guarantee like a CD player or a walk-man? A guarantee is a promise that the item will work. When you receive Jesus as your Savior, God gives you a guarantee of eternal life with Him in Heaven someday. This guarantee is the Holy Spirit.

The Holy Spirit is a person not a force. He has feelings just like a person. He can choose and decide things because He has a will. He has a mind and is able to teach. He is a Person and He is God. Our God is a three-in-one person. He is God the Father, God the Son and God the Holy Spirit.

When you receive Jesus as your Savior, the Holy Spirit comes to live inside you. Since He is God, your body becomes the house where God lives. The Bible says, "Don't you know that . . . God's Spirit lives in you?" (1 Corinthians 3:16). Even though you cannot see Him, He is very real. The Holy Spirit is your reminder that God is always with you! He is your guarantee of eternal life!

GOD THE HOLY SPIRIT

Write down three things you have learned about the Holy Spirit.

_____

_____

_____

You can pray:

Dear God, thank You for giving me Your Holy Spirit as a guarantee so I can know I have eternal life. In Jesus' name. Amen.

What Does the Holy Spirit Do?

61

Don't you know that you yourselves are God's temple and that God's Spirit lives in you? **1 Corinthians 3:16**

GOD THE HOLY SPIRIT

The Holy Spirit lives in people who have trusted Jesus as their Savior. But what does the Holy Spirit do for people who have not trusted Jesus? The Bible says, " . . . he [the Holy Spirit] will convict the world [everyone] of guilt in regard to sin and righteousness and judgment" (John 16:8). The Holy Spirit uses God's Word to show people that they are sinners. He helps them see that they need Jesus to forgive their sins.

Maybe you've never trusted Jesus as your Savior. Has the Holy Spirit spoken to you? Admit to God that you are a sinner. Tell Him that you trust in Jesus, who died on the cross for your sins. He will forgive you today.

If you do know Jesus as your Savior, the Holy Spirit can help you tell others about Jesus. You can share Bible verses about Jesus with them. The Holy Spirit will use those verses to help them understand that they are sinners and need to be forgiven. Can you think of someone who does not know Jesus as his Savior? Will you let the Holy Spirit use you to show that person how to trust in Jesus? Share the truth about Jesus and then let the Holy Spirit do His work.

 What does the Holy Spirit do for those who do not know Jesus as their Savior?

_____

_____

_____

You can pray:

 Dear God, thank You for the Holy Spirit. Help me to share about Jesus' forgiveness with someone who does not know You. In Jesus' name. Amen.

How Does the Holy Spirit Work in My Life?

Don't you know that you yourselves are God's temple and that God's Spirit lives in you? **1 Corinthians 3:16**

Maps are used to give directions. Often maps are hard to understand. You need someone to show you how to read them. The Bible is like a map. It gives you directions for how to get to Heaven. It shows you how to live for Jesus. The Holy Spirit is the person who helps you read this map.

If you have trusted Jesus as your Savior, the Holy Spirit lives inside you. The Holy Spirit helps you understand the Bible. He also helps you to know God. He gives you strength to do right and say "no" to sin. When you sin, the Holy Spirit lets you know you have done wrong. He helps you understand that you need to tell God what you have done wrong.

The Bible calls the Holy Spirit your counselor, which means helper. Before Jesus left this Earth to return to Heaven, He told His followers, "And I will ask the Father, and he will give you another Counselor to be with you forever" (John 14:16). Jesus called this Counselor, or Helper, the Spirit of truth who will live in God's children forever (John 14:17). Isn't it wonderful to know that God's Holy Spirit will live in you forever? He is your helper!

GOD THE HOLY SPIRIT

Can you think of three ways the Holy Spirit helps you? Write them here:

_____

_____

_____

You can pray:

Dear God, thank You for Your Holy Spirit who is my Helper. I will listen to Him as I learn more about You. In Jesus' name. Amen.

What Does It Mean to Be Filled with the Spirit?

Don't you know that you yourselves are God's temple and that God's Spirit lives in you? **1 Corinthians 3:16**

GOD THE HOLY SPIRIT

When you receive Jesus as your Savior, the Holy Spirit comes to live in you forever. This is called His indwelling. God also wants you to be filled with the Holy Spirit. Let Him control your life. The Bible says, " . . . be filled with the Spirit" (Ephesians 5:18). When the Holy Spirit fills you, He controls your thoughts, words and actions. The Holy Spirit will indwell you forever, but you need to ask God to fill you with His Spirit each day. Then you can live to please Him.

How do you know if you're filled with the Holy Spirit?

When the Holy Spirit fills you, He gives you power to win over sin. He controls your thoughts, words and actions so they are pleasing to God. Do your thoughts, words and actions show that you are filled with the Holy Spirit? If not, you need to ask God to fill you again.

God wants to fill you with His Spirit each day. But did you know you can ask God to fill you with His Spirit for special jobs that He wants you to do? God's Spirit dwells in you always. But don't forget that He wants to fill you each day so you can serve Him better.

How can you tell if you're filled with the Holy Spirit?

_____

_____

_____

You can pray:

Dear God, please fill me with Your Holy Spirit today. I want Your Spirit to control every area of my life. Thank You. In Jesus' name. Amen.

Can the Holy Spirit Help Me Not to Sin?

Don't you know that you yourselves are God's temple and that God's Spirit lives in you? **1 Corinthians 3:16**

Amanda stood looking at the computer. Mom had told her, "No computer games until after your homework is done." Mom will be gone for another hour, she thought. Amanda was tempted (had a strong desire) to play just one game but knew that would be sinning.

Before you trusted Jesus as your Savior, you were under the power and control of sin. But now the Holy Spirit dwells in you. The Bible says you are His living temple. The Holy Spirit wants to help you to keep that temple clean from sin. He dwells in you to set you free from sin's power and control. The Bible says, "For sin shall not be your master . . ." (Romans 6:14).

However, that doesn't mean you'll never be tempted to sin. When you are tempted to sin, the Holy Spirit convicts you. He helps you to know that your behavior is wrong. But it's up to you to choose to obey God. Pay attention to what He is showing you. The Holy Spirit is working in you. He will give you the ability to choose to obey God and not to sin. Will you choose to listen to the Holy Spirit and do what is right?

GOD THE HOLY SPIRIT

What does the Holy Spirit do when you are tempted to sin?

_____

_____

_____

You can pray:

Thank You, God, that the Holy Spirit convicts me before I sin. Help me to listen to Him and not sin. In Jesus' name. Amen.

What Happens If I Sin?

Don't you know that you yourselves are God's temple and that God's Spirit lives in you? **1 Corinthians 3:16**

GOD THE HOLY SPIRIT

Have you ever done something wrong to a friend and wanted to hide it from him? Were you sad and afraid he would find out? Did you stay away from him? Because you did something wrong to your friend, you have broken your fellowship (friendship) with him. However, when you tell your friend what you did, it makes everything right. You want to spend time with him again.

If you sin against God, it is the same. You do not want to talk to Him in prayer. You do not want to read your Bible. Sin spoils your fellowship (friendship) with God. He will never leave you, but sin makes Him sad. Sin will also make you sad. It will take away your peace and joy. Sin also blocks your prayers so that God will not answer. The Bible says, "If I had cherished [kept] sin in my heart, the Lord would not have listened . . ." (Psalm 66:18).

If you sin, you are no longer allowing the Holy Spirit to control your life. It is then that He begins to convict you (points out your sin). He causes you to want to make things right with God. You need to confess your sins to God (agree with Him that you've sinned), to make things right again.

How does sin affect your friendship with God?

_____

_____

_____

You can pray:

Dear God, Thank You for the Holy Spirit, who convicts me when I sin. Help me to listen to Him and do what is right. In Jesus' name. Amen.

66 How Do I Confess My Sins to God?

Don't you know that you yourselves are God's temple and that God's Spirit lives in you? **1 Corinthians 3:16**

Tamika sat in the principal's office. She was in big trouble. Her teacher caught her writing on the bathroom wall. The principal came into his office and closed the door. "Tamika," he said, "I am disappointed in you."

"I'm sorry," Tamika said.

"Are you really?" He asked. "Are you sorry because you did something wrong, or are you sorry because you got caught?"

When you sin, the Holy Spirit living inside you convicts you. He lets you know that things are no longer right between you and God. You should feel sorry because you sinned against God, not because you were caught. Confessing your sins to God makes things right again.

Confess means to name your sins, that is, to agree with God that you did wrong. God already knows, but He wants you to tell Him. The Bible says, "If we confess our sins, he is faithful and just and will forgive us our sins . . ." (1 John 1:9). Tell God, "I admit I was wrong when I (name the sin)." God promises to forgive you. Thank Him for His forgiveness and ask Him to help you not to sin that way again. You may also need to say "I'm sorry" to someone else who has been hurt by your sin.

What does God promise to do when you confess your sins to Him?

_____

_____

_____

You can pray:

Dear God, Thank You for Your forgiveness. Help me to do right and not give in to sin. In Jesus' name. Amen.

GOD THE HOLY SPIRIT

What Happens When I Confess My Sins?

 Don't you know that you yourselves are God's temple and that God's Spirit lives in you? **1 Corinthians 3:16**

When you come in from playing outside and are dirty what do you do? You take a bath. The "real you" inside gets dirty when you sin. It needs to be cleaned. Confessing your sins to God is like taking a spiritual bath for the "real you."

Do you remember what you have been learning about the Holy Spirit? When you receive Jesus as your Savior, the Holy Spirit comes to live inside you. Your body is the temple where He lives. He is your helper. And when you give in to sin, He convicts you.

God promises to forgive you if you confess your sins to Him. "If we confess our sins, he is faithful and just and will forgive us our sins and purify [cleanse] us from all unrighteous-ness [sin]" (1 John 1:9). Confessing your sins to God is like taking a spiritual bath.

When you confess your sins, your relationship with God is made right again. Your peace and joy returns. God hears and answers your prayers. You are once again filled by Him. He is in control.

Taking a bath and being clean feels great, but taking a spiritual bath and being forgiven feels even better!

 Write down three things the Holy Spirit does after you confess your sins to God.

_____

_____

You can pray:

 Dear God, help me to listen to the Holy Spirit and not give in to sin when I am first tempted. Thank You for Your promise to forgive me when I confess my sin. In Jesus' name. Amen.

GOD THE HOLY SPIRIT

How Does the Holy Spirit Teach Me?

But when he, the Spirit of truth, comes, he will guide you into all truth. **John 16:13**

Do you have a favorite teacher? Why do you like this teacher the best? Is it because he or she helps you learn new things? Is it because he or she helps you understand what is being taught? Good teachers make you think. They make learning fun and interesting.

The Holy Spirit is your teacher, also. The Bible says, " . . . the Holy Spirit . . . will teach you all things . . ." (John 14:26). The Bible is the textbook the Holy Spirit uses to teach you. When you read God's Word, the Holy Spirit helps you understand what is being said. He helps you learn about God. He helps you to grow in your Christian life and to please God.

Before you read God's Word, it is important to stop and pray. Ask the Holy Spirit to help you understand what you are about to read. When you are finished reading, ask God to help you obey what you have just read. Don't be upset if you do not understand everything that is written in the Bible. Even adults do not understand everything. But the Holy Spirit will teach you just what He wants you to know right now.

GOD THE HOLY SPIRIT

Write down two things the Holy Spirit helps you to learn or to understand.

_____

_____

_____

You can pray:

Dear God, thank You for the Holy Spirit who is my teacher. Help me to obey what he teaches me. In Jesus' name. Amen.

How Does the Holy Spirit Guide Me?

 But when he, the Spirit of truth, comes, he will guide you into all truth. **John 16:13**

The Holy Spirit is not just a teacher; He is also your guide. The Holy Spirit will direct you in little things. He will help you to speak to a friend about Jesus. He will show you how to help someone who is hurting. He will also guide you in big things like what you should do when you grow up and who you should marry.

If you know Jesus as your Savior, you need to ask God for guidance. Then listen quietly for His plan. One way the Holy Spirit may guide you is through God's Word. Reading the Bible will help you to know God's thoughts. A second way He guides is through things that happen. Look for ways God is working things out. God will cause things to happen that will show you His plan step by step. A third way the Holy Spirit guides is through other Christians. He may use your parents or others who love God to give you good advice.

God promises, "I will instruct you and teach you in the way you should go" (Psalm 32:8). You don't know what will happen in the future, but God does. He knows what's best for you. You can trust the Holy Spirit to guide you.

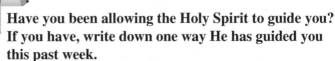 **Have you been allowing the Holy Spirit to guide you? If you have, write down one way He has guided you this past week.**

_____

_____

_____

You can pray:

 Dear God, help me to trust in You and allow the Holy Spirit to guide me each day. In Jesus' name. Amen.

GOD THE HOLY SPIRIT

What Does It Mean to "Quench" the Spirit?

... when he, the Spirit of truth, comes, he will guide you into all truth ... **John 16:13**

The Bible uses symbols to help you understand how the Holy Spirit works in your life. One symbol of the Holy Spirit is fire. Fire makes things pure. The Holy Spirit cleans away things in your life God does not like. He convicts you when you do wrong. He helps you and guides you.

Have you ever watched a campfire or leaves burning? The fire grows stronger when it is fanned with air. It is quenched, or put out, with water. The Holy Spirit's fire grows stronger in your life when you pray, witness, read the Bible and obey God. When you disobey, you quench the Spirit. You also quench Him when you refuse to allow Him to guide you and lead you in serving God. Without the Spirit's leading, you have no joy or inner peace.

The Bible says, "Do not put out the Spirit's fire" (1 Thessalonians 5:19). This does not mean the Holy Spirit will leave you. He is your guarantee of eternal life! It means you are not controlled and filled by Him. Confess your sins. Start obeying God and allow the Holy Spirit to do His work in your life.

GOD THE HOLY SPIRIT

Name two ways you might quench the Holy Spirit.

_____

_____

_____

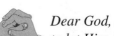

You can pray:

Dear God, help me not to quench the Holy Spirit, but to let Him do His work in my life. In Jesus' name. Amen.

What Does It Mean to "Grieve" the Spirit?

... when he, the Spirit of truth, comes, he will guide you into all truth. ... John 16:13

G O D   T H E   H O L Y   S P I R I T

Have you ever heard the word "grieve?" It means to have deep feelings of pain or sadness. There are many different experiences in our lives that cause us to grieve. When someone you love–or maybe your pet–dies, or when you have to say good-bye to a good friend who moves away, you grieve over your loss. Did you know that your actions or attitudes might cause others to grieve over you? You grieve your parents when you disobey.

In your Christian life, there may be times you grieve the Holy Spirit–cause Him pain and sadness. You grieve the Holy Spirit when you are mean, or when you talk in a harsh or angry way. Fighting and arguing also grieve the Holy Spirit. You cause Him sadness when you do not confess your sins to God. You grieve Him when you doubt God's care for you or when you doubt God's Word about your being saved from sin.

God says, " . . . do not grieve the Holy Spirit of God, with whom you were sealed for the day of redemption" (Ephesians 4:30). You are still God's child. You still have God's promise of eternal life, but it hurts Him when you grieve the Holy Spirit. Grieve is a love word. God loves you and is sad when you grieve His Spirit. Confessing your sins to God allows the Holy Spirit to have control of your life once again.

What are three ways you might grieve the Holy Spirit?

_____

_____

You can pray:

Dear God, thank You for forgiving me. Help me not to grieve the Holy Spirit. In Jesus' name. Amen.

How Does the Holy Spirit Change Me?

. . . when he, the Spirit of truth, comes, he will guide you into all truth . . . John 16:13

When you were born, you could not feed yourself. Someone had to take care of you. As time passed, you began to crawl and then walk. Soon you began to talk. You were growing and changing.

When you trust in Jesus as your Savior, you are born into God's family. You are changed into a new person on the inside. The Bible says, "Therefore, if anyone is in Christ, he is a new creation; the old has gone, the new has come!" (2 Corinthians 5:17). You are a new-born baby in Christ with a new "want to" to please God. Now you need to grow up in your new life. Jesus is your example of how God wants His children to grow and live. It pleases God when you act like His Son.

The Holy Spirit living in you helps you grow and change so you can live to please God. He teaches you and guides you through the Bible. He helps you pray and gives you power to obey God. When you do sin, He convicts you so you will confess your sins to God. Little by little the Holy Spirit is working in your life to change you.

GOD THE HOLY SPIRIT

Write three ways the Holy Spirit is changing you.

_____

_____

_____

You can pray:

Dear God, I want the Holy Spirit to work in my life to change me and help me grow. In Jesus' name. Amen.

What Is the Fruit of the Spirit**?**

73

But the fruit of the Spirit is love, joy, peace, patience, kindness, goodness, faithfulness, gentleness and self-control. Galatians 5:22

G O D   T H E   H O L Y   S P I R I T

Have you ever seen bananas growing on an apple tree? It's impossible! Apple trees produce (grow) apples, and banana trees produce bananas. When you become God's child, He wants to produce fruit in you. This is not fruit like apples or bananas. This is spiritual fruit. This fruit shows in your actions and words. It is what you are on the inside–your character. Obeying and serving God is what you do, but spiritual fruit is produced by what you are.

The Bible lists the fruit you should produce. "But the fruit of the Spirit is love, joy, peace, patience, kindness, goodness, faithfulness, gentleness and self-control" (Galatians 5:22).

This fruit is produced in your life when you listen to the Holy Spirit and allow Him to be in control. What is the result of controlling your own life? Bad fruit like jealousy, anger and selfishness are produced. When you obey the Spirit and allow Him to control you, good fruit is produced. The more you obey the Holy Spirit, the more the fruit of the Spirit grows and develops. What kind of fruit is seen in your life? Is it good fruit or bad fruit?

Can you list the fruit of the Spirit that God wants to produce in you?

_____

_____

_____

You can pray:

Dear God, help me to give my life to the Spirit and allow Him to produce good fruit in my life. In Jesus' name. Amen.

Can the Holy Spirit Help Me Love Others?

But the fruit of the Spirit is love, joy, peace, kindness, goodness, faithfulness, gentleness and self-control. Galatians 5:22

Do you know what love means? You may think that love is just a feeling, but that is not true love. If you love someone only because that person loves you, you are not showing true love. True love comes from God.

The Bible says that "God is love" (1 John 4:8). God loves you even though you are a sinner. God showed His love by sending His Son to die on the cross for your sin. When you trust in Jesus as your Savior, God fills you with His love. The Bible says, " . . . God has poured out his love into our hearts by the Holy Spirit, whom he has given us" (Romans 5:5). When the Holy Spirit is in control, He will produce love for others in your life.

True love is loving others like Jesus does. This means to think of others more highly than yourself. True love is to want God's best for others. When the fruit of love is produced in your life, you will not expect to receive anything in return for the love you give. Is the Holy Spirit producing the fruit of love in your life?

GOD THE HOLY SPIRIT

List two ways you can show the spiritual fruit of love to others.

_____

_____

_____

You can pray:

Dear God, thank You for loving me with Your true love. Please produce the fruit of love in my life. In Jesus' name. Amen.

ow Does the Holy Spirit Give Me Joy Inside? 75

> But the fruit of the Spirit is love, joy, peace, patience, kindness, goodness, faithfulness, gentleness and self-control. **Galatians 5:22**

GOD THE HOLY SPIRIT

It was midnight. All the prisoners were locked in their jail cells. Suddenly there was singing! Two prisoners, Paul and Silas, were singing praises to God. They had been beaten and thrown into jail because they were telling others about Jesus. How could Paul and Silas praise God at a time like this? They had joy inside. (Acts 16:16-40)

Joy is a fruit the Holy Spirit produces in your life when you allow Him to be in control. You can have joy even when things are not going well. This joy is not a happiness that comes and goes. It is a deep inner gladness and delight that you know God is faithful and keeps His promises.

Even when problems come, the Holy Spirit can produce joy in your life. Joy comes when you obey God and trust in His promises. God gives you joy and strength to handle problems. The Bible says, " . . . Do not grieve [be sad], for the joy of the LORD is your strength" (Nehemiah 8:10). When you remember that God is in control, you will have a song of joy in your heart. You will be able to praise God like Paul and Silas.

How can you have joy in your life even when things are not going well?

_____

_____

_____

You can pray:

 Dear God, thank You for the strength and joy You give to handle my problems. In Jesus' name. Amen.

76 How Can I Have Peace on the Inside?

> But the fruit of the Spirit is love, joy, peace, patience, kindness, goodness, faithfulness, gentleness and self-control.
> **Galatians 5:22**

Megan looked out the window. It was raining. "When will Mom get home?" she asked softly. Thoughts raced through her mind. *What if lightning strikes the house? What if Mom dies in a car accident?* Then Megan remembered her Grandmother's words. "Trust in the Lord and give Him your fears. Keep your thoughts on Him and He will give you peace."

Have you ever been afraid or worried? Jesus said, "Peace I leave with you; my peace I give you . . ." (John 14:27). When you trust in Jesus as your Savior, you have peace with God. Sin no longer makes you God's enemy. You have forgiveness because Christ paid for your sin when He died and came back to life. Jesus has become your peace.

Not only do you have peace with God, but you also have the peace of God. Peace is a fruit of the Spirit. It is an inner quietness in your heart and mind that comes as you trust God and keep your thoughts on Him. (Isaiah 26:3) When the Holy Spirit is in control, He produces peace in your life. When worries or fears come, you can pray to God and depend on Him to give you peace.

What should you do when worries or fears come into your life?

_____

_____

_____

You can pray:
Dear God, help me to keep my thoughts on You so the fruit of peace is produced in my life. In Jesus' name. Amen.

GOD THE HOLY SPIRIT

How Does the Holy Spirit Give Me Patience?

> But the fruit of the Spirit is love, joy, peace, patience, kindness, goodness, faithfulness, gentleness and self-control. **Galatians 5:22**

GOD THE HOLY SPIRIT

"Hurry up, I can't wait any longer." "Why is she taking so long?" "When will we get there?" Do you ever talk like this? Talking this way shows you do not have patience. Patience is the ability to go through hard or boring times calmly. It is being able to wait without getting restless or upset. If you have trusted in Jesus as your Savior, the Holy Spirit can produce the fruit of patience in your life.

Patience is produced as you wait for the Lord to work and allow the Holy Spirit to be in control. As you go through hard things in life, the Holy Spirit will give you strength to have patience. He will help you accept trouble or pain, even for a long time. God says, "Be joyful in hope, patient in affliction [trouble], faithful in prayer" (Romans 12:12). The Holy Spirit will also help you show patience to others who do wrong to you or are unkind.

The next time you find yourself thinking, *I can't wait any longer*, stop and pray. Thank God for the Holy Spirit who is living in you. Ask Him for the strength to show patience.

Write down a time when you have trouble being patient.

_____

_____

You can pray:

Dear God, I have trouble being patient when (name the situation). Please produce the fruit of patience in me. In Jesus' name. Amen.

Can the Holy Spirit Help Me to Be Kind?

But the fruit of the Spirit is love, joy, peace, patience, kindness, goodness, faithfulness, gentleness and self-control. **Galatians 5:22**

Jake sat all alone in the lunchroom. Ever since his father had gone to jail, the other boys made fun of him. They called him names. They said he would end up in jail, too. Their words hurt Jake. He wanted to say unkind words in return but knew that it would not be right.

It surprised Jake as Jerome sat down beside him. Jerome had made fun of him earlier that day. "Jake. I've been watching you," Jerome said. "You never get mad when we laugh at you. In fact, you are nice to us. I saw you help Desmond pick up the books he dropped the other day. What's with you?"

"Well," Jake said, "I know it pleases God when I am nice to others even when they are unkind to me." I'm a Christian, and God's Spirit living in me helps me to be kind."

God was producing the fruit of kindness in Jake's life. Instead of getting mad, he showed kindness. The Bible says, "Be kind and compassionate [caring] to one another, forgiving each other, just as in Christ God forgave you" (Ephesians 4:32). Are you letting God produce the fruit of kindness in your life?

GOD THE HOLY SPIRIT

Write something you can do to show kindness to someone else.

_____

_____

_____

You can pray:

Dear God, thank You for giving me strength to show kindness to someone today. In Jesus' name. Amen.

What Does It Mean to Be Good?

But the fruit of the Spirit is love, joy, peace, patience, kindness, goodness, faithfulness, gentleness and self-control. **Galatians 5:22**

GOD THE HOLY SPIRIT

"Wait up!" Jerome called as he ran towards Jake. "I didn't get my homework done. Can I copy yours?"

"Sorry." Jake answered, "That would be cheating."

Later as Jake was going out to recess, he saw Jerome sitting at his desk. Jake ran to talk with his teacher. Minutes later he walked up to Jerome's desk. "Mrs. Snow said I could help you learn your spelling words."

Yesterday Jake showed kindness to Jerome. Today he is showing the fruit of goodness. Goodness is doing what is right. Jake knew it was wrong to help Jerome cheat. He chose to do right. He was being good.

God is the only one who is perfectly good. God wants His children to be like Him. You should do good. The Bible says, "The good man brings good things out of the good stored up in his heart . . ." (Luke 6:45). When the Holy Spirit is in control, the fruit of goodness will show in your life.

Goodness is more than doing what is right. Goodness is shown in your words and actions. Jake decided to give up his recess and help Jerome. He spoke kind words. Goodness is love in action.

Write two ways you could show the fruit of goodness in your life.

_____

_____

_____

You can pray:

Dear God, thank You for being good to me. Help me to be good in all I think, say and do. In Jesus' name. Amen.

How Can the Holy Spirit Help Me to Be Faithful?

But the fruit of the Spirit is love, joy, peace, patience, kindness, goodness, faithfulness, gentleness and self-control . . .
Galatians 5:22-23

Do you keep your promises? A faithful person is someone you can depend on and who keeps his promises. God always keeps His promises. He is faithful. When you trust the Lord Jesus Christ as your Savior, His Holy Spirit wants to produce the fruit of faithfulness in your life. Faithfulness means to be true to God in your thoughts, words and actions. The Bible says, "The one [God] who calls you is faithful and he will do it" (1 Thessalonians 5:24).

As God develops the fruit of faithfulness in your life, others will see it in what you do and say. They will notice that you keep your promises. They know that you do things on time and to the best of your ability. They will notice that you put God first in everything you do. Most importantly, God will notice your faithfulness and He will be pleased. When God sees that you are faithful with a few things, He will put you in charge of many things (Matthew 25:21).

When you keep your promises, you are allowing the fruit of faithfulness to be seen in your life. Will you be someone others depend on and trust?

List three ways the Holy Spirit can help you be faithful.

_____

_____

_____

You can pray:

Dear God, thank You for Your faithfulness to me. Help me be faithful to You and others in my life. In Jesus' name. Amen.

GOD THE HOLY SPIRIT

Am I a Gentle Person?

But the fruit of the Spirit is love, joy, peace, patience, kindness, goodness, faithfulness, gentleness and self-control . . . **Galatians 5:22-23**

GOD THE HOLY SPIRIT

Chris was a gentle person. He was kind and respectful of others. He did nice things for people whenever he could. He didn't allow anger to control his words and actions. Do you think Chris had many friends? Yes! People enjoy being around a gentle person.

Gentleness is treating others with love, kindness and respect because you appreciate them and understand their needs. When you allow the Holy Spirit to be in control, He produces the fruit of gentleness in your life. You may think that gentleness is being weak, but it's not. It shows great inner strength.

Jesus showed gentleness many times when He lived on earth. He accepted and helped many people who others rejected. He welcomed children, showed kindness to the poor and healed the sick. Jesus' life is an example of how you should show gentleness to others.

When you say, "Excuse me," "Please" and "Thank you," you show gentleness. When you quietly do kind things for others, you show gentleness. When you respond to people with gentle words instead of being rude or shouting angrily, you show gentleness. God tells us in the Bible, "Let your gentleness be evident [shown] to all . . ." (Philippians 4:5). Will you respond to others with gentleness?

What are some ways you can show gentleness to someone today?

_____

_____

You can pray:

Dear God, thank You for Jesus Christ who shows me how to be gentle. Please help me to be gentle with others. In Jesus' name. Amen.

How Can the Holy Spirit Help Me to Control Myself?

But the fruit of the Spirit is love, joy, peace, patience, kindness, goodness, faithfulness, gentleness and self-control . . .
Galatians 5:22-23

Have you ever watched a star athlete receive a medal or trophy? What did the athlete do to win? He trained hard. He disciplined himself. He spent many hours getting his body under control.

The Bible compares the Christian life to running a race (1 Corinthians 9:24-27). If you are God's child, your spiritual life needs a workout. Exercising self-control is like training to be a spiritual star athlete.

Self-control means staying in charge of your thoughts, feelings and actions instead of them controlling you. It is being disciplined. The Bible says, " . . . but let us be alert and self-controlled" (1 Thessalonians 5:6).

The Holy Spirit living in you can produce the fruit of self-control in your life. Through His power, you can have self-control in what you eat. He can help you have self-control in what you say or do. Your thoughts and the things you look at can be under His control. When He is in control, instead of getting angry and losing your temper, you respond with gentleness. Will you be a spiritual star athlete by allowing the Holy Spirit to produce the fruit of self-control in your life?

GOD THE HOLY SPIRIT

When are some times that you need the Holy Spirit to give you self-control?

_____

_____

You can pray:

Dear God, thank You for the Holy Spirit's power to give me self-control. Please produce this fruit in my life each day. In Jesus' name. Amen.

What Are Spiritual Gifts?

 You are the body of Christ, and each one of you is a part of it. **1 Corinthians 12:27**

If you have trusted the Lord Jesus as your Savior, you are part of the Body (family) of Christ. The Bible says, "You are the Body of Christ, and each one of you is a part of it" (1 Corinthians 12:27). Each member of God's family is special. He has given each one at least one special gift. It is not a natural talent, like the ability to play an instrument or be a star athlete. It is a spiritual gift. This gift is given to you by God to help you serve Him and others in the Body of Christ.

We all have times when we need help. Sometimes we feel sad or discouraged or have physical problems. As members of the Body of Christ, we all need to work together and look after each other. We can use our spiritual gifts in many ways to meet each others' needs.

Some of the spiritual gifts God gives are helping, giving, showing mercy, teaching and leading. In the next few devotionals, you will learn more about these spiritual gifts. You'll also learn how to discover what your gifts are and how to use them for God.

 Why does the Holy Spirit give each Christian a spiritual gift?

_____

_____

_____

You can pray:

 Dear God, thank You for giving Your children spiritual gifts. Help me to learn what my gift is, and to use it to help others. In Jesus' name. Amen.

Do I Have a Spiritual Gift?

You are the body of Christ, and each one of you is a part of it.
1 Corinthians 12:27

When you choose a gift for someone, you think about what that person is like. The better you know the person, the better you know the right gift to give. God knows you best of all. He made you! His plan for you is to serve Him and build up the Body of Christ. To help you fulfill God's plan, the Holy Spirit gave you at least one spiritual gift. How do you know what your spiritual gift is?

Once you know what the spiritual gifts are, you need to pray and ask God to show you what gift (or gifts) He has given to you. Then, as you are serving God, notice what you are good at. What do you enjoy doing the most? These things are evidence that God has most likely given you spiritual gifts in these areas. Also, others may point out to you areas where God is using you in a special way.

Pay special attention to the next few devotionals. See if you can identify your spiritual gifts among those mentioned. Ask God to help you discover your spiritual gift and how you can best use it to serve Him.

GOD THE HOLY SPIRIT

How can you know what your spiritual gift is?

_____

_____

_____

You can pray:

Dear God, thank You for giving me a spiritual gift. Help me to learn what it is and to be willing to use it to serve You and others. In Jesus' name. Amen.

What Is the Gift of Serving?

You are the body of Christ, and each one of you is a part of it. **1 Corinthians 12:27**

GOD THE HOLY SPIRIT

Trisha likes to help. Without being asked, she runs to help her mother bring in the groceries from the car. At school, she helps the teacher put away books. At church, she picks up the papers left in the benches and throws them away. Trisha has trusted in the Lord Jesus Christ as her Savior. The Holy Spirit has given her the spiritual gift of serving.

Serving is one of the spiritual gifts the Holy Spirit gives God's children. Spiritual gifts are used to help others who are in the Body of Christ. Serving is the ability to see jobs that need to be done and to do them. People with the gift of serving help in a way that frees others to use their own gift for the Lord.

Do you like to help others? When you see a need, do you often help without being asked? If you have answered "yes", you may have the gift of serving. The Bible says, "Serve wholeheartedly [willingly], as if you were serving the Lord, not men" (Ephesians 6:7). If you have the gift of serving, will you use it to help others in the Body of Christ?

How can you tell if someone has the gift of serving?

_____

_____

_____

You can pray:

Dear Lord, please show me my spiritual gift. If I have the gift of serving, help me use it to help others in the body of Christ. In Jesus' name. Amen.

What Is the Gift of Giving?

You are the body of Christ, and each one of you is a part of it.
1 Corinthians 12:27

Austin knocked on the door of Mr. Young's house. Mr. Young opened the door and smiled at him. "What can I do for you today, Austin?" Mr. Young asked.

"I was wondering if you have any jobs I could do to earn some extra money?" Austin replied. "There's a new kid at school named Todd. He only has one pair of shoes, and they are full of holes. I want to earn some money to buy him a new pair."

"That's so nice of you!" Mr. Young replied. "I think I can find something for you to do."

Austin saw that Todd had a need and wanted to give to meet this need. Austin has the spiritual gift of giving. You do not need lots of money to have the gift of giving. You can use your time and talents to give to others. Austin was willing to give his time and talents to earn money for Todd's new shoes.

The Bible says, "We have different gifts . . . If [a person's gift] is contributing [giving] to the needs of others, let him give generously [joyfully]" (Romans 12:6, 8). If you have the gift of giving, will you give joyfully?

GOD THE HOLY SPIRIT

Write two things, besides money, that you could give.

_____

_____

You can pray:

Dear God, please show me my spiritual gift. If I have the gift of giving, help me to give joyfully to meet the needs of others. In Jesus' name. Amen.

What Is the Gift of Mercy?

You are the body of Christ, and each one of you is a part of it. **1 Corinthians 12:27**

GOD THE HOLY SPIRIT

Kim could tell that something was wrong with Ann. She walked over to where Ann was sitting and sat beside her. "Is there something wrong?" Kim asked. "My grandma is very sick," Ann said. "God can help," Kim encouraged her. "Let's talk to Him right now." The two girls bowed their heads and Kim prayed.

If you are quick to sense the hurts of others, you may have the spiritual gift of mercy (showing kindness). This gift of the Spirit causes you to comfort a friend who gets a bad grade or loses a pet. If you have the gift of mercy, you quickly offer help and pray for others.

People with the gift of mercy comfort others in a way that gives them strength to go on. The Holy Spirit living in you gives you wisdom to use this gift. The Bible says, "But the wisdom that comes from heaven is . . . full of mercy . . ." (James 3:17). Since people with this gift want to help, the Spirit can also give wisdom not to do things for others they should do for themselves. If you feel you have the gift of mercy, ask God to use you to help others who are hurting.

List two ways that show that someone has the gift of mercy.

_____

_____

_____

You can pray:

Dear God, please show me my spiritual gift. If I have the gift of mercy, give me wisdom to use it to comfort others. In Jesus' name. Amen.

What Is the Gift of Teaching?

You are the body of Christ, and each one of you is a part of it.
1 Corinthians 12:27

After his teacher had given an assignment, Terrance asked to use the computer. He could hardly wait to search for the answers himself. Whenever Terrance learned something new, he was eager to share it with his friends. Terrance has the spiritual gift of teaching.

Teaching is another spiritual gift given by the Holy Spirit. If you find yourself asking questions like, "Why?" or "Is this correct?" you may have the gift of teaching. People with this gift like to search for answers for themselves. When they find the answer, they enjoy sharing what they learned with others.

If you have the gift of teaching, you will want to know if something is true or not. You will want to learn more about God's Word and share what you learned with others. One day, you might become a teacher of God's Word! The Bible says, "We have different gifts . . . if [a person's gift] is teaching, let him teach" (Romans 12:6, 7).

Each person who trusts in the Lord Jesus as his Savior receives at least one spiritual gift. These gifts are used to help others in the Body of Christ. If your gift is teaching, will you use it to help others learn more about God?

How can you tell if someone has the gift of teaching?

_____

_____

_____

You can pray:

Dear God, please show me my spiritual gift. If I have the gift of teaching, help me use it so others can learn more about you. In Jesus' name. Amen.

GOD THE HOLY SPIRIT

What Is the Gift of Leading? 89

You are the body of Christ, and each one of you is a part of it. **1 Corinthians 12:27**

GOD THE HOLY SPIRIT

"Mom!" Ryan called as he ran into the house. "My teacher made me the leader of our class project!" Ryan's mother smiled. "That's great!" she said. "You'll make a good leader."

Do you like to be in charge of projects? Are you quick to come up with a plan to get a job done? Is it easy for you to get others involved so they can help, too? If you have answered "yes," you may have the spiritual gift of leading.

The Bible tells us that the Holy Spirit gives different gifts. It says, " . . . if [a person's gift] is leadership, let him govern diligently" (Romans 12:7). To govern diligently means to lead carefully–to do your best and not quit.

The church needs people with the gift of leading to serve the Lord Jesus Christ. People with this gift are not afraid to stand alone for something they believe is right. Leaders are people who come up with a plan and get things done. A good leader does not stand back and give orders but gets involved and helps with the job. If you have the gift of leading, ask God to help you use it to serve the Body of Christ.

List three ways that show you that someone has the gift of leading.

_____

_____

_____

You can pray:

Dear God, please show me my spiritual gift. If I have the gift of leading, help me to use it to serve the body of Christ. In Jesus' name. Amen.

How Can I Use My Spiritual Gift**?**

You are the body of Christ, and each one of you is a part of it.
1 Corinthians 12:27

As you have been reading about some of the spiritual gifts, have you discovered your gifts? The Bible says that spiritual gifts are given "to prepare God's people for works of service, so that the Body of Christ may be built up" (Ephesians 4:12). Let's review the gifts you've been reading about:

Serving – Seeing jobs that need to be done and doing them.

Giving – Finding joy in giving to others.

Mercy – Noticing when others are hurting and comforting them.

Teaching – Enjoying the study of God's Word and helping others understand it.

Leading – Organizing others and helping them get a job done.

Are you like Trisha, who enjoys serving others? Maybe you're like Austin, who gave to help a friend in need. Perhaps you're like Kim, who was quick to comfort a friend who was hurting. Are you like Terrance? He has the gift of teaching and enjoyed sharing what he learned with others. Maybe you're like Ryan, who liked being in charge of a project and getting it done.

Will you use your spiritual gift to build up others in the Body of Christ? God will bless you and give you joy as you use your gift for Him.

GOD THE HOLY SPIRIT

List the spiritual gifts you feel you have.

_____

_____

You can pray:

Dear God, thank You for giving me the spiritual gift of (list the gifts you feel you have). Help me to use them to serve You and others. In Jesus' name. Amen.

THE MEMORY ZONE

Here are some great Bible verses about what you've learned so far. Put a check mark in the box as you memorize each one!

☐ **1 John 1:9** "If we confess our sins, he is faithful and just and will forgive us our sins and purify us from all unrighteousness."

☐ **Psalm 32:8** "I will instruct you and teach you in the way you should go; I will counsel you and watch over you."

☐ **Psalm 66:18** "If I had cherished sin in my heart, the Lord would not have listened."

☐ **John 14:26** "But the Counselor, the Holy Spirit, whom the Father will send in my name, will teach you all things and will remind you of everything I have said to you."

☐ **2 Corinthians 5:17** "Therefore, if anyone is in Christ, he is a new creation; the old has gone, the new has come!"

☐ **Ephesians 4:30** "And do not grieve the Holy Spirit of God, with whom you were sealed for the day of redemption."

☐ **Luke 6:45** "The good man brings good things out of the good stored up in his heart, and the evil man brings evil things out of the evil stored up in his heart. For out of the overflow of his heart his mouth speaks."

☐ **Ephesians 4:3** "Make every effort to keep the unity of the Spirit through the bond of peace."

This is the end of the section of "God the Holy Spirit" devotionals.

It is time to do the next activity sheet that came in the mail. Remember to add your prayer request so your mailbox friend can pray for you. When you finish the whole page, fold it on the lines so the Mailbox Club address shows. Put a small piece of tape on the bottom to keep it folded. Add a stamp and mail your activity page.

Your work will be marked and sent back to you, along with a personal note. The activity sheet for the next set of lessons will be sent to you, too.

Enjoy getting to know God better with your next group of devotionals!

Victory!

Are Angels Real?

Be self-controlled and alert. Your enemy the devil prowls around like a roaring lion looking for someone to devour.
1 Peter 5:8

Have you ever watched a movie or TV program about angels? Do you wonder if they are real? Most of what you see in the movies or on TV about angels is not true. However, it is true that God made angels, and they are very real.

Angels are special creations of God and each one is different. We don't know exactly what angels look like. We do know they are not people—people who die don't become angels. We do know that some angels have wings and some look like us. God made these wonderful, strong, heavenly creatures to worship, praise, obey and serve Him. Angels also watch over God's children. Angels are more powerful than men, but not as powerful as God. Angels can appear and disappear very quickly. They do not die. Some people pray to angels, but that is wrong. Only God can answer prayers.

One angel, named Lucifer, was called an angel of light. At some time Lucifer turned against God. Now we call him Satan—the devil. Some of the angels followed Satan. They are called "fallen angels" or demons. Satan and his demons are God's enemies. They are also the enemies of God's people. In the next few days, you'll learn more about your enemy, Satan.

VICTORY

What are two things you learned about angels?

_____

_____

_____

You can pray:

Dear God, thank You for creating angels to serve and obey You. In Jesus' name. Amen.

Who Is Satan?

92

VICTORY

Be self-controlled and alert. Your enemy the devil prowls around like a roaring lion looking for someone to devour. **1 Peter 5:8**

Some people think Satan wears a red suit and has horns and a tail. That is not what he looks like. The Bible tells us that when God first made him he was one of the most beautiful angels. He was called Lucifer. He probably watched as God made the first man and woman. One terrible day he chose to turn against God and become His enemy. He became Satan.

The Bible calls Satan "the god of this world" (2 Corinthians 4:4). He is completely bad and evil. His plan is to trick people.

He wants them to turn against God like he did. He wants to ruin God's plan for you. It may seem that Satan can do whatever he wants. But he is still under the control of God, who is all-powerful. When Jesus returns to Earth, Satan will be punished. When the judgment is over, Satan will be thrown into the lake of fire where he will stay forever.

Satan wants you to think he is just a pretend character in a funny red suit. Remember, he is real, and he is your enemy. But the Bible says, " . . . the one who is in you [God] is greater than the one who is in the world [Satan]."

Why is Satan God's enemy?

_____

_____

_____

You can pray:

Dear God, thank You that You are more powerful than Satan. Help me to be careful not to be tricked by Satan, but to obey You. In Jesus' name. Amen.

93 How Did Satan Become God's Enemy?

Be self-controlled and alert. Your enemy the devil prowls around like a roaring lion looking for someone to devour.
1 Peter 5:8

"I will do what I want, not what you want me to do." Have you ever said or thought something like that? Do you know where that sort of thought comes from?

One day Lucifer, God's special angel, had that thought. He decided he wanted to be like God. His thoughts may have been, "I will put my throne above the stars of God. I will be higher than the clouds. I will make myself like God" (Isaiah 14:12-14). Do you hear the words, "I will?" Only God could truly speak with that authority because only God is all-powerful.

What caused Lucifer to turn against his Creator? It was pride. Pride is thinking more highly of yourself than you should. Lucifer thought he was as good as God. His sinful pride separated him from God. When Lucifer rebelled, God had to separate Himself from Lucifer. Lucifer and his angel followers had to leave Heaven. Now Lucifer is known by a different name—Satan or the devil. He is God's enemy, and he is your enemy.

The Bible says, " . . . God opposes [goes against] the proud . . ." (1 Peter 5:5). Don't let pride take control of you and turn you away from God. Remember that God is your Creator. Worship and obey Him only.

How can you guard against pride taking control of your life?

_____

_____

_____

You can pray:

Dear God, thank You for being my great Creator. Help me to guard against pride that would turn me against You. In Jesus' name. Amen.

VICTORY

Why Is Satan My Enemy?

Be self-controlled and alert. Your enemy the devil prowls around like a roaring lion looking for someone to devour. **1 Peter 5:8**

What does the word enemy mean? An enemy is someone who hates you and wants to hurt you. Satan hates God and wants to hurt Him. Because you are God's child, Satan hates you and wants to hurt you, too. He wants to destroy everything that belongs to God.

Satan shows that he is your enemy in many ways. He lies to you. The Bible says he is "the father of lies" (John 8:44). He tries to trick you into doing wrong things so you will disappoint God. He tries to get you to sin against God. What does the Bible verse at the top of this page tell you about Satan? He is your enemy; he prowls around like a lion looking for someone to devour (destroy).

Is Satan always successful in finding someone to destroy? Does Satan always win? No! You can escape the danger and guard against Satan's attacks. When you obey God, Satan loses. If you have trusted Jesus as your Savior, you have God's Holy Spirit living in you. God is greater than Satan. When you let the Holy Spirit control you, you will obey God and do what is right. You need to be alert, listening to God and watching out for Satan's attacks.

What are two things you can do to guard against Satan's attacks?

_____

_____

_____

You can pray:

Dear God, thank You for loving me. Please help me to listen to You and to watch out for Satan's attacks. In Jesus' name. Amen.

What Are Some of Satan's Tricks?

Be self-controlled and alert. Your enemy the devil prowls around like a roaring lion looking for someone to devour.
1 Peter 5:8

"Come on Jeron! All you have to do is watch for the store clerk," Sam said. "You don't have to take anything. You won't be stealing. You are just watching. If you want to be my friend you will help me." Sam didn't care about being Jeron's friend. He just wanted to trick Jeron into helping him do wrong.

Satan doesn't want you to love and obey God. He tries to trick you into doing wrong things. One of his tricks is to tell you the lie that you won't have any friends if you don't do drugs or drink. Another of his tricks is to get you to want new things so much that you would do something wrong to get them. Have you ever thought that God isn't real? Have you ever thought that God doesn't really love you? Those are other lies that Satan tells.

Satan would like to trick you into believing that Jesus did not die on the cross to pay for your sins. Satan doesn't want you to know how much God loves you. He wants you to believe you can take care of yourself and don't need Jesus. Watch out for Satan's tricks. Remember that he is a liar.

VICTORY

Can you think of one way Satan has tried to trick you?

_____

_____

_____

You can pray:

Dear God, please help me to see when Satan is trying to trick me. Help me to believe Your Word instead. In Jesus' name. Amen.

Is Satan As Powerful As God?

> Be self-controlled and alert. Your enemy the devil prowls around like a roaring lion looking for someone to devour.
> **1 Peter 5:8**

V I C T O R Y

Satan is very powerful. He is more powerful than we are. Who do you think has more power, God or Satan? God made the world in six days. God made our bodies. God raised Jesus from the dead. Satan cannot do anything like that. God is much more powerful than Satan.

However, Satan has power. His attacks on God's people are powerful and hard to fight, but Satan is not as powerful as God. Satan tried with all of his might to stop Jesus from paying for your sins. He may have thought he had won when Jesus died on the cross. People took Jesus' body from the cross and buried Him. But, on the third day, God raised Jesus back to life again! God is always the winner over Satan.

God is sovereign. He is the highest ruler, and He is always in control. Our God is above all and rules over all; He has all power. God has the power to hear and answer your prayers. Only He has the power to forgive your sins and make you His child. God even has control over Satan. One day God will punish Satan by putting him and his followers into the lake of fire forever.

 What are three things that show you God's power?

_____

_____

_____

 ### You can pray:

Dear God, thank You that You are more powerful than Satan. Thank You for loving me. In Jesus' name. Amen.

97 Why Does God Allow Satan to Tempt Me?

Be self-controlled and alert. Your enemy the devil prowls around like a roaring lion looking for someone to devour.
1 Peter 5:8

Think of your very best friend. Do you love that person because you have to or because you want to? Love is something you choose to give.

God chose to love you, and He wants you to choose to love Him. When God allows Satan to tempt you (try to get you to disobey), He is allowing you to choose who you will love and serve. God wants you to obey Him because you love Him.

One of the ways you obey God is by saying "no" when Satan tempts you to do something wrong. You can't do that by yourself—you need God's help. That is another reason why God allows you to be tempted. He wants you to learn to depend on Him to give you strength to say "no" to Satan. The Bible says, " . . . The Lord is my helper . . ." (Hebrews 13:6). You can ask God to help you be a winner over Satan's temptations.

When you ask God for help and you obey Him, you get to know Him better. The better you know someone, the more you love him. God wants you to choose to love Him. Do you?

What are two reasons why God allows Satan to tempt you?

_____

_____

_____

You can pray:

Dear God, please help me to say "no" to Satan's temptations. Help me to show that I love You by obeying You. In Jesus' name. Amen.

Can I Really Win over Satan?

 Be self-controlled and alert. Your enemy the devil prowls around like a roaring lion looking for someone to devour.
1 Peter 5:8

V I C T O R Y

If you were in a battle with a very strong enemy all by yourself, do you think you could win? No! However, if you were in a battle with that same enemy and had the biggest and the strongest helper, could you win? Yes!

The Bible tells us about a man who lived a long time ago. His name was Elijah. One day, God asked Elijah to do something very scary. God asked Elijah to go to the king and tell him God was going to punish all the people because they were do-ing very bad things. The people were serving Satan, not God. The king got very angry and tried to kill Elijah, but Elijah escaped. Elijah continued living and serving God. How did that happen? What made it possible for Elijah to win? He didn't have any super power. The Bible says he was just like you and me. He won because he had God on his side. If you know Jesus as your Savior, He is on your side, too. When you have Jesus, the Bible says, " . . . the one who is in you [Jesus] is greater than the one who is in the world [Satan]" (1 John 4:4). With Jesus you can win.

 What made it possible for Elijah to win?

_____

_____

_____

 You can pray:

Dear God, thank You that because of Jesus I can win over Satan. In Jesus' name. Amen.

What Is God's Battle Plan for Me?

Be self-controlled and alert. Your enemy the devil prowls around like a roaring lion looking for someone to devour. **1 Peter 5:8**

Soldiers need a battle plan to tell them the best way to fight. God has a battle plan for you. You are in a war every day because Satan hates you. It is a war you can win because you have the biggest and strongest helper—God. If you follow God's battle plan, you will win.

Here's the plan. It has four parts: (1) Believe Jesus died for your sins. (2) Remember you don't have to sin. God says, if you will obey Him and refuse to listen to the devil, Satan will run away from you (James 4:7). (3) Obey God. Sin makes God sad and it can keep God from hearing your prayers. If you do sin, you need to confess your sin to God. (4) Thank God for victory over Satan. The Bible says, "But thanks be to God! He gives us the victory through our Lord Jesus Christ" (1 Corinthians 15:57).

God has given you special protection in your battle against Satan. It's called the armor of God. This armor can't be seen, but it defends you against Satan's attacks. If you use it correctly, God will help you to defeat Satan in every battle. You'll read more about this armor in the next few days.

VICTORY

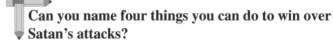

Can you name four things you can do to win over Satan's attacks?

_____

_____

_____

You can pray:

Dear God, thank You that You are my helper. Please help me to remember how to win over Satan. In Jesus' name. Amen.

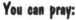

What Must I Do Before I Can Have Victory over Satan?

 Put on the full armor of God so that you can take your stand against the devil's schemes. **Ephesians 6:11**

V
I
C
T
O
R
Y

Do you want to be a winner (have the victory)? Before you can have victory over Satan, you need to receive Jesus as your Savior.

The Bible says, "Yet to all who received him, to those who believed in His name, he gave the right to become children of God" (John 1:12). You receive Him (Jesus) by admitting you have sinned. You were born with a "want to" to sin. You sin when you lie, steal, hurt someone or even think bad things. Everyone sins (Romans 3:23), and God must punish sin. The pun-

ishment for sin is to be away from God forever.

What does it mean to believe in His name? It means you believe that Jesus is God and never sinned. He died on the cross to be punished for your sins. He died willingly because He loves you. Jesus did not stay dead; on the third day He came alive again. He is in Heaven now, praying for you. You receive Him by telling God you have sinned. Tell Him you believe Jesus was punished for your sins. Ask Him to forgive you. Then, you become God's child. Once you are God's child, you can begin to have victory over Satan.

 What does it mean to receive Jesus as your Savior?

_____

_____

_____

You can pray:

 Dear God, I have sinned. I believe Jesus died to take the punishment for my sins. Please forgive me and make me Your child. In Jesus' name. Amen.

101

How Can I Be Prepared for the Battle?

Put on the full armor of God so that you can take your stand against the devil's schemes. **Ephesians 6:11**

Every day you are in a battle against Satan. He hates God and wants you to sin against Him. You need to be prepared for the battle, because you can't win over Satan in your own strength.

An important part of being prepared for the battle is to confess your sins to God. God is with you to help you say "no" to sin. However, sometimes you don't accept His help. Sometimes Satan tricks you into sinning. And sometimes you just choose to sin. Whenever you realize you have sinned, you should confess that sin to God. That means agree with God that what you did was sin. The Bible says, "If we confess our sins, He is faithful and just and will forgive us our sins . . ." (1 John 1:9).

Another important part of being prepared for battle is to watch out for Satan's attacks. He always looks for ways to cause you to sin. Be careful to avoid places, people or things that often tempt you to sin.

To be strong for the battle, you need to spend time with God each day. Reading His Word and praying will strengthen you against Satan's attacks.

VICTORY

How can you be prepared for your battle against Satan?

_____

_____

_____

You can pray:

Dear God, help me to remember to confess my sins and to watch out for Satan's attacks so I will be ready for battle. In Jesus' name. Amen.

What Is the Armor of God?

Put on the full armor of God so that you can take your stand against the devil's schemes. **Ephesians 6:11**

VICTORY

Do you know what armor is? Maybe you've seen suits of armor that soldiers used to wear into battle. Police officers today also wear armor to protect them–bullet proof vests and helmets. Firemen wear helmets and heavy coats and boots as protective armor.

If you know Jesus as your Savior, God has given you armor to protect you in your battle against Satan. You can't see this armor–it's invisible. But it is described in the Bible in Ephesians 6:13-17. The "helmet of salvation" protects your mind. The "breastplate of righteousness" protects your heart so that you will do what's right. The "belt of truth" helps you to learn God's Word and to tell the truth. The "shoes of the Gospel of peace" help you stand firm in your battle with Satan. The "shield of faith" protects you from Satan's attacks that would cause you to doubt God. The "sword of the Spirit" is the Word of God. It is your weapon against Satan.

The armor God has given you will never wear out or break. In the next few days, we will talk more about what each piece of the armor means and how it can help you.

Why is the armor of God important to you?

_____

_____

_____

You can pray:

Dear God, thank You for giving me Your armor so I can win when Satan attacks me. In Jesus' name. Amen.

163 Why Do I Need God's Armor?

Put on the full armor of God so that you can take your stand against the devil's schemes. **Ephesians 6:11**

Why would someone need armor? Armor is designed to protect something. A soccer goalie wears armor–shin guards to protect his legs. A baseball catcher wears armor–a mask and chest guard so he won't be hurt if the ball hits him. Did you know that Christians need armor, too?

Christians need armor to protect us from Satan's attacks. Satan is God's enemy. Because you are God's child by trusting in Jesus as your Savior, Satan is your enemy, too. The Bible says that Satan is sneaking around looking for someone to destroy (1 Peter 5:8). There are many ways Satan tries to destroy you. He attacks your mind, tempting you to believe his lies and doubt God's love and care. He attacks your heart, tempting you to do things your own way instead of God's way.

You are not strong enough to fight against Satan yourself. God knows that, so besides giving you His armor, He has promised to be your helper. The Bible says, "The Lord is my helper; I will not be afraid" (Hebrews 13:6). A good soldier knows that without his armor the enemy can destroy him. You need God's armor for your protection.

VICTORY

What are two things God has given to help you win against Satan?

_____

_____

_____

You can pray:

Dear God, help me to remember I have Your armor and You as my helper. In Jesus' name. Amen.

How Do I Use the Belt of Truth? 164

Put on the full armor of God so that you can take your stand against the devil's schemes. **Ephesians 6:11**

V I C T O R Y

We have talked about your enemy, Satan, and his attacks. God has given you armor for protection, but armor won't help you unless you use it. For the next few days, we're going to talk about each piece of the armor and how it can help you.

One of the pieces of armor God has given you is the "belt of truth." This important piece helps you to know what is true and not to be fooled by Satan's lies. How do you use the belt of truth? There are two ways: First, you use the belt of truth by learning as much as you can from God's Word. You can do this by reading the Bible and memorizing Bible verses from this devotional book. Remembering truths from God's Word will help you when Satan tempts you to doubt God.

Another way to use the belt of truth is to be sure that you are always truthful in everything you do. One of Satan's names is the "father of lies." Satan is happy when you tell even a small lie. The belt of truth will protect you against Satan's temptations to lie. God can help you remember to use the belt of truth each day.

Name two ways to use the belt of truth.

_____

_____

_____

You can pray:

Dear God, please help me to use my belt of truth every day by reading Your Word and telling the truth. In Jesus' name. Amen.

165 What Is the Breastplate of Righteousness?

Put on the full armor of God so that you can take your stand against the devil's schemes. **Ephesians 6:11**

One of the most important parts of the body that a soldier must protect in battle is his heart. As a child of God, you also need protection for your heart. Not the organ in your body that keeps you alive, but your feelings, attitudes and emotions. For this reason, God has given you the breastplate of righteousness.

Righteousness is a big word. It means being right before God and doing right. None of us is perfect or righteous all the time. But, since you trusted Jesus as your Savior, God no longer sees you as a sinner. He sees you through His perfect Son, Jesus, who died for your sin.

Satan may try to attack you by reminding you of your sin. He wants you to think that God rejects you. When you have your breastplate of righteousness on, you know Satan is lying. God says in the Bible, "I have loved you with an everlasting [forever] love" (Jeremiah 31:3).

Living the right way is a protection to you, just like a shield. Only God can help you have a right attitude and the strength to do right. Choosing God's way–being truthful, obedient and kind–shows that you are using the breastplate of righteousness.

VICTORY

How do you use the breastplate of righteousness?

_____

_____

_____

You can pray:

Dear God, thank You for the breastplate of righteousness that helps me have right attitudes and to do the right thing. In Jesus' name. Amen.

Why Do I Need the Helmet of Salvation?

Put on the full armor of God so that you can take your stand against the devil's schemes. **Ephesians 6:11**

V
I
C
T
O
R
Y

What do motorcycle riders, skateboarders and soldiers all wear to protect their heads? Yes, a helmet. As God's child, your head needs protection, too–especially your mind.

Satan wants to attack your mind and lead you away from God. He may put wrong thoughts in your mind like, "I hate you!" or "Nobody loves me." Satan can use things like TV, music, or the Internet to put wrong thoughts in your mind. That is why you need to use your helmet of salvation. It helps you to believe God's promise that you are saved from the punishment of your sin. It also gives you confidence that God can guard your mind from Satan's attacks.

How do you use the helmet of salvation? When you read your Bible and think about good things, you are using your helmet to guard your mind. Be careful what enters your mind–what you think about, read, watch and listen to. The Bible tells you to "take captive [guard] every thought" (2 Corinthians 10:5). You need the helmet of salvation to help you choose right things to look at and listen to. Remember that God is more powerful than Satan. Use your helmet and trust God to guard your thoughts!

How will you use the helmet of salvation today?

_____

_____

_____

You can pray:

Dear God, thank You for the helmet of salvation that guards my mind. Please help me choose good things to look at and listen to. In Jesus' name. Amen.

167 What Are the Shoes of the Gospel of Peace?

Put on the full armor of God so that you can take your stand against the devil's schemes. **Ephesians 6:11**

Firefighters wear special shoes to protect their feet. These shoes are made of rubber, and they have metal inside for extra protection. They also have sturdy soles to keep them from slipping on wet floors.

Special shoes are part of the armor God has given you. Satan, wants you to slip and fall. He wants you to worry about whether you truly belong to God. He doesn't want you to tell others about Jesus or to let them see God's peace in your life. That's why you need to use the shoes of the Gospel of peace every day!

Peace is a calm and quietness on the inside. It is a steady confidence that everything is okay. The Bible says that ". . . he [Jesus] himself is our peace . . ." (Ephesians 2:14). You have peace with God when you trust Jesus as your Savior. God also gives you peace with yourself because He helps you to see yourself as He sees you. You are loved by Him, forgiven and accepted into His family! In addition, God gives you peace with others. He helps you to share His love with others. Are you using your special shoes today?

V I C T O R Y

What will the shoes of the Gospel of peace do for you?

_____

_____

_____

You can pray:

Dear God, thank You for the shoes of the Gospel of peace. Help me to use them every day so that I can share Your peace and love with others. In Jesus' name. Amen.

How Do I Use the Shield of Faith? 168

Put on the full armor of God so that you can take your stand against the devil's schemes. **Ephesians 6:11**

VICTORY

Soldiers from years ago often went into battle carrying a shield. Usually the shields were large and heavy. They covered almost every part of the soldier's body to protect against the enemy's arrows. The sides of the shield were often made to hook together with the shields of other soldiers. The soldiers could join together to form a wall of protection against the enemy.

If you are God's child, He has given you a shield of protection against the attacks of Satan. It's called the shield of faith. Faith is believing that what God says, He will do. Faith is also acting on what you believe, even when you have doubts. Satan is constantly firing arrows of doubt at you. He wants you to doubt God's promises, doubt God's faithfulness, doubt God's goodness and doubt God's power.

You need to hold your shield of faith up high by trusting God's Word. Trust the truths you know about God. Trust the words you have memorized from the Bible. Even when things seem to be going wrong, trust that God is with you and is in control of everything. Like soldiers, join together with your Christian friends. You can encourage each other to stand strong.

What are two ways you can use your shield of faith?

_____

_____

_____

You can pray:
Dear God, thank You for my shield of faith. Help me to trust You, no matter what. In Jesus' name, Amen.

169 What Is the Sword of the Spirit?

Put on the full armor of God so that you can take your stand against the devil's schemes. **Ephesians 6:11**

**V
I
C
T
O
R
Y**

Do you know what a sword is? It's like a huge knife. It was a weapon with sharp edges that could cut and stab the enemy. All the rest of your armor is something you put on to protect yourself. Your sword is a weapon you use to attack your enemy. The sword of the Spirit is the Word of God.

The Lord Jesus used the sword of the Spirit when Satan attacked Him. Three times Satan came and tried to get Jesus to sin. Each time, Jesus quoted words from the Bible. Satan finally went away.

You can use your sword when Satan tries to get you to sin. You need to be learning verses from the Bible by memory. If you don't have a Bible, learn some of the verses in this devotional book. God's Holy Spirit, will bring these verses to your mind when Satan tempts you to sin. These verses will help you remember what God wants you to do–or what He doesn't want you to do. Each time you remember and use a verse from God's Word, you are becoming skillful in using your powerful weapon, and keeping Satan far away.

How can you use the sword of the Spirit?

_____

_____

_____

You can pray:

Dear God, please help me to memorize at least one Bible verse each week so I will be able to use the sword of the Spirit to keep Satan away. In Jesus' name. Amen.

How Do I Put on God's Armor?

 Put on the full armor of God so that you can take your stand against the devil's schemes. **Ephesians 6:11**

VICTORY

If you were a soccer goalie, would you be ready to play if you did not have your shin guards on? As a Christian, you're not ready to fight your enemy without your armor.

In today's Bible verse, God says to put your armor on. You need to be constantly aware that you have God's armor of protection. When you have your quiet time with God, think about the armor and what it is for. It might help you to "put on" each piece by talking to God about it. Thank Him for the helmet; ask Him to protect your mind. Thank Him for the belt; ask God to help you be truthful. Thank Him for your breastplate; ask God to guard your feelings and help you to do right. Thank Him for your shoes; ask God to give you His peace on the inside. Thank Him for your shield and trust that God will be with you and help you. Practice using your sword by saying a Bible verse aloud as you get dressed. Remember that your armor is invisible to you, but God sees it and so does Satan.

 Why do you need God's armor each day?

_____

_____

_____

You can pray:

 Dear God, Thank You for giving me Your armor to protect me today. In Jesus' name. Amen.

Did Jesus Use God's Armor?

Put on the full armor of God so that you can take your stand against the devil's schemes. **Ephesians 6:11**

Throughout His earthly life, the Lord Jesus Christ gave us the example of how to use God's armor. If you read about Him in the first four books of the New Testament, Matthew, Mark, Luke and John, you will see how he perfectly used the armor of God.

Jesus used the breastplate of righteousness by always doing what was right. He used the shield of faith, believing the promises of His Father, God. Jesus used the helmet of salvation by keeping his thoughts focused on doing His Father's will. He used the belt of truth by speaking only what was true. He used the shoes of peace by demonstrating how we could have peace with God. Jesus also used the sword of the Spirit as he resisted temptation by quoting verses from God's Word.

Did the Lord Jesus use God's armor? Yes–in fact, He is the armor! He is your righteousness (Philippians 3:9), your salvation (Psalm 27:1) and your peace (Ephesians 2:14). He is the Truth (John 14:6), and He is the Word of God (John 1:1). As you put your faith in the Lord Jesus and use His Word, you can be a winner over sin and Satan.

V I C T O R Y

Write a thank-you note to Jesus for showing you how to use the armor.

_____

_____

_____

You can pray:

Dear God, thank You for the Lord Jesus, who showed me how to use the armor. Help me to follow His example. In Jesus' name. Amen.

What If I Forget to Use the Armor? 112

 Put on the full armor of God so that you can take your stand against the devil's schemes. **Ephesians 6:11**

VICTORY

Imagine a fireman carrying his protective equipment to the fire, but then trying to fight the blaze without using it. That wouldn't be a very good idea. He would get seriously hurt–possibly even killed!

You have been learning all about the protective armor that God gives to His children. You have that armor in the Lord Jesus Christ. He is with you all of the time. But, what if you choose not to let the Lord Jesus give you the strength to resist the temptations to do wrong? Maybe you think you are strong enough to fight the battle against sin and Satan without God's help. But, you cannot win without God.

If you don't use your armor, how will you say "no" when that bad thought comes to you? What will you do when something makes you afraid? You won't have the strength on the inside to be a winner over sin.

God never meant for you to fight your battles alone. He is with you every day and everywhere you go to help you and to make you a winner. When temptations to do wrong come, remember your armor. Thank God for each piece and use it. You will win the battle!

What happens if you don't use your armor?

_____

_____

_____

 You can pray:
Dear God, please remind me each morning to use my armor throughout the day. In Jesus' name. Amen.

Is Prayer Part of My Protection?

Put on the full armor of God so that you can take your stand against the devil's schemes. **Ephesians 6:11**

How would you like to have a super weapon that no one could resist or defend against? Did you know you do have one? It is called prayer. The Lord Jesus used the weapon of prayer many times in His earthly life. He wanted always to do His Father's will. He also took time to thank His Father, God.

Jesus told His followers to always pray and not give up. Prayer is an important part of your protection against the enemy. Each day your enemy, Satan, prowls around looking for someone to hurt (1 Peter 5:8). You can try to fight him, but you would not win by yourself. You need to pray and ask your Heavenly Father for help.

Prayer is talking to God. Satan trembles when God's children pray. He knows that if you pray, God listens, and Satan will lose. Part of prayer is learning to listen and obey. It's not just a time for you to talk to God, it's also a time for Him to talk to you. Prayer is a super weapon, but it won't help you if you don't use it. You can pray any time, any place, about anything. Just do it!

VICTORY

Why is prayer an important part of your protection?

_____

_____

_____

You can pray:

Dear God, please help me to remember to talk to You every day. Help me to listen to You and obey. In Jesus' name. Amen.

Did People in the Bible Face Temptation? 114

Submit yourselves, then, to God. Resist the devil, and he will flee from you. **James 4:7**

VICTORY

Sometimes we think that the people in the Bible were super people. We think they had some kind of special power that we don't have. Maybe you've read the stories of Noah and the ark, David and Goliath and Daniel in the lion's den. Perhaps you wonder how they had such courage. You wish you were as brave as they were! Maybe you are! The people we read about in the Bible were just like us. They had many problems, and they also had temptations to sin.

Everyone faces temptation to do wrong. Satan attacks everyone. He wants the whole world to serve him and turn against God. Satan attacked the people you read about in the Bible, too. God put their stories in His Word so you and I could learn from them. Some of the people in the Bible were true heroes. They trusted God for the strength to say "no" to the temptation to sin and "yes" to obeying God. The people you read about in the Bible had to make hard choices. Not all of them chose to trust and obey God. When you are tempted, what will you choose to do?

What should you do when you are tempted to sin?

_____

_____

_____

You can pray:

Dear God, please help me to be like heroes in the Bible who trusted and obeyed You when tempted to sin. In Jesus' name. Amen.

How Did Joseph Handle Temptation?

Submit yourselves, then, to God. Resist the devil, and he will flee from you. **James 4:7**

The Bible tells about a young man named Joseph and what he did when he was faced with temptation (Genesis 37-47). He submitted to (trusted and obeyed) God. He resisted (said "no" to) the devil. God helped Joseph to be a winner over temptation.

Joseph had ten brothers who hated him. They sold him as a slave. He was taken far away from his family. He was probably tempted to hate his brothers, but he didn't. Years later when Joseph saw his brothers again, he was a very important man in Egypt. His brothers came

there to buy food for their families because there was a famine–no food was growing in their land. There was food in the land of Egypt because God had told Joseph to save it. The king put Joseph in charge of selling food to the people. When his brothers knew it was Joseph, they were afraid. Joseph could have given in to the temptation to get revenge, but he didn't. He told them, "It was not you who sent me here, but God" (Genesis 45:8). Joseph submitted to God and resisted the devil. God helped Joseph to be a winner over temptation.

VICTORY

How can you resist temptation?

_____

_____

_____

You can pray:

Dear God, please help me to resist the temptation to be angry and want to get revenge. In Jesus' name. Amen.

How Did Daniel and His Friends Take a Stand for God?

 Submit yourselves, then, to God. Resist the devil, and he will flee from you. **James 4:7**

V I C T O R Y

The Bible tells about a group of young men who were taken as captives to a foreign land. They were to be trained for service to a king who did not worship the true and living God. Unlike the other young men, Daniel and his three friends decided to take a stand for God and honor Him by doing what was right. Their first test came at mealtime. They knew that the food had probably not been prepared according to the laws God had given His people. Also, it had most likely been offered to false gods.

Daniel determined he would not dishonor God by eating this food. God gave Daniel courage and wisdom to ask the guard for permission to eat vegetables and drink water for ten days. Afterward, Daniel and his friends were healthier than the other men were. From that time on, God helped them in their training, giving them special wisdom and knowledge. Daniel and his friends were determined to take a stand for God. God gave them strength to do what was right. (Daniel 1:6-20)

The next time you are in a hard situation, remember that God can give you strength and courage to stand for Him and do what's right.

 How can you have courage to stand for God?

_____

_____

_____

 You can pray:
Dear God, please give me strength and courage to take a stand for You and do what's right, no matter what others may do. In Jesus' name. Amen.

117 **W**hat Happened When David Failed to Resist Temptation❓

Submit yourselves, then, to God. Resist the devil, and he will flee from you. **James 4:7**

King David wanted something that was not his. He wanted another man's wife for his own. He knew that what he wanted was wrong and sinful, but the temptation was strong. Instead of submitting to God (obeying God), King David gave in to the temptation and took the other man's wife. He even purposely sent the other man into battle so he would be killed. Then, David was free to marry the woman. But the Bible says that God knew what David had done, and God was not pleased.

Several terrible things happened because David failed to resist temptation. First, an in-nocent man died. Then, the baby that was born to David and his new wife also died. But, even worse than these things, David knew that he had sinned against God. David finally confessed his sin to God, and his relationship was healed. However, David must have never forgotten the danger of failing to resist temptation. (2 Samuel 11-12)

God will not let you get away with sin. Failing to resist temptation hurts your relationship with Him. It may hurt others, too. When temptation comes, submit to God and He will help you to resist!

VICTORY

What might happen if you fail to resist temptation?

_____

_____

_____

You can pray:

Dear God, when temptations come, please help me submit to You. Please give me the strength to resist. In Jesus' name. Amen.

How Did Gideon Have Courage to Stand for God?

Submit yourselves, then, to God. Resist the devil, and he will flee from you. **James 4:7**

V
I
C
T
O
R
Y

Gideon was scared! His country, Israel, was being overrun by its enemy. Gideon was so afraid that he hid so the enemy couldn't find him. God sent an angel who told Gideon that God had chosen him to lead his country in battle against the enemy! Gideon was doubtful, but God said, "I will be with you . . ." (Judges 6:16). God was reminding Gideon that he would not have to stand alone.

As Gideon prepared for the coming battle, God gave him some very strange instructions. Gideon and his small army did exactly what God

had told them to do. The night of the battle, they circled the enemy camp, blew trumpets and broke clay pitchers. Then, holding blazing torches high in the air they cried out, "For the LORD and for Gideon" (Judges 7:16-25). As they watched in amazement, the startled enemy ran away in fear and confusion. Gideon's army chased and defeated their enemy! How did Gideon have courage to stand for God? He remembered God's promise and obeyed what God said. (Judges 6-7)

You can do the same! When you need courage to stand for God, submit to Him. Remember His promise to be with you and obey Him. He will give you victory!

 How did Gideon have courage to stand for God?

_____

_____

You can pray:

 Dear God, I need courage to stand for You. Help me to remember that You are with me, and help me to obey You. In Jesus' name. Amen.

How Did Rahab Use the Shield of Faith?

Submit yourselves, then, to God. Resist the devil, and he will flee from you. **James 4:7**

A woman named Rahab lived in Jericho. The people in her city didn't believe in the true and living God and had done many evil things. God had commanded His people, Israel, to conquer Jericho. The Israelite leader sent spies into the city, but the king of Jericho found out and was searching for them. (Joshua 2)

Rahab helped the spies to hide. She told them that she believed in the God of Israel. Later, she helped them escape by lowering them down the high stone wall by a rope. Before they left, they made a promise to Rahab. Because of her faith, God would save her during the battle. They told her to tie a red rope in her window and gather her family inside. They promised that when the day of battle came, she and her family would be safe (Joshua 2:17-20).

It may have seemed strange to Rahab and her family, but she believed God's promise, and did exactly as she was told. Because of her faith, Rahab and her family were saved. In another part of the Bible, God lists Rahab as a hero of faith (Hebrews 11:31). Trust and obey God–that's how you use your shield of faith!

VICTORY

How did Rahab use her shield of faith?

_____

_____

_____

You can pray:

Dear God, I want to trust and obey You. Please help me to remember to use my shield of faith. In Jesus' name. Amen.

What Happened When Peter Failed the Lord Jesus?

Submit yourselves, then, to God. Resist the devil, and he will flee from you. **James 4:7**

V I C T O R Y

Have you ever told someone you would do something? If you don't keep your word, how do you feel? How would you feel if your close friend pretended he didn't even know you?

When the Lord Jesus told His disciples that He was going to die, Peter promised Jesus he would always be there for Him. Peter said, "Even if I have to die with you I will never disown you" (Matthew 26:35). But, Peter failed the Lord Jesus. For three years, they had been close friends. However, when Jesus needed Peter, Peter pretended he didn't know him.

I am sure Jesus felt just as bad as you would, but He didn't stop loving Peter. Jesus died before Peter had a chance to say he was sorry. Peter must have felt awful. But, Jesus didn't stay dead. When He came back to life, He forgave Peter and gave him another chance. He even gave him a very special job. You can read about it in John 21:15-19. You can't make Jesus stop loving you, even if you fail Him. If you know Jesus Christ as your Savior, He is always ready to forgive you and give you another chance.

What should you do if you fail the Lord Jesus?

_____

_____

_____

You can pray:

Dear God, thank You for always loving me. I am sorry when I fail You. Thank You for forgiving me. In Jesus' name. Amen.

This is the end of the section of "Victory" devotionals.

It is time to do the next activity page that came to you in the mail. Remember to add your prayer request so your mailbox friend can pray for you. When you finish the whole page, fold it on the lines so the Mailbox Club address shows. Put a small piece of tape on the bottom to keep it folded. Add a stamp and mail your activity page.

Your work will be marked and sent back to you, along with a personal note. The activity sheet for the next set of lessons will be sent to you, too.

Enjoy getting to know God better with your next group of devotionals!

GOD's
Word
and
Me

What Is the Bible?

All Scripture is God-breathed and is useful for teaching, rebuking, correcting and training in righteousness. **2 Timothy 3:16**

You may have wondered what makes the Bible special. It is a book from God. It isn't like any other book you can read. Other books have the thoughts and ideas of people, but the Bible is God's own Word. Every single word in the Bible is true.

The Bible is one way God tells us what He wants us to know. The Bible says it " . . . is useful for teaching, rebuking, correcting and training in righteousness" (2 Timothy 3:16). The Bible tells what God is like. It shows you what you are doing wrong, and how God can take care of those things. The Bible will train you to live in the way God says is right.

Do people ever call you by other names? Your name might be Robert, but you may be called Bob or Robbie. The Bible is sometimes called by different names, too. It may be called "God's Word" or "Holy Bible." That is because it comes from our perfect, holy God. The Bible is also called the "Scripture," which means writing. Even though it is called by other names, it is still God's book, His message to us.

GOD'S WORD & ME

What are some ways the Bible can help you?

_____

_____

_____

You can pray:

Dear God, thank You for giving us the Bible. Help me to use it to learn more about how You want me to live. In Jesus' name. Amen.

Where Did the Bible Come From?

122

All Scripture is God-breathed and is useful for teaching, rebuking, correcting and training in righteousness.
2 Timothy 3:16

GOD'S WORD & ME

You already know the Bible came from God. Our Bible verse says, "All Scripture is God-breathed." But how did God give us the Bible? Did it just fall from Heaven? No, God's Spirit told 40 different men what to write. God used their own style and personality to write His Words. The Holy Spirit inspired and guided them in such a way that there were absolutely no mistakes in any of the words as they were originally written.

This didn't happen all at once. It took 1,600 years for the whole Bible to be finished!

Just think about taking that long to write a book! No man could ever live 1,600 years, but time isn't a problem for God. He has always lived and will live forever. He told men at different times in history what to write. Sometimes they wrote what was happening right then. Other times they wrote about what had already happened. God even had them write what would happen in the future.

The men wrote what God told them to write in their own languages. Later, the Bible was put into many other languages as well. That way people all over the world could read it and learn about God.

How does having the Bible in your own language help you?

_____

_____

_____

You can pray:

Dear God, thank You for the Bible. Thank You that it is in my language so I can read it and learn what You want me to do. In Jesus' name. Amen.

Is the Bible True?

All Scripture is God-breathed and is useful for teaching, rebuking, correcting and training in righteousness. **2 Timothy 3:16**

How can you tell if something you read is true? One way is to compare it with other things you know are true. The Bible says, " . . . your word is truth" (John 17:17). The facts prove that. Much of the Bible was written by eyewitnesses. They were people who actually saw the things they wrote about. Archaeological and historical writings from Bible times agree with what the Bible says. That helps you know it is true.

The Bible told about many things hundreds of years before they happened. These are called prophecies. Many of those things have already come true. God said something would happen and it did. You can be sure all the other prophecies will come true, too. God knows what will happen in the future. He knew just what to tell the men to write.

God has protected the Bible for thousands of years. Many people in history have tried to destroy the Bible. God didn't let that happen. He kept His true Word safe so you can have it today. The Bible says, "The grass withers and the flowers fall, but the word of our God stands forever" (Isaiah 40:8).

GOD'S WORD & ME

 What helps you believe the Bible is God's true Word?

_____

_____

_____

You can pray:

Dear God, thank You for protecting the Bible so I can read it today. Help me to remember that everything in Your Word is true. In Jesus' name. Amen.

Why Are There Two Parts to the Bible?

All Scripture is God-breathed and is useful for teaching, rebuking, correcting and training in righteousness.
2 Timothy 3:16

Did you know that our calendar tells something about Jesus? Each year tells about how long it's been since Jesus was born. The years before Jesus was born have "before Christ," or "BC" numbers. The years after He was born have "in the year of our Lord," or "AD" numbers. All the years are numbered starting with Jesus' birth!

The parts of the Bible are divided by Jesus' birth, too. The Bible is made up of 66 books. Each book is part of either the Old Testament or the New Testament. The Old Testament is in the front of the Bible. It tells about creation and other things that happened before Jesus became a man.

The New Testament is in the back part of the Bible. The books in it were written after Jesus was on Earth. It tells about Jesus' life. You can find out how to have your sin forgiven by believing in Him. The New Testament also tells what Jesus' followers did after He returned to Heaven.

Knowing the Bible is divided by time will help you find things in it more easily.

What are three things you could find in the New Testament part of the Bible?

_____

_____

_____

You can pray:

Dear God, thank You for giving us both parts of the Bible. Help me find out more about You by reading it. In Jesus' name. Amen.

125 How Does the Bible Fit Together?

All Scripture is God-breathed and is useful for teaching, rebuking, correcting and training in righteousness. **2 Timothy 3:16**

Have you ever tried to write a story or report? Sometimes it's hard to get it just right. What if lots of people tried to write a book together? What if they lived in different times and places? Would it be likely to fit together right? Amazingly enough, that is the way the Bible was written.

It is wonderful that the Bible fits together the way it does. It was written by 40 men over hundreds of years. It is hard to believe all those authors could agree on everything! That's just what happened though. The later authors agree exactly with the earlier ones.

Another way the Bible fits together is in telling about Jesus. In the Old Testament God promised He would send a Savior. This Savior would take the punishment for sin. People waited hundreds of years for God to keep His promise. In the New Testament God sent Jesus as our Savior. That was His plan all along.

Why does the Bible fit together? "All Scripture is God-breathed" (2 Timothy 3:16). Only God could make all the parts of the Bible fit together perfectly! You can always trust God's Word. It will never change.

GOD'S WORD & ME

Why is it important that the Bible all fits together?

_____

_____

_____

You can pray:

Dear God, thank You for making the Bible all go together just right. Help me trust You to take care of my life just right, too. In Jesus' name. Amen.

All Scripture is God-breathed and is useful for teaching, rebuking, correcting and training in righteousness.
2 Timothy 3:16

GOD'S WORD & ME

You already know that Jesus died for sin. You can have your sin forgiven by believing in Him as your Savior. What happened before Jesus came? Could those people have their sins forgiven?

God's people often chose to disobey Him. God is perfectly fair. He couldn't ignore the people's sin. The Bible says, " . . . without the shedding of blood there is no forgiveness" (Hebrews 9:22). God made a way for the people to have their sin covered (forgiven). God told them to bring animals to sacrifice for their sin. The people deserved to be punished, but the animals were killed instead. The people knew they had done wrong. The animals died in their place. The blood of the animals covered the people's sin. Someday a Savior would come to take away that sin forever. The people needed to believe that promise.

Jesus was that Savior. He took the punishment for sin forever. Now animals don't have to be sacrificed. Jesus is the perfect Son of God. He took the punishment for sin for everyone in the whole world. The Bible says, "For Christ died for sins once for all . . ." (1 Peter 3:18).

 Why don't you have to sacrifice animals to pay for your sins?

_____

_____

_____

You can pray:

 Dear God, thank You for making the way for sin to be forgiven through Your Son, Jesus. I love You because of what You did for me. In Jesus' name. Amen.

Why Is the Old Testament Important for Me?

All Scripture is God-breathed and is useful for teaching, rebuking, correcting and training in righteousness. **2 Timothy 3:16**

Some people think it isn't important to read the Old Testament. They think only the New Testament is important. That is not true! The Bible says, "All Scripture is God-breathed and is useful for teaching, rebuking, correcting and training in righteousness" (2 Timothy 3:16). The whole Bible is important for you!

The Old Testament is helpful for teaching. The Bible says, "For everything that was written in the past was written to teach us . . ." (Romans 15:4). Reading the Old Testament will train you to live the right way. It will show you how to think and act to please God. He knows what is best for your life. When you live to please Him, you will have true happiness on the inside. You can see this as you read about the lives of people in this part of the Bible.

Many of God's laws are in the Old Testament. These laws help you see your sin. God rebukes, or scolds you, by helping you see what you have done wrong. Remembering God's laws can help keep you from sin. The Bible says, "I have hidden your word in my heart that I might not sin against you" (Psalm 119:11).

GOD'S WORD & ME

What are some ways the Old Testament can help you?

_____

_____

_____

You can pray:

Dear God, thank You that the Old Testament can still help me today. Please help me obey Your laws and stay away from sin. In Jesus' name. Amen.

What Is the New Testament About? 128

All Scripture is God-breathed and is useful for teaching, rebuking, correcting and training in righteousness.
2 Timothy 3:16

The word "testament" means promise. The New Testament tells about how God kept His promise to send a Savior. This Savior was Jesus. Jesus came from Heaven and was born as a baby. He grew up without ever sinning. He was the perfect Son of God. Jesus taught the people about His Father. Then, He died on a cross, taking the punishment for sin. The Bible says, " . . . Christ died for our sins . . ." (1 Corinthians 15:3).

Jesus was buried, but He didn't stay dead! On the third day He came alive again. He spent time with many of His followers. He told them to tell people all over the world about Him. Jesus said, "Go into all the world and preach the good news to all creation" (Mark 16:15). Then, He was taken back up to Heaven.

God sent the Holy Spirit to help Jesus' followers. They told people everywhere that Jesus had died for their sin. Many believed in Him and were saved. Groups of new believers met together to worship God and serve Him. Each of these groups was called a church. The New Testament tells of many new churches that started during the first years after Jesus went back to Heaven.

Why is it important that Jesus' followers told other people about Him?

_____

_____

_____

You can pray:

Thank You, God, for keeping Your promise to send a Savior. Help me to be like Jesus' followers and tell other people about Him. In Jesus' name. Amen.

Why Is the New Testament Important for Me?

All Scripture is God-breathed and is useful for teaching, rebuking, correcting and training in righteousness. **2 Timothy 3:16**

If something could save your life would you think it was important? What God says in the New Testament can save your life! The New Testament tells how God sent His only Son to Earth to die for your sin. When Jesus came back to life, He proved He is the winner over sin and death.

The Bible says, " . . . believe in the Lord Jesus, and you will be saved . . ." (Acts 16:31). You need to trust in Jesus, who died for you! He took the punishment you deserve. When you trust that Jesus is the only one who can forgive you, you will be saved. You can live with God in Heaven forever. That is very important news!

Most of the New Testament has been written to people who already believe in Jesus. The New Testament tells us how to live as God's children. It shows us how to love and serve God and how to treat other people. The things written there are still important for you today. If you read and obey them, you will get to know God better. You will be able to live to please Him. The New Testament is from God and is important in helping you live for Him.

GOD'S WORD & ME

What is one important way the New Testament can help you?

_____

_____

_____

You can pray:

Dear God, thank You for sending Your Son, Jesus, to die for my sin. Help me read and obey the New Testament so I can live to please You. In Jesus' name. Amen.

What Is a Quiet Time?

 . . . present yourself to God as one approved, a workman who does not need to be ashamed and who correctly handles the word of truth. **2 Timothy 2:15**

GOD'S WORD & ME

Who are your good friends? Do you spend lots of time with them and talk to them often? God wants to be your friend and helper. He is the very best friend you could ever have! The only way to become best friends with Him, though, is to spend time with Him.

Talking to God in prayer only once in a while isn't enough. Learning about God with other people is good, but you shouldn't stop there. You need to spend time alone with God each day to get to know Him well. Even Jesus took time alone to talk to God. The time you set aside to be alone with God is called your quiet time.

When you start your quiet time, ask God to teach you and to help you obey Him. Then read God's Word, the Bible, and think about what it means. Spend some time memorizing a Bible verse, too. If you don't have a Bible, you can read Bible verses in this book. End your quiet time with prayer. Talk to God about what He has shown you in the Bible and about everything else in your life. Having a quiet time is one way you can "present yourself to God as one approved" like our verse says.

 What should you do in your quiet time with God?

_____

_____

_____

You can pray:

 Thank You, God, that I can talk to You. Thank You for talking to me through the Bible. Help me spend time alone with You each day. In Jesus' name. Amen.

Should I Have a Quiet Time?

. . . present yourself to God as one approved, a workman who does not need to be ashamed and who correctly handles the word of truth. **2 Timothy 2:15**

Josh and Juan were best friends before Josh moved away. They wrote to each other often at first. Juan kept writing to Josh, but Josh quit answering. Soon their friendship wasn't very important to him.

That same thing can happen with you and God. If you don't have a quiet time with Him each day, He will become less important to you. Through His Holy Spirit, God will remind you to spend time with Him, but what will you do? Will you take time to be with Him, or will you ignore Him?

When you do spend time with God, you'll get to know Him. The Bible says, "Come near to God and He will come near to you" (James 4:8). You will learn what God is really like. You will become close friends and you'll want to know Him even better. When you read the Bible, God will teach you things that will help in your life. He will give you the strength you need each day. He will give you power to obey Him so you won't have to be ashamed of the things you do. Will you show God how much you love Him by having a quiet time?

GOD'S WORD & ME

How can having a quiet time help you?

_____

_____

_____

You can pray:

Dear God, thank You for being willing to let me know You. Help me remember each day to spend time alone with You. In Jesus' name. Amen.

What Do I Need to Have a Quiet Time?

. . . present yourself to God as one approved, a workman who does not need to be ashamed and who correctly handles the word of truth. **2 Timothy 2:15**

GOD'S WORD & ME

Are you more likely to do the things you have a set time to do, or those you do whenever you happen to think about it? Having a quiet time is important! Set aside a regular time for it each day. Maybe you will need to get up earlier in the morning. Maybe night will be best for you. The important thing is to set a time and stick to it.

Find a place for your time alone with God where others won't bother you. It is important to be able to think about what God is saying to you in the Bible. You need to be able to talk to Him quietly. Let the people around you know you need that time alone each day.

When you have your quiet time, you will need your Bible, some paper and a pen or pencil. It is also good to use a devotional book like this one. When God shows you something, write it down. Make a list of the things you are praying about. Be sure to write down the answers to your prayers, too. Then, you will be able to remind yourself of how faithful God is to you.

When and where will you have your quiet time?

_____

_____

_____

You can pray:

Dear God, thank You that I can spend time with You. Help me be faithful in having my quiet time with You each day. In Jesus' name. Amen.

ow Will Studying the Bible Help Me?

. . . present yourself to God as one approved, a workman who does not need to be ashamed and who correctly handles the word of truth. **2 Timothy 2:15**

Learning all you can at school is important. You won't have to be ashamed when you get your grades. Learning will help you prepare for life. Studying the Bible is even more important. It will help you be approved, or pleasing, to God like our verse says.

Studying the Bible will help you in other ways, too. You will find many promises from God that you can believe. They will help you when you are having problems or are afraid. You will learn what God is like. You will see that you can trust Him completely.

Studying the Bible and obeying it can change your life! The Bible says, "For the word of God is living and active . . ." (Hebrews 4:12). It has the power to change you on the inside. It shows you how to get to Heaven and how to live here on Earth. If you read God's Word and think about it often, your life will be happier. You will learn to make wise choices that keep you from sin. You will have God's peace on the inside, no matter what happens around you. Will you let God's Word change you? Others will see the difference!

GOD'S WORD & ME

What changes do you want the Bible to make in your life?

_____

_____

_____

You can pray:

Dear God, thank You that Your Word is alive and can change me. Help me to be willing to obey what You tell me when I study the Bible. In Jesus' name. Amen.

How Is the Bible a Sword?

 ... present yourself to God as one approved, a workman who does not need to be ashamed and who correctly handles the word of truth. **2 Timothy 2:15**

Can you imagine why the Bible would be called a sword? It doesn't look like one! A sword is long and pointed with sharp edges. A sword can make deep cuts, slicing things apart. Sometimes God's Word can slice through your thoughts and feelings, cutting apart the good from the bad. " ... it judges the thoughts and attitudes of the heart" (Hebrews 4:12). The Bible will show you what you need to confess to God and let Him change in your life.

We learned earlier that a sword is also a weapon. Remember that it's part of the armor that God has given to you. The Bible is your weapon for fighting against Satan. He will tempt you to do things you know are wrong. Satan even tempted Jesus! Do you remember what Jesus did? He quoted God's Word, and Satan had to leave Him. If Satan tries to get you to steal something, you can use the Bible, too. You can quote, "You shall not steal" (Exodus 20:15). Say this verse aloud or to yourself, then obey it. This is how you resist Satan. He can't stand up to the Bible! Will you use the sword God has given you to fight against Satan?

When are some times you need to use the Bible as a sword?

_____

_____

_____

You can pray:

Dear God, thank You for making the Bible my sword. Help me learn to use it to fight against Satan's temptations. In Jesus' name. Amen.

How Do I Study the Bible?

. . . present yourself to God as one approved, a workman who does not need to be ashamed and who correctly handles the word of truth. **2 Timothy 2:15**

The Bible is a very long book, isn't it? It may even seem like too much for you to read. Don't worry though. God doesn't expect you to read and obey everything in His Word all at once. You need to read a little bit at a time and think about it.

You could start with one of the first four books in the New Testament–Matthew, Mark, Luke or John. They tell you about Jesus' birth and death. You will also learn many things Jesus did while He was here on Earth. The large numbers in the Bible are the chapters. The smaller numbers are the verses. Start at the beginning of the book with chapter one and just read a few verses. Most Bibles have titles that tell about different parts of the chapter. It would be a good idea to read one of these parts of a chapter each day. The next day you can start where you left off.

As you read your Bible, God will teach you things. Think about what He says. Then, you need to do it. When you obey God's Word, you will be correctly handling the word of truth, like our verse says.

GOD'S WORD & ME

How can reading just a little of the Bible each day help you?

_____

_____

_____

You can pray:

Dear God, thank You that You will teach me when I read the Bible. Help me remember to stop and think about what You say to me. In Jesus' name. Amen.

What Should I Look for as I Study the Bible?

. . . present yourself to God as one approved, a workman who does not need to be ashamed and who correctly handles the word of truth. **2 Timothy 2:15**

How will you find out what God wants to teach you in the Bible? Pray and ask for His help first. Then, read a few verses and ask yourself these three questions:

1. "What does it say?" Put the ideas in your own words. For the first part of the verse above you might say, "Do everything you can to make God happy."

2. "What does it mean?" If there are words you don't understand, look them up in a dictionary or ask someone what they mean. Are the verses telling you something about God? Is there a promise for you? Do they say something you should or should not do?

3. "What is God saying to me?" How does God want you to use these verses in your own life? Maybe you need to tell God how great He is. Thank Him for His promises. Ask Him to remind you of them when you are lonely or afraid. Maybe you need to admit that something you are doing is wrong. Learn the verse so you can use it as a sword to help you fight against sinning again. Write down what God shows you so you won't forget it.

What is God saying to you through your memory verse above?

_____

_____

_____

You can pray:

Dear God, I know You have a lot to teach me. Help me understand what You want me to see as I read the Bible. In Jesus' name. Amen.

How Can I Memorize God's Word?

... present yourself to God as one approved, a workman who does not need to be ashamed and who correctly handles the word of truth. **2 Timothy 2:15**

Do you remember your best weapon to fight against sin? It is the Bible. What can you do when you don't have your Bible? If you memorize verses from God's Word, you will always have them with you. They will be ready like a sword to help you fight temptation. The Bible says, "I have hidden your word in my heart that I might not sin against you" (Psalm 119:11). Start by learning the verses in this devotional book. Then, memorize other special verses God shows you.

Read aloud the verse you want to memorize several times. Think about what it says. Write it and take it with you to look at often during the day. Say the first part of the verse to yourself over and over until you can do it without looking. Add another part, and do the same thing. Keep adding parts until you can say the whole verse without help. Say it to someone else and tell him or her what it means. Remember to do what the verse says! Learn other verses, but keep reviewing the first ones too. Then, when you need them, God's Spirit can bring them back to your mind.

GOD'S WORD & ME

How will memorizing parts of the Bible help you?

_____

_____

_____

You can pray:

Thank You, God, for giving me a mind that can learn. Help me memorize Bible verses and use them to fight against sin. In Jesus' name. Amen.

What Is Prayer?

Call to me and I will answer you and tell you great and unsearchable things you do not know. **Jeremiah 33:3**

What would it be like to have a king for your best friend? What if you could talk to the Creator of the universe whenever you want to? If you know the Lord Jesus as your Savior, you can do these things! The one, true God is the Creator–the King of kings. He has made a way for you to talk to Him! That is called prayer.

You don't have to have a telephone or e-mail to talk to God. Even though you can't see Him, He is everywhere all the time.

You can talk to Him aloud or quietly in your mind. He can always hear you. He wants you to talk to Him often. In our Bible verse today, God says, "Call to me and I will answer you . . ." Will He answer you aloud? No, but He will talk to you through the Bible, or quietly in your heart.

Sometimes people think they have to memorize prayers and say them over and over again. Saying a memorized prayer is fine if you really mean it, but don't stop there. God wants you to talk to Him with your own thoughts or words. He is never too busy to listen.

 What do you want to talk to the Creator of the universe about?

_____

_____

_____

You can pray:

 Dear God, thank You for making a way for me to talk to You! Help me remember to do it often. In Jesus' name. Amen.

139 Why Should I Pray?

Call to me and I will answer you and tell you great and unsearchable things you do not know. **Jeremiah 33:3**

GOD'S WORD & ME

God knows everything about you. He knows what you need before you even tell Him. Why, then, do you need to pray? One important reason is that God created you to love Him and be His friend. Friends talk to each other. The way you talk to God is through prayer. You can tell Him how much you love Him and how wonderful He is. You can also tell Him what you need.

Another good reason to pray is because you need God's help. Prayer is the way God made for you to ask for His help. The Bible says, " . . . You do not have, because you do not ask God" (James 4:2). Maybe you are having trouble at school or don't know what to do about a problem. God has the power to help you, and He can show you what to do. Our verse says, He will "answer you and tell you great and unsearchable things you do not know." God's answer may be something you would never have thought about. Answers to prayer help you remember that God is really the one who gives you everything. They help you remember to depend on Him.

Why do you think God wants you to pray?

_____

_____

_____

You can pray:

Dear God, I need Your help every day. Thank You that I can call on You and You will answer. In Jesus' name. Amen.

Why Does God Hear My Prayers? 140

Call to me and I will answer you and tell you great and unsearchable things you do not know. **Jeremiah 33:3**

The Bible tells about Elijah, a prophet of the one true God. Elijah was in a contest with 450 prophets of a false god named Baal. First, the prophets of Baal prayed to their god to send down fire from Heaven. They screamed and danced for many hours, but no fire came down. Why? Because the god they served wasn't alive! He couldn't even hear them! Then, Elijah prayed to the one true God. Immediately, fire came down from Heaven! God was proving that He is the one true God. He showed everyone that He hears and answers prayer!

The one true God is still alive and listening today! That is why He can hear and answer your prayers. The Bible says, "Call to me and I will answer you . . ." (Jeremiah 33:3). When you pray to God as His obedient child, He will hear you. If you have never believed in Jesus, His son, the first prayer God wants to hear from you is to admit your sin and believe in Jesus, who died to take your punishment. You can talk to God right now. He loves you and is waiting to hear from you!

How do you know God hears your prayers?

_____

_____

_____

You can pray:

Dear God, help me never to forget that You are always listening and ready to answer my prayers. In Jesus' name. Amen.

141

When and Where Can I Pray?

Call to me and I will answer you and tell you great and unsearchable things you do not know. **Jeremiah 33:3**

Jamie and Karl were out on the lake in a small boat. Suddenly, a big motorboat cut right in front of them! Big waves rocked their boat violently and they tipped over into the water. Jamie couldn't swim well and found himself going under in the waves. "God," he prayed, "help me!" Just then, something bumped into him. It was their boat! It was upside down but floating on the waves. Quickly Jamie grabbed hold of it. Then, he saw Karl. "Thank you, God!" Jamie said. He and Karl were able to float with the boat until help came.

Should Jamie have waited to pray until bedtime or until he was at church? No! He did exactly what he should have. He prayed right there where he was when he needed help. God is everywhere all the time, so you, too, can call to Him any time. People in the Bible prayed all times of the day and night wherever they were. The Lord Jesus even prayed to God while He was hanging on the cross. You can talk to God any time, at any place. If you are His child, He is always with you and ready to listen.

GOD'S WORD & ME

Name some times and places you can talk to God.

_____

_____

_____

You can pray:

Dear God, thank You that I can talk to You any time at any place. Remind me to pray often, wherever I am. In Jesus' name. Amen.

What Should I Pray to God About?

 Call to me and I will answer you and tell you great and unsearchable things you do not know. **Jeremiah 33:3**

Do you always have your hand with you? It can remind you who to pray for. Hold it so your thumb points towards you. Your thumb can remind you to pray for the people who are close to you. That might be your family and good friends.

Now turn your hand so it faces you. After your thumb comes your pointer finger. It can remind you to pray for the people who point you to the Lord Jesus. That might be your pastor or a teacher. It could be the people who write things to help you learn about God.

Then, comes your tallest finger. It reminds you to pray for the people who have authority over you. That would include your parents, teachers and government leaders. Your ring finger is the weakest. It has trouble working by itself. It can remind you to pray for those who are weak. You can pray for the sick, the elderly or very young children. You could also pray for those who've never trusted Jesus as their Savior.

Last comes your little finger. It helps you remember to put others first and then pray for yourself. The Bible says, "Be ... faithful in prayer" (Romans 12:12).

Write the names of three people you should pray for.

_____

_____

_____

You can pray:

 Dear God, thank You for showing me I should pray for others. Help me think about them more than I think about myself. In Jesus' name. Amen.

GOD'S WORD & ME

143

Does God Always Answer Prayer?

Call to me and I will answer you and tell you great and unsearchable things you do not know. Jeremiah 33:3

When you pray about something, will God answer you? He promises to answer if you are His child. God says, "Call to me and I will answer you . . ." God doesn't say, "I might answer," but "I will answer." Does that mean He will always give you what you want? No. God will do what He knows is best for you.

Sometimes in the Bible God gave people what they prayed for. He gave Hannah a baby son when she asked (1 Samuel 1:20). Other times God's answer was "no." Paul wanted God to take away a problem he had (2 Corinthians 12:7-9). God said, "no."

Instead, He helped Paul deal with the problem. The third answer God gave was "wait." Two sisters wanted Jesus to heal their sick brother, Lazarus. The Lord Jesus waited until Lazarus had died. Then, Jesus brought him back to life! People realized that Jesus really was the Son of God! (John 11:5, 32, 43-44)

God gives those same answers to prayer today. He may say "yes," He may say "no" or He may say "wait." Your job is to keep praying, believing God will answer your prayers in the way He knows is best for you.

GOD'S WORD & ME

Write about a time God answered your prayer "yes."

_____

_____

_____

You can pray:

Dear God, help me trust You to answer my prayers in the way You know is best. Thank You for hearing and answering me. In Jesus' name. Amen.

Should I Have Others Pray with Me**?**

Call to me and I will answer you and tell you great and unsearchable things you do not know. **Jeremiah 33:3**

GOD'S WORD & ME

How would you feel if you were put in prison for telling others about the Lord Jesus? That's exactly what happened to a man in the Bible. Peter was thrown into prison. He had four soldiers at a time to guard him. Two of them were even chained to him! Do you think Peter was praying for help? Probably! He wasn't the only one praying though. The other Christians were praying for Peter, too. They knew God was the only one who could help him.

God did one of those "great and unsearchable things" our verse talks about. He sent an angel right into that prison. Peter's chains fell off. He and the angel walked out of the prison right past all the guards! God heard and answered the Christians' prayers in a very special way! (Acts 12:6-10)

Prayer brings God's power to help you, too. It is very important to pray yourself, but you need to have others pray for you and with you, too. That multiplies the power of your prayer. Jesus said, " . . . if two of you on earth agree about anything you ask for, it will be done for you by my Father in heaven" (Matthew 18:19).

What do you need someone else to pray with you about?

_____

_____

_____

You can pray:
Dear God, thank You for answering prayer. Help me share my needs with others so they can help me pray. In Jesus' name. Amen.

145 What Do I Need to Include in My Prayers?

. . . The prayer of a righteous man is powerful and effective.
James 5:16

There are many things you could pray about. Sometimes it is hard to remember them all. The letters in the word "ACTS" can help you.

"A" stands for adoration. Tell God how much you love and respect Him. Praise Him for how wonderful and mighty He is. You could even sing your praise to God!

"C" is for confession. You need to tell God about the wrong things you do. Name your sin and admit it is wrong. God promises to forgive you when you confess your sin. Then, your prayer will be "powerful and effective" like our verse says.

"T" is for thanksgiving. If someone gives you a gift or does something nice for you, don't you usually thank that person? God has done a lot for you! Remember to tell God thank you for what you have, who you are and what He has given you.

"S" stands for supplication. That means to ask God for things. Talk to God about the things other people need. Pray about the things you want and need, too.

Remember what the letters in the word "ACTS" mean when you pray. They will help you talk to God the way you should.

GOD'S WORD & ME

Name one thing you can say to God for each letter of the word "ACTS."

_____

_____

_____

You can pray:

Dear God, You are so good to me! Help me remember to do more than just ask You for things when I pray. In Jesus' name. Amen.

How Do I Praise God?

. . . The prayer of a righteous man is powerful and effective. **James 5:16**

GOD'S WORD & ME

How do you feel when someone praises you? Maybe you wrote a great story or did something kind. If others notice and say something about it, you feel good inside. God deserves to be praised far more than you or I do! He is pleased when you tell Him how wonderful He is. The Bible says over and over to praise God. In fact, it says, "Let everything that has breath praise the LORD" (Psalm 150:6). Praising God is one way to show how much you love Him.

You can praise God by telling Him how much you admire Him. Talk to Him about His greatness, power, wisdom and love. Praise Him for the things He has done, like creating the huge mountains and mighty oceans. Praise Him for keeping the stars and planets moving just right. Only our great God could do those things!

The Bible says, "Sing to the LORD a new song . . ." (Psalm 149:1). That is another way to praise God. Maybe you know songs that tell about God's greatness. Sing them to Him. You can even make up your own songs to praise God. He is listening and loves to hear your praise!

Write three things you can praise God for today.

_____

_____

_____

You can pray:

Dear God, You are so awesome! Remind me every day to spend time praising You for who You are and what You do. In Jesus' name. Amen.

147

How Do I Confess My Sins to God?

... The prayer of a righteous man is powerful and effective.
James 5:16

Kirsten was God's child. She knew she should obey. She didn't think her mom would let her go to her friend's house. She said she needed to study at the library but went to her friend's house instead. Later, when she started to pray, things just didn't seem right. She needed to confess her sin to God and to her mother.

As God's child, if you choose to sin, things won't be right between you and God. Your prayer won't be powerful because you haven't acted in a way that is right and good. As soon as you know you have sinned,

confess it to God. Admit what you did and agree with God that it was wrong. The Bible says, "If we confess our sins, he is faithful and just and will forgive us our sins and purify us from all unrighteousness" (1 John 1:9). You can know God has forgiven you because He always keeps His promises. Make things right with the people you have sinned against, too.

Should you keep choosing to sin and asking forgiveness? No! Be willing to stop doing the wrong things. Ask God to help you do what's right.

GOD'S WORD & ME

Why is it important to confess your sins to God right away?

_____

_____

_____

You can pray:

Dear God, thank You for Your forgiveness. Show me when I sin and remind me to confess it to You right away. In Jesus' name. Amen.

What Should I Thank God For?

... The prayer of a righteous man is powerful and effective. **James 5:16**

Suppose you spent a lot of time doing something really special for a friend. How would you feel if your friend didn't even thank you? You might wonder if he or she cares about you or what you do. God is disappointed when you don't remember to thank Him for the things He does for you, too.

The most important thing you should thank God for is sending His Son, Jesus, to die on the cross for you. He forgave your sin and is getting a place in Heaven ready for you! There are many other things to thank God for as well. Do you know that all the good things you have really came from God? He owns the world and everything in it. Thank Him for what He has given you. Thank Him for the people He has put into your life to help you.

God gives you the strength you need for each day. When problems come, He is right there helping you. Have you thanked Him for His help and strength? The Bible says, "Give thanks to the LORD, for he is good . . ." (1 Chronicles 16:34). Thanking God should be a big part of your prayer time.

 List three things or people you need to thank God for.

_____

_____

_____

You can pray:
 Dear God, please forgive me for not remembering all You do for me. Thank You for loving me and taking care of me in so many ways. In Jesus' name. Amen.

GOD'S WORD & ME

149 How Should I Pray for Others?

. . . The prayer of a righteous man is powerful and effective.
James 5:16

If your friend was hurt in a car wreck, would you know how to pray for him? You could pray that God would heal him, but that is just a start. If the friend has never trusted the Lord Jesus as his Savior, pray that he will. If he has trusted Jesus, pray that he will grow closer to God while he is healing. Ask God to help him show others that he has Jesus in his life by the way he acts.

Maybe a person is tempted to do something wrong. Pray that God would show that person how to escape the temptation. Maybe a friend doesn't get along with his parents. Pray that his actions will show respect and love for them. Ask God to help you be a good listener and helper for your friend.

Sometimes it is hard to know how to pray for the needs of others. Ask God to help them in the way He knows is best. The important thing is to pray for others. Our verse says, "The prayer of a righteous man [woman, boy or girl] is powerful and effective." Confess your own sins, then put God's power to work in the lives of others through your prayers.

Choose three people and write one thing you could pray for each of them.

_____

_____

_____

You can pray:

Dear God, thank You for letting me pray for others! Help me see their needs and remember to pray for them. In Jesus' name. Amen.

GOD'S WORD & ME

Why Should I Pray for Those in Charge?

 . . . The prayer of a righteous man is powerful and effective. **James 5:16**

GOD'S WORD & ME

Think of the people in your life who are in charge. That might include your parents, teachers, government leaders and others. God chooses who will be in charge. The Bible says, " . . . The authorities that exist have been established by God" (Romans 13:1). The things these people do are important! The decisions they make affect many lives. That is why God tells you to pray for them. The Bible says prayers should be "made for everyone–for kings and all those in authority" (1 Timothy 2:1-2). Those who are in charge need God's help to make wise choices.

Sometimes these people are Christians. Pray that God will show them what to do. Pray that they will depend on God to help them do what is right. Some of the people in charge are not Christians. Pray that they will believe in the Lord Jesus. Ask God to help them make choices that please Him. God has more power than any person. He can even work through people who don't know Him!

You may think your prayers won't make a difference, but they do! God says that when you live His way, your prayers will be powerful and effective!

 Write something you could pray for your parents or teacher this week.

_____

_____

_____

You can pray:

 Dear God, thank You that no one can be in charge unless You allow it. Remind me to pray for the authorities in my life every day. In Jesus' name. Amen.

Is It Okay to Pray for Myself?

. . . The prayer of a righteous man is powerful and effective.
James 5:16

Is it selfish to talk to God about your own problems? Should you pray for others and ignore your own needs? No! God wants you to pray for others, but He wants you to pray for yourself, too. God loves you so much! He wants to take care of you in every way. When you pray about your own needs, you show God you are trusting Him to help you.

Talk to God about physical needs like your health, food and clothes. Tell Him what you are feeling. Sometimes there are things you can't talk to anyone else about. Tell God. You can always trust Him to understand and help you. The Bible says, "Cast [put] all your anxiety [troubles] on him because he cares for you" (1 Peter 5:7). When you are worried about something, give it to God. He can take care of it far better than you can!

When you pray for yourself, don't just ask for things. Pray that God will help you fight temptation and live the way He wants you to live. Ask Him to help you get to know Him better. Those kinds of prayer for yourself will please God.

Why does God want you to pray about your own needs?

_____

_____

_____

You can pray:

Dear God, remind me to bring all of my needs and troubles to You. Thank You for loving me and taking care of me. In Jesus' name. Amen.

GOD'S WORD & ME

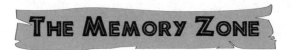

THE MEMORY ZONE

Here are some great Bible verses about what you've learned so far. Put a check mark in the box as you memorize each one!

☐ **Isaiah 40:8** "The grass withers and the flowers fall, but the word of our God stands forever."

☐ **Romans 15:4** "For everything that was written in the past was written to each of us, so that through endurance and the encouragement of the Scriptures we might have hope."

☐ **Psalm 119:11** "I have hidden your word in my heart that I might not sin against you."

☐ **Hebrews 4:12** "For the word of God is living and active. Sharper than any double-edged sword, it penetrates even to dividing soul and spirit, joints and marrow; it judges the thoughts and attitudes of the heart."

☐ **Psalm 119:105** "Your word is a lamp to my feet and a light for my path."

☐ **Hebrews 4:16** "Let us then approach the throne of grace with confidence, so that we may receive mercy and find grace to help us in our time of need."

☐ **Psalm 34:4** "I sought the LORD, and he answered me; he delivered me from all my fears."

☐ **Philippians 4:6-7** "Do not be anxious about anything, but in everything, by prayer and petition, with thanksgiving, present your requests to God. And the peace of God, which transcends all understanding, will guard your hearts and minds in Christ Jesus."

This is the end of the section of "God's Word and Me" devotionals.

It is time to do the next activity page that came to you in the mail. Remember to add your prayer request so your mailbox friend can pray for you. When you finish the whole page, fold it on the lines so the Mailbox Club address shows. Put a small piece of tape on the bottom to keep it folded. Add a stamp and mail your activity page.

Your work will be marked and sent back to you, along with a personal note. The activity sheet for the next set of lessons will be sent to you, too.

Enjoy getting to know God better with your next group of devotionals!

Witnessing

152 What Is a Witness?

**Go into all the world and preach the good news to all creation.
Mark 16:15**

Have you ever seen a witness in a court case? A witness tells the judge or jury what he knows to be true. A Christian witness tells what he knows to be true about Jesus. If you have trusted the Lord Jesus as your Savior, you can be a witness. You can tell others how they can trust Him, too.

Erin told her friend, Travis, that God loves him. She told him how God sent His Son, Jesus, to die on the cross for his sins and how He came alive again. Travis made an important decision that day. He trusted Jesus to forgive his sins and be his Savior.

Erin is a witness. She knows the truth from the Bible. Jesus said, "I am the way and the truth and the life. No one comes to the Father except through me" (John 14:6). Erin wants other people to know the truth about Jesus.

You can be a witness, too. First, be sure you have trusted Jesus as your Savior from sin. Then, you can tell others who Jesus is and how He died on the cross for their sins. Encourage them to trust Jesus as their Savior.

WITNESSING

What should you tell others if you are a witness for Jesus?

_____

_____

_____

You can pray:

Dear God, help me to be a true witness for You. In Jesus' name. Amen.

Why Should I Witness?

 Go into all the world and preach the good news to all creation. **Mark 16:15**

Suppose your mom or dad had to go away on a long trip. Would you remember their last words to you? If they gave you some special instructions, would you obey?

Just before Jesus, God's Son, left this Earth to go back to Heaven, He spoke some last words to His disciples. His words were a command. He said, "Go into all the world and preach [tell] the good news [that Jesus died and rose again] to all creation"(Mark 16:15). Jesus told them to go and tell others about Him. Do you think they did? Yes! They obeyed Jesus because He had commanded them. They also obeyed because they loved Him.

If you know Jesus as your Savior, His command is for you, too. When you go and tell about Jesus, you are being a witness. Jesus wants you to go and tell as many people as you can what He has done for you. Why should you witness? One reason is that God has commanded it. Another reason is that you love Jesus and want to obey Him. Jesus wants you to go and tell. Will you obey His command? Will you be a witness for Him because you love Him?

 Can you think of two reasons why it is important to be a witness?

_____

_____

_____

You can pray:

 Dear God, I love You. I want to obey You every day. Help me to obey Your command to go and tell others about You. In Jesus' name. Amen.

154 What Do I Say When I Witness?

Go into all the world and preach the good news to all creation.
Mark 16:15

Have you ever wanted to tell someone about Jesus, but you didn't know what to say? Begin by telling about God. He is the Creator, who made us special. Tell how God loves us and how He is perfect and lives in Heaven.

Then, talk about sin. Sin is when we disobey God. The Bible says, "For all have sinned . . ." (Romans 3:23). We were all born with a "want to" to sin. Our sin separates us from God. Someday, everyone that is separated will be punished forever in a terrible place called Hell.

Next, talk about Jesus, God's only Son. Tell how Jesus, who was perfect, died on the cross to take our punishment for sin. He was buried, and three days later He came back to life again. When you believe [trust completely] in Jesus, you can be saved from the punishment of your sin. Then, you can ask: "Would you like to believe in Jesus today?"

Before you can tell someone else how to believe in Jesus, you need to be sure that you have done so. If you've never told Jesus that you believe He died for you, do that right now. Then, you can tell others how to believe in Jesus, just like you did!

WITNESSING

What could you tell someone about God, about sin and about Jesus?

_____

_____

_____

You can pray:

Dear God, thank You for the good news I can tell others about how You love them and how Jesus died for their sins and came alive again. In Jesus' name. Amen.

What If I'm Afraid to Witness?

> Go into all the world and preach the good news to all creation. **Mark 16:15**

WITNESSING

The Bible tells about a time when God gave a special assignment to the leader of Israel named Moses. His assignment was to tell God's message to the elders of Israel and to Pharaoh, king of Egypt. Moses didn't want to do it. He was afraid. He said to God, " . . . what if they do not believe me or listen to me?" (Exodus 4:1).

Have you ever felt like Moses? God has given you a special assignment. You are to tell God's message to other people. You are to be a witness. Like Moses, do you make excuses such as, "I'm afraid I might say the wrong thing;" or "I'm afraid people will not listen to me;" or "I'm afraid people will make fun of me?" God said to Moses, "Who gave man his mouth? . . . Is it not I, the Lord? Now go, I will help you speak and will teach you what to say" (Exodus 4:11,12).

God promises the same to you. He is the one who made you. He will be with you. He will give you the words to say. You don't have to be afraid. Trust God to help you be a witness for Him.

What can you do if you are afraid to witness?

_____

_____

_____

You can pray:

Dear God, when I'm afraid to witness, help me to remember the promises in Your Word and give me courage to tell others about You. In Jesus' name. Amen.

156 How Can My Life Be a Witness?

 Go into all the world and preach the good news to all creation.
Mark 16:15

When Maria became angry, she often got in trouble with her words. Sometimes she said bad words. Sometimes she said things that were mean or talked back to her parents.

One day Maria heard the good news about Jesus. She believed in Jesus as her Savior. Then, Maria prayed, "Dear Jesus, when I am tempted to sin with my mouth, help me to remember what You did on the cross for me."

God helped Maria control her anger and her words. Soon her friends at school began to see a change in Maria's life. Two of them asked her why she was different. Maria was able to tell them about Jesus. Maria was witnessing, not only by her words, but by her changed life.

Your life can be a witness, too. If you know Jesus as your Savior, others should see a difference in you. Ask God to help you change those areas that need to be changed. The Holy Spirit, who lives in you, can help you stop saying bad words you used to say. He can help you to be kind instead of being mean. When others see that your life is different, they will want to know why. Then, you can tell them the good news!

WITNESSING

What are some things in your life that may keep you from being a good witness?

_____

_____

_____

 ### You can pray:
Dear God, may my words and my life be a witness for You today. In Jesus' name. Amen.

Who Can I Witness To?

Go into all the world and preach the good news to all creation. **Mark 16:15**

WITNESSING

Did you read the verse at the top of this page? It says that we are to go into all the world and tell the good news about Jesus to everyone. God has put you in a very special part of His world. He wants you to be a witness for Him right now—right where you are.

Think about those people who live around you who do not know Jesus. They could be friends at school or in your neighborhood. Maybe it's a brother or sister or your grandparent. Perhaps even your mom or dad needs to hear about Jesus. Do you know that God might want you to be the one to tell them about Him? Maybe God even wants you to be a witness to someone who has been mean to you. That would not be easy, would it?

God didn't promise that being a witness would be easy, but He has promised that He will always be with you. He has promised He will help you know what to say. God has brought certain people into your life who need to hear about Him. He wants to help you to be a witness to those you meet every day.

 List three people you could witness to.

_____

_____

_____

You can pray:

Dear God, I pray for the three people on my list. Give me the courage and the words to tell them about You. In Jesus' name. Amen.

158 Where Can I Witness?

Go into all the world and preach the good news to all creation.
Mark 16:15

Stephen hated riding the school bus mostly because Anthony rode the same bus. Anthony was a bully. He was always making trouble, especially for Stephen. Stephen talked to his mother about the problem. She suggested that they pray.

Later, Stephen's mother asked him if he would be interested in having a Bible club in their home. Stephen thought that was a great idea. Then, his mother suggested he invite Anthony. She told Stephen to pray and ask God what he should do. Stephen prayed. He knew what God wanted him to do. He asked God for courage to be a witness to Anthony on the school bus.

One day, God gave Stephen that courage. Stephen told Anthony how he had received Jesus as his Savior. Then he invited Anthony to the Bible club. The first day of club, who do you suppose came? Anthony! That day Anthony received Jesus as his Savior.

Like Stephen, you could be a witness on your way to school. Maybe you can tell the good news to a friend during lunch at school. Perhaps you can be a witness right in your own home. Can you think of other places where you can be a witness?

WITNESSING

Write down three places where you can be a witness.

_____

_____

_____

You can pray:

Dear God, help me think of places where I can be a witness for You; then, help me to do it. In Jesus' name. Amen.

Did People in the Bible Witness to Others?

Yet to all who received him, to those who believed in his name, he gave the right to become children of God.
John 1:12

WITNESSING

Here is a "W" test for you: Who, in the Bible, were witnesses? What did they say? Where did they go to witness?

Who, in the Bible, were witnesses? God used people just like you. He used a young servant girl to tell her master about Him. Perhaps she was even your age. Isn't that encouraging! God will use you, if you are willing. The Bible also tells us about a blind man, some followers of Jesus and two prisoners who were witnesses.

What did witnesses in the Bible say? Perhaps you thought they used big, hard words. No, they just told others what they knew about Jesus. One man named Paul told someone, "Believe in the Lord Jesus and you will be saved . . ." (Acts 16:31). Ask God to give you the words to share what you know about Him.

Where did they witness? They witnessed wherever God placed them. One was a witness in another country, and one was a witness in his home. Another was a witness on a desert road. Two others were witnesses in jail. Where has God placed you so that you can be a witness?

Why do you think God uses people like you to be His witnesses?

_____

_____

_____

You can pray:

Thank you, Lord, that You are willing to use even me to be a witness for You. In Jesus' name. Amen.

160 Should I Witness to People in Authority over Me?

Yet to all who received him, to those who believed in his name, he gave the right to become children of God.
John 1:12

In 2 Kings chapter 5, the Bible tells about an army captain named Naaman. He was sick with a terrible disease that no one could cure. Also, he didn't know the true and living God.

Naaman's country went to war. A young girl was captured and brought to his house to be a servant. This young girl knew the true and living God. She learned about Naaman's disease. She knew her God could help him.

The young girl bravely witnessed to Naaman's wife. She politely told about a prophet of God named Elisha. She knew he could tell Naaman how to be healed by God's power. Naaman went to see Elisha and heard how to be healed. Naaman followed Elisha's instructions. God healed his disease! Naaman now believed in the true and living God.

Was it scary for that girl to witness to someone in authority (in charge) over her? It probably was! But God gave her courage. Are there people in authority over you who need to hear about Jesus? Maybe it's your parents or your teacher. Be polite and respectful when you tell them about Jesus. God will give you courage!

WITNESSING

How can you have courage to witness to people in authority over you?

_____

_____

_____

You can pray:
Dear God, may my words and my actions be a witness to those who are in authority over me. In Jesus' name. Amen.

Does God Have Certain People Ready to Listen?

161

Yet to all who received him, to those who believed in his name, he gave the right to become children of God. **John 1:12**

WITNESSING

Philip loved God and told others about Him. The Bible says that one day an angel spoke to him. The angel told Philip to go to a certain place on a desert road. Philip obeyed.

Another man was traveling on that same road. This traveler was from Ethiopia. He was an important man in his country. He was the queen's treasurer. This man wanted to worship God.

God made sure that Philip and the Ethiopian man met on that desert road. Philip heard the man reading God's Word. He was reading Old Testament promises about Jesus. Philip asked him if he understood what he was reading. The Ethiopian man said, "How can I unless someone explains it to me" (Acts 8:31).

Philip told the man who Jesus is. He told how Jesus died on the cross for sin and rose again. That day the Ethiopian man believed in Jesus. Philip was a good witness. He obeyed God. God had someone ready to listen to him.

God may have someone ready to listen to you, too. Maybe it's a family member. Maybe it's a friend who needs to hear about Jesus. Maybe it's someone you've never met before. Will you be ready and willing to go where God sends you to tell someone about Him?

Who do you think God may be preparing for you to talk to?

_____

_____

_____

You can pray:

Dear God, may I be ready always to witness for You to anyone, any place and at any time. In Jesus' name. Amen.

162 How Can I Witness in Hard Times?

Yet to all who received him, to those who believed in his name, he gave the right to become children of God. **John 1:12**

"**Throw them in jail,**" the angry mob probably shouted that day as they attacked Paul and Silas. The officials ordered them to be beaten many times with a rod. With their backs bleeding, they were thrown in prison. How easy it could have been for them to grumble and complain in that dark prison, but they didn't.

The Bible says that Paul and Silas began praying and singing hymns to God. The other prisoners and the jailer heard them. Paul and Silas were witnesses during their hard time to those around them. It was midnight. Suddenly, an earthquake shook open the jail doors. The jailer was afraid they had escaped, and he was about to kill himself, but Paul called out to him. The jailer asked, "What must I do to be saved?" They witnessed to him, and that night he and his family believed in Jesus Christ. (Acts 16:25-31)

Are you going through a hard time in your life? Remember what Paul and Silas did. They prayed and praised God. Their right attitudes were a witness to those around them. What about your attitude? Will you let God use you to be a witness during your hard time?

WITNESSING

How can God use you to be a witness during a hard time?

_____

_____

_____

You can pray:

Dear God, help me to have a right attitude so that I can be a good witness for You. In Jesus' name. Amen.

Should I Witness to My Brothers and Sisters?

163

Yet to all who received him, to those who believed in his name, he gave the right to become children of God. **John 1:12**

WITNESSING

Antonio came from a large family. He had four brothers and two sisters. Their family never went to church. One day Mrs. Roberts, invited Antonio to a Bible club at her home. There Antonio heard about Jesus for the first time, and he believed in Jesus as his Savior.

The next week the teacher told the children about a man in the Bible named Andrew. Andrew believed Jesus was the Savior God promised to send. He wanted his brother, Peter, to know Him, too. Andrew brought his brother to Jesus. The teacher said Andrew was a witness.

Antonio wanted to be like Andrew. He thought about his brothers. The next week he brought his four brothers to club. He wanted them to hear about Jesus. The following week, he brought his two sisters to club!

Andrew was a witness. Antonio was a witness. What about you? Do you have brothers and sisters who need to hear about Jesus? Although it's sometimes hardest to witness to someone in your own family, God can help you do it. Maybe there's no Bible club in your neighborhood, but you can tell them what Jesus has done for you. God wants you to be a witness.

What are different ways you can be a witness to a sister or brother?

_____

_____

You can pray:

Dear God, help me to be like Andrew. Show me how I can be a witness to my brother or sister. In Jesus' name. Amen.

164 How Do I Begin a Conversation about God?

Yet to all who received him, to those who believed in his name, he gave the right to become children of God. **John 1:12**

In Jesus' day, everyone got water from a well. The Bible tells us about a woman from Samaria who came to get water from a well. The Lord Jesus began to talk with her. He asked her for a drink of water. They talked about the "living water." He told her He was the "living water," and that He was the One who could forgive her sins. (John 4:7-15)

What can we learn from Jesus Christ about witnessing? He showed us to look for everyday opportunities to talk to people about Him. Also, Jesus used what the woman was talking about to begin a conversation with her about spiritual things. You can do the same. Maybe a friend at school tells you his parents are getting a divorce. You could be a good listener. Then, at the right time, you could tell him that Jesus loves and cares about him.

Maybe another friend wants you to do something wrong, like stealing something from the store or watching a dirty video. That could be your opportunity. You could tell him why you don't do these things. Then, talk to him about Jesus.

Every day God gives you opportunities to witness. Don't miss out on them!

WITNESSING

Write an everyday opportunity you could use to tell someone about Jesus.

_____

_____

You can pray:
Dear God, thank You for the opportunities You give to tell others about You. In Jesus' name. Amen.

Do I Have to Know a Lot to Be a Witness?

Yet to all who received him, to those who believed in his name, he gave the right to become children of God.
John 1:12

WITNESSING

The Bible tells us about a man who was blind from birth. As Jesus walked by him, he reached down to the ground and made clay. With the clay, he touched the eyes of the blind man. Jesus then told the man to go wash his eyes. The blind man went immediately and washed, and when he came back, he could see!

The religious leaders, who were called Pharisees, were not happy about what had happened. They even called Jesus a sinner because He healed the man on the Sabbath Day (the day of rest). The man who had been blind said, "Whether he is a sinner or not, I don't know. One thing I do know. I was blind, but now I see!" (John 9:25). This man did not know a lot about Jesus, but he eagerly told them what He did know. He knew what Jesus had done for him.

What about you? Maybe you don't think you can be a witness because you don't know a lot about Jesus. If Jesus Christ has changed your life, then you have a lot to tell others. Tell them what He has done for you!

Describe what Jesus has done for you.

_____

_____

_____

You can pray:
Dear God, help me to be willing to tell others what I know about You. In Jesus' name. Amen.

166 Will Everyone I Witness to Believe?

Yet to all who received him, to those who believed in his name, he gave the right to become children of God. **John 1:12**

These are true stories about a man in the Bible named Paul and a boy in New York named Nathan. The Bible tells us Paul was a witness wherever he went. But not everyone he witnessed to believed. One time Paul witnessed to an important King named Agrippa. After listening to Paul, Agrippa asked, "Do you think . . . you can persuade me to be a Christian?" (Acts 26:28). There is no record that King Agrippa ever became a Christian.

Nathan is eight years old. He wants to be a witness wherever he goes. One day he witnessed to a friend at school. His friend listened for awhile. Then, he told Nathan that Jesus is just pretend, and he walked away. Nathan was discouraged. Nathan's dad reminded him that all God is asking him to do is to tell his friends the truth about Jesus. They must decide for themselves to believe in Jesus or to reject Him.

Have you been discouraged in witnessing? Have people walked away from you? Remember that not everyone you witness to will believe. But God wants you to keep on telling others about Him. Don't give up. Trust God and be a faithful witness.

WITNESSING

What can you remember when you are discouraged in witnessing?

_____

_____

You can pray:

Dear God, Help me to be a faithful witness even if others refuse to believe. In Jesus' name. Amen.

What Is the Wordless Book?

But God demonstrates his own love for us in this: While we were still sinners, Christ died for us. **Romans 5:8**

WITNESSING

Have you seen the *Wordless Book*? It has no words or pictures. Instead, it has five colors. They are gold, black, red, white and green. Each color tells a special part of the Gospel message–the good news about Jesus.

Missionaries (Christians who spend their lives telling others about Jesus) have used the *Wordless Book* in many countries to share the Gospel with many people. Several years ago, a missionary went to a country where it was difficult to be a witness for Jesus. There were people in that country who hated Christians. Soldiers broke into the home of the missionary. They took all her Bible materials and burned them. She lost everything–well, almost everything. She had a pile of *Wordless Books*. The soldiers picked up a *Wordless Book* and looked at it. Then, they threw it down. Because it had no words, they thought it was not important. They didn't burn one *Wordless Book*! They didn't know how special that little book was!

The *Wordless Book* has been used to tell many people about Jesus. It is a book you can use to be a witness to others. In the following devotionals, you will learn how to use the *Wordless Book* yourself.

List three people who need to hear the message of the *Wordless Book*.

_____

_____

_____

You can pray:

Dear God, help me to learn the message of the Wordless Book *so I can share it with these three people. In Jesus' name. Amen.*

What Can I Tell on the Gold Page about God?

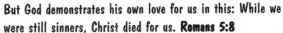

But God demonstrates his own love for us in this: While we were still sinners, Christ died for us. **Romans 5:8**

Each of the five colors of the *Wordless Book* tells a special part of the Gospel. We begin with the gold page. This is what you can tell about God as you witness to a friend:

"This gold page reminds me of a place with a street of gold. It's called Heaven and it is God's home. God is the Creator of this world. He made the sky, trees, flowers, birds and the animals. God made everything, and He made you. God loves you. The Bible says, "For God so loved the world" (John 3:16). That means God loves you. Isn't that good news!

"Because God made you and loves you, He wants you to be a part of His family and be with Him in Heaven someday. Heaven is a perfect place, and God is perfect. That means He has never thought, said or done anything wrong. God wants you to be with Him in Heaven someday, but there's one thing that will never be in Heaven and that is sin."

This is the first part of the message you can share with someone. Practice telling the message of the gold page aloud until you can say it smoothly.

WITNESSING

What are three things you can tell a friend about God on the gold page?

_____

_____

_____

You can pray:

Dear God, thank You for loving me. Help me to tell others about Your love with the gold page of the Wordless Book. *In Jesus' name. Amen.*

What Can I Tell on the Dark Page about Sin?

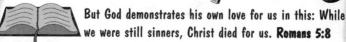

But God demonstrates his own love for us in this: While we were still sinners, Christ died for us. **Romans 5:8**

WITNESSING

Many boys and girls where you live do not know who God is. They don't know that He created them, that He loves them, and that He has a plan for their lives. Perhaps no one has told them that the wrong things they do are called sin and that God hates sin. Turn to the dark page in your *Wordless Book.* Here are some important things you can tell a friend about sin.

"Sin is anything you think, say or do that displeases God. Lying, stealing, or disobeying are things that God calls sin. Having a bad attitude, saying mean, angry words, or destroying someone else's property, is also sin. God's Word says, "All have sinned" (Romans 3:23). That means you and I have sinned. You were born with a "want to" to sin.

"God says that sin must be punished. That punishment is to be separated from God forever in a terrible place of darkness and suffering. But God has a wonderful plan so that you don't have to be punished for your sin."

Be sure to practice telling this part of the message, so you can tell it to a friend.

 Name three things God tells us about sin.

_____

_____

_____

You can pray:
Dear God, help me realize the seriousness of sin. Help me to be able to explain about sin to others. In Jesus' name. Amen.

170

What Can I Tell on the Red Page about Jesus?

But God demonstrates his own love for us in this: While we were still sinners, Christ died for us. **Romans 5:8**

The red page of the *Wordless Book* tells about the Lord Jesus, God's perfect Son, and what He did so our sins could be forgiven. This is what you can say to a friend:

"God loved you and me so much that He didn't want us to be separated from Him. In God's perfect plan, He sent His only Son, the Lord Jesus Christ, to be born on Earth. Jesus lived a perfect life. He never sinned. When He grew to be a man, He allowed wicked men to put Him to death on a wooden cross. This red page reminds that as Jesus suffered, bled and died on that cross, He was taking the punishment you and I deserve for our sin. The Bible says, "... without the shedding [giving] of blood there is no forgiveness" (Hebrews 9:22).

"After Jesus died, He was buried. But Jesus, the all-powerful Son of God, did not stay dead. On the third day He came alive again. Now He is alive in Heaven. Because of what Jesus has done for you, you can have your sins forgiven."

You'll want to practice the red page so you can tell your friends about God's wonderful plan to forgive their sins.

 How did God show His love for us?

_____

_____

_____

You can pray:

 Dear God, help me to learn the message of the red page so I can tell others what Jesus did for them. In Jesus' name. Amen.

How Do I Use the Clean Page to Help Someone Believe in Jesus?

But God demonstrates his own love for us in this: While we were still sinners, Christ died for us. **Romans 5:8**

Jesus has the power to forgive sin. That's the good news of the Gospel that you can share on the clean page. You can share this verse from the Bible with your friend. "Believe in the Lord Jesus, and you will be saved . . ." (Acts 16:31). To explain this verse, remember three key words: Admit, Believe, and Choose. Here's what you can say:

"This verse (read Acts 16:31) means you need to admit you are a sinner. You need to tell God you believe (trust completely) in Jesus, who died for you, and came alive again. Then, you need to choose to let Jesus Christ be your Savior from sin. When you do this, the Lord Jesus promises He will forgive your sin. One day you will go to Heaven to be with Him. Would you like to believe in Jesus as your Savior?"

If your friend says "yes," you can help him pray, just like you did. If he says "no" or "I want to think about it," don't be discouraged. Pray for him, and remember that God has been pleased with your faithful witness. Practice this clean page so you can help your friend believe in Jesus.

 What does someone need to do to be saved from sin?

_____

_____

You can pray:

Dear God, help me to learn the message of the clean page so I can help someone else to believe in Jesus. In Jesus' name. Amen.

172

How Can I Help Someone Know He's Been Saved?

But God demonstrates his own love for us in this: While we were still sinners, Christ died for us. **Romans 5:8**

Has someone ever made a promise to you, then, at the last minute, he couldn't keep his promise? Our God never breaks a promise. He is a promise keeper!

The verse you shared on the clean page with your friend was Acts 16:31. Do you remember it? That verse is a promise from God. If your friend trusted the Lord Jesus Christ as his Savior, then God made him a promise. God promised in Acts 16:31 that your friend is saved. "Saved" means that God has forgiven his sin. God lives in your friend through His Holy Spirit to help him do right. One day,

your friend will go to Heaven to be with Jesus. That's a never-to-be-broken promise.

There's another promise you can share with your friend. It's found at the end of Hebrews 13:5 where Jesus says, "I will never leave you." Jesus promises to always be with you. You can talk to Him any time and any place. He is there to give you power to do what is right. Look at your hand. You can remember each word of Jesus' promise by your five fingers, "Jesus-will-never-leave-you." You can trust God to keep His promise!

WITNESSING

What can you say to someone to help him know he's saved?

_____

_____

_____

You can pray:

Thank You, God, that You are the great promise keeper! In Jesus' name. Amen.

How Can I Help Someone to Grow in Christ?

But God demonstrates his own love for us in this: While we were still sinners, Christ died for us. **Romans 5:8**

WITNESSING

If your friend asked Jesus to forgive his sins and be his Savior, he needs to grow in God's family. This is what you can share on the green page of the *Wordless Book.*

"This green page reminds me of things that grow, like the grass, flowers and trees. Now that you are part of God's family, He wants you to grow by learning more about Him. You have His power and strength to do what is right. When you do something that is sin, God tells you in the Bible what you need to do. He says, 'If we confess our sins, he is faithful and just and will forgive us our sins . . .' (1 John 1:9). 'Confess' means to name your sin and agree with God that you've done wrong. He will forgive you because that is what He promised to do. Ask Him to give you the power and strength to obey Him and do what is right.

"There are four things you can do to learn more about the Lord Jesus:

1. **Pray (talk) to God every day.**
2. **Read and obey the Bible.**
3. **Witness by telling others what Jesus has done for you.**
4. **Go to church and Sunday school."**

What are some things you can say to help someone grow in Christ?

_____

_____

_____

You can pray:

Dear God, help me learn how to use the green page of the Wordless Book *to show others how they can grow in Christ. In Jesus' name. Amen.*

Who Could I Share the *Wordless Book* With?

But God demonstrates his own love for us in this: While we were still sinners, Christ died for us. **Romans 5:8**

Stop! The first thing you need to do before you share the *Wordless Book* is to pray. Make a list of people who don't know the Lord Jesus as Savior. Pray for each one by name. Ask God to make them ready to hear the Gospel. If you don't have your *Wordless Book* with you, look around to see if you can find the colors in something else–maybe even your clothes!

Katie is nine years old. She has just learned how to use the *Wordless Book*. She began praying for the first person on her list, her cousin, Lisa. One day Katie showed Lisa her *Wordless Book*.

She asked her if she had ever seen a book like that. Lisa said, "No." Katie asked Lisa what makes this book different from other books. Lisa looked at it carefully and said, "It has no words or pictures." Katie said, "But it has colors, and the colors tell the most wonderful true story from the Bible. Do you want to hear it?" Lisa said, "Sure!" Katie shared the *Wordless Book* with her, and Lisa trusted Jesus as her Savior! Now, Katie is praying for the next person on her list. What about you? Have you made your list?

Write a prayer to God for one friend who needs to hear about Jesus.

_____

_____

_____

You can pray:

Thank You, God, for the Wordless Book. *Help me to share it with the people on my list. In Jesus' name. Amen.*

How Do I Give a Testimony?

. . . Always be prepared to give an answer to everyone who asks you to give the reason for the hope that you have. But do this with gentleness and respect . . . 1 Peter 3:15

WITNESSING

"Sara, would you be willing to give your testimony at church next Sunday night?" Pastor Carson asked. Giving a testimony means telling others how you came to trust the Lord Jesus as your Savior and what He means to you. Sara was a little scared about being asked to share her testimony, but when she thought about her wonderful Savior, she was willing to do it. She had never given a testimony before. Sara's Sunday school teacher helped her prepare.

They prayed and asked God for help, and then her teacher suggested she write her testimony. Sara wrote what her life was like before she trusted Jesus Christ as her Savior. Then she wrote where and how she made the decision to believe in Him. Sara thought it would be important to include a Bible verse. She wrote out the verse, John 1:12. The last thing Sara wrote was how much Jesus means to her. She wrote about how He helps her to say "no" to sin and to obey God.

Sara then practiced saying what she had written. Now she was ready to share her testimony at any time with others. What about you? Would you be ready to share your testimony?

Write two important things you would want to include in your testimony.

_____

_____

_____

You can pray:

Dear God, help me to prepare my testimony and then be willing to share it with others. In Jesus' name. Amen.

Should I Give My Friend a Tract?

. . . Always be prepared to give an answer to everyone who asks you to give the reason for the hope that you have. But do this with gentleness and respect . . . **1 Peter 3:15**

"A paper missionary"– that's what Carlos' Sunday school teacher called a tract. His teacher said that one way to be a witness for Jesus was to give tracts. Tracts are pieces of paper that tell people about sin and their need to trust the Lord Jesus as their Savior. Carlos' teacher set out some tracts and challenged the Christian kids to give one to a friend.

Carlos prayed for the courage to give his friend, Luis, the tract. Then, he prayed that Luis wouldn't throw it away. Luis wanted Carlos to play street ball with some of the other kids. Af- ter the game, Carlos asked Luis if he wanted some lemonade. As they went into the kitchen, Carlos quietly prayed, "God, help me." Just before Luis left, Carlos ran to get his Bible. He took out the tract, and told Luis to read it sometime. To Carlos' sur- prise, Luis sat down and read it. Luis asked, "Who is Jesus?"

For Carlos, giving a tract to Luis was one way of introduc- ing him to Jesus. Do you know someone you could share a tract with? If you don't have a tract to share, maybe you could make one of your own!

WITNESSING

Why should I give my friend a tract?

_____

_____

_____

You can pray:

Dear God, help me to use tracts as a witness to others. In Jesus' name. Amen.

How Can I Tell the Gospel with My Hand?

177

. . . Always be prepared to give an answer to everyone who asks you to give the reason for the hope that you have. But do this with gentleness and respect . . . 1 Peter 3:15

WITNESSING

You can use your hand to share the Gospel with others. Here's how! Hold your hand up, point your thumb to yourself and say, "God loves me. God says in the Bible, 'I have loved you with an everlasting love'" (Jeremiah 31:3).

Then go to your pointer finger and say, "I am a sinner. The Bible says, 'For all have sinned . . .' (Romans 3:23). My sin separates me from God."

Point to your tallest finger and say, "Jesus, God's Perfect Son, died and came alive for me. The Bible says, ' . . . Christ died for our sins according to the Scriptures, that he was buried, that he was raised on the third day . . .' (1 Corinthians 15:3-4). Jesus paid the payment for my sin."

Go on to the next finger and say, "I believe in the Lord Jesus as my Savior. The Bible says, 'Believe in the Lord Jesus, and you will be saved' (Acts 16:31). I believe Jesus died for me."

Point to your little finger and say, "I am saved. The Bible says, 'Whoever believes in the Son [Jesus] has eternal life . . .' (John 3:36). I know that I will live forever with God."

Learn these Bible verses and practice sharing the Gospel with your hand!

What are the five important truths you can share on your hand?

_____

_____

_____

You can pray:

Dear God, help me learn the important truths and verses I can share on my hand so that I will always be ready to be a witness. In Jesus' name. Amen.

Where Could I Invite My Friend to Come Hear the Gospel?

. . . Always be prepared to give an answer to everyone who asks you to give the reason for the hope that you have. But do this with gentleness and respect . . . **1 Peter 3:15**

Can you think of three places where you could take a friend to hear the Gospel? Sunday school should be on the top of your list. If your church has a children's program, you could invite a friend to go with you. In the summer, a great place to bring a friend is to vacation Bible school. Another great place is a Christian camp. Some churches have programs especially for kids during their missionary conference. Sometimes, churches will have children's rallies or fairs.

Is there a Bible club in your neighborhood? If not, maybe your family could start one!

What a great witness that would be. Is there a Christian radio program in your area? You could invite a friend to listen with you.

Maybe you live in a place where people are not allowed to openly worship God and talk about the Gospel. Perhaps people are even punished for following the Lord Jesus Christ. Pray and ask God to help you find ways to share about Him with your friends. Even if you can't invite them to a special place to hear the Gospel, you may be able to share with them from your own life.

Where could you invite a friend to hear the Gospel?

_____

_____

_____

You can pray:

Thank You, God, for places where I can invite my friends to hear the Gospel. In Jesus' name. Amen.

Is My Life a Good Witness to Others? 179

. . . Always be prepared to give an answer to everyone who asks you to give the reason for the hope that you have. But do this with gentleness and respect . . . **1 Peter 3:15**

Witnessing is not just the words that you say. God says that the light of His love should shine through your life. Then others will be drawn to Him (Matthew 5:16). Are your actions and attitudes a good witness to those around you, or do they keep others from wanting to believe?

Todd is a Christian. He's usually fun to be around. However, at home, whenever Todd doesn't get his way, he has a bad attitude. He becomes mean and angry. He makes his family miserable. What kind of a witness is Todd to his family? God can use your good attitudes and actions to show your family how the Lord Jesus controls your life. But bad attitudes or selfish behavior can ruin your witness.

Marissa was always inviting her friend, Tina, to Sunday school. She wanted Tina to hear about Jesus Christ. One day at school during a test, Marissa looked at someone else's paper for an answer. When she turned around, Tina was watching her. What kind of witness was Marissa's life?

If you want to be a good witness to your family and friends, remember that your actions and attitudes speak louder than your words. What kind of witness is your life?

How can your life be a good witness?

_____

_____

_____

You can pray:

Dear God, help me to be a good witness for You by my actions and attitudes. In Jesus' name. Amen.

180 How Can I Help Others Go with the Gospel?

... Always be prepared to give an answer to everyone who asks you to give the reason for the hope that you have. But do this with gentleness and respect ... **1 Peter 3:15**

You can't witness to everybody in the world! However, there is a way you can share the Gospel with people you will never meet. You can help to send a missionary. A missionary is a Christian whose life's work is telling others about the Lord Jesus. Some missionaries work in their own country. Others go to foreign countries.

How can you help missionaries to go with the Gospel? First, pray for them. Ask God to send people that He chooses to be missionaries. When you pray for missionaries, think of the many needs they may have. Just like you, missionaries need food, clothing and a place to live. They need medicine when they are sick. They need fuel for their cars. They need safety in dangerous places. Missionaries also need encouragement to face loneliness or other difficulties. They need courage to tell others about Jesus.

Another way you can help missionaries to go is to give money. You could give some of the money you have earned as an offering to the missionaries at your church. When you give your money to help missionaries, you are giving to God! What are you doing to help missionaries to go with the Gospel?

Write three things you can do to help missionaries go with the Gospel.

_____

_____

You can pray:

Dear God, thank you for missionaries who take the Gospel to many places. Help me to pray and give so that missionaries can go. In Jesus' name. Amen.

WITNESSING

Could I Be a Missionary Someday?

> ... Always be prepared to give an answer to everyone who asks you to give the reason for the hope that you have. But do this with gentleness and respect ... **1 Peter 3:15**

WITNESSING

Many missionaries knew when they were children that God wanted them to do that work. How did they know? They spent time with God each day to read His Word and pray. They attended church where they could learn more about God. Perhaps they read missionary stories. They were faithful witnesses right where they lived. Little by little, God put a strong desire in their hearts to do His work as a full-time missionary. Perhaps He even gave them a deep concern for a particular place or people.

Someday, God may ask you to be a missionary. You can prepare now by learning all you can about God. Read His Word and pray. Go to church whenever you can. Also, you can pray for and give to missionaries. Read missionary stories. Most importantly, be a faithful witness where God has placed you.

Don't worry that God will ask you to do something you don't like or something you can't do. If God wants you to be a missionary, He will give you the desire and the ability to do it. Ask God to give you a willing heart to obey Him. Maybe one day, God will ask you to be a missionary!

How might you know that God wants you to be a missionary?

_____

_____

_____

You can pray:

Dear God, please help me to know if You want me to be a missionary someday, and then please give me a willing heart to obey You. In Jesus' name. Amen.

This is the end of the section of "Witnessing" devotionals.

It is time to do the next activity page that came to you in the mail. Remember to add your prayer request so your mailbox friend can pray for you. When you finish the whole page, fold it on the lines so the Mailbox Club address shows. Put a small piece of tape on the bottom to keep it folded. Add a stamp and mail your activity page.

Your work will be marked and sent back to you, along with a personal note. The activity sheet for the next set of lessons will be sent to you, too.

Enjoy getting to know God better with your next group of devotionals!

Worshiping GOD

182 What Is Worship?

Come near to God and he will come near to you. **James 4:8**

The young boy worked hard almost every afternoon, shining shoes for the people who passed by. No one ever paid him much, only a few cents for a good shine, but the boy didn't complain. He wanted to buy a bicycle! No matter how hard he had to work, it was worth it!

What is "worth it" to you? Take a look at how you spent your time last week, and you'll get a pretty good idea. Did you spend most of your time with friends? Watching TV? Playing on the computer? How much time did you spend with God? Did you worship Him?

What is worship? Some people think worship is only what Christians do at church on Sundays, but worship is much more! Worship is showing God He is "worth it" to you. You can worship God as you sing praise songs, pray and give money at church. You can also worship when you do ordinary things like obeying your parents. However, just doing those things isn't worship. Worship is doing those things in a way that shows God you think He's awesome. It's something you can and should do every minute of your life!

WORSHIPING GOD

What will you do to show God He is "worth it" to you?

_____

_____

_____

You can pray:

Dear God, You are worth it! Help me love and worship You more each day. In Jesus' name. Amen.

Who Can Worship God? 183

Come near to God and he will come near to you.
James 4:8

On the outside, some things look almost the same. For example, how can you tell the difference between a raw egg and a hard-boiled one? Or between a dry orange and a juicy one? Sometimes you can only tell the difference by looking on the inside.

When God looks at those who worship Him, He looks on the inside—He looks at their hearts. Only those who have received Jesus as their Savior can truly worship Him. True worshippers are those who know that Jesus is the one and only way to God the Father.

What does God see when He looks at your heart? Does He see someone whose sins are forgiven? Or does He see someone who needs to become His child? The Bible says, "Yet to all who received him [Jesus], to those who believed in his name, he gave the right to become children of God" (John 1:12). To become a child of God you must have your sin forgiven. You can pray right now and believe in Jesus, who died and rose again for you.

If you have already received Jesus, you are God's child. The Holy Spirit lives in you. Now you can truly worship God as part of His family!

Are you in God's family? How do you know?

_____

_____

_____

You can pray:

Dear God, I'm so glad I'm Your child. Thank You for sending your Holy Spirit to always live inside me. In Jesus' name. Amen.

184 Why Should We Worship God?

Come near to God and he will come near to you. **James 4:8**

The candle was sad. Everything else in the house seemed useful, but not him. He had tried everything from propping open a door to stirring a pot of soup, but everything he did failed. Then, one dark day the master of the house struck a match and applied it to the little candle's wick. Instantly, a small flame took hold and filled the house with light! Wow! thought the candle. Now I know what I was made for!

Do you know what you were made for? The Bible teaches that God made you for Himself—He made you to love, worship and glorify Him. His Word says, " . . . whatever you do, do it all for the glory of God" (1 Corinthians 10:31). Although this world is full of things to enjoy, God wants you to enjoy Him most of all.

The Bible says, "Come near to God and he will come near to you" (James 4:8). You can come near to God by obeying His Word, the Bible, and spending time with Him. God wants you to come near and worship Him. God wants you to know Him as a Father and a special friend, but God won't force you to come. It's your choice, and it's the best choice you'll ever make.

What one thing will you do right now to come near to God?

_____

_____

_____

You can pray:

Dear God, help me to love and worship You more each day. In Jesus' name. Amen.

Where Is God? 185

Come near to God and he will come near to you.
James 4:8

WORSHIPING GOD

Have you ever looked up to see the stars so high in the sky? God created each one—even the stars billions of light-years away! Isn't that amazing? You could never live long enough to visit just one of those far-away stars, but God can! In fact, God is there right now, just as He is here with you.

The Bible teaches that God is omnipresent. "Where can I go from your Spirit? Where can I flee from your presence?" (Psalm 139:7). He is there and here and everywhere else all at once! God is caring for hungry people in a distant country. He's also guiding presidents, and God is taking care of you.

Nothing is too big or too small for God to pay attention to. You may think you're not very important, but to God you are. He's been with you every second of your life! He's always been there loving you just as He is loving you now.

The next time you look at the stars, think about how God is omnipresent. You can be in only one place at a time, but God is everywhere, all the time! The more you realize that God is omnipresent, the more you'll want to worship Him.

As God watches over you today, what's one thing He'd like to see you doing?

_____

_____

_____

You can pray:
Dear God, I praise You for being omnipresent. It's good to know You always watch over me. In Jesus' name. Amen.

186 How Much Does God Know?

Come near to God and he will come near to you. **James 4:8**

Can you keep a secret? When someone tells you to be quiet about something, can you do it? Even if you're good at keeping secrets, there is always someone who knows. That someone is God!

God is not only omnipresent (everywhere), He is also omniscient (om - NISH - ent) God is all-knowing! God knows everything. He knew when and where you would be born. He knew who your parents would be. He knows easy things like your name and how old you are. He knows difficult things like how many hairs you have on your head. He even knows private things like your thoughts and your feelings.

Nothing can ever surprise God. He knows what will happen long before it does. He even knows the future! The Bible says God knew how you would live every day of your life "before even one of them came to be" (Psalm 139:16). God is there guiding and loving you as you live through each one!

Aren't you glad you don't need to hide things from God? You can come to Him in worship and be who you really are. The more you realize that God is omniscient, the more you'll want to worship Him.

WORSHIPING GOD

Write down two things you're glad God knows about you.

_____

_____

_____

You can pray:

Dear God, I praise You for being omniscient. I'm glad You know everything there is to know. In Jesus' name. Amen.

How Much Can God Do?

Come near to God and he will come near to you
James 4:8

Have you ever thought of what you could do if you had more power? What if you were stronger or quicker? What if you could stay awake all the time and never have to sleep? What if you could do anything you wanted to do?

Power can sometimes be a bad thing. Some people use their power to break the law or hurt others, but power can also be a good thing. Think of how God made this world in just six days. He made all the mountains, streams, animals and people. Now that's power! The Bible teaches that God is omnipotent (om - NIP - oh - tent). He is all-powerful. He has power to do absolutely anything! And because God is good, He will never use His power to do wrong.

You can worship and thank God in every situation because He has power to help you. The Bible says, " . . . If God is for us, who can be against us?" (Romans 8:31). God has power to help you make right choices. He has power to help you be joyful even in hard times. The more you realize that God is omnipotent, the more you'll want to worship Him.

What's one way God has shown His power in your life?

_____

_____

_____

You can pray:

Dear God, I praise You for being omnipotent. Thank You for always using Your power for good. In Jesus' name. Amen.

WORSHIPING GOD

188 Am I a Friend of God?

Come near to God and he will come near to you. **James 4:8**

How can you tell if someone is your friend? That person likes to spend time with you, to talk and listen to you. He says good things about you to others. You are important to him. Did you know that God wants you to be His friend? What does it mean to be a friend of God?

The Bible tells about a man named Abraham. He once worshiped false gods—gods that weren't real. Then, one day the true God spoke to him. Abraham believed in God and chose to obey Him. Abraham was changed from a sinful man who didn't know God to one who knew Him in a special way. The Bible says Abraham was a friend of God (Isaiah 41:8).

Maybe you're like Abraham. There was a time when you didn't know or worship God, but now you do. Would others say you're a friend of God? Do you love spending time with God each day? Do you say good things about Him to others? Is He more important to you than anything else? When you know God as your friend, you'll want to worship Him.

The Bible says, "Come near to God and he will come near to you" (James 4:8). Come near to God today, and be His friend!

WORSHIPING GOD

 What's one thing you will do to be a friend of God?

_____

_____

_____

 You can pray:
Dear God, I want to be Your friend. Help me love You more than anyone or anything else. In Jesus' name. Amen.

Can I Worship God When I'm All Alone?

189

Come near to God and he will come near to you.
James 4:8

W O R S H I P I N G   G O D

Do you remember what worship is? Worship is showing God He is "worth it" to you. You were made to worship God. He is omnipresent (everywhere), omniscient (all-knowing) and omnipotent (all-powerful)! He is more awesome than you could ever imagine, yet He loves you and wants to be your friend.

Can you worship God on your own? Yes! The Bible says, "For Christ died for sins . . . to bring you to God" (1 Peter 3:18). Because Jesus died for your sins and rose again, you can talk directly to God through prayer. You can worship Him even when no one else is there.

It's good to sing praise songs while someone plays music, but you can also sing to God all by yourself. You can even write your own songs like David. He wrote many of the psalms (poems or songs) in the Bible! We can learn a lot from David's life. He loved and worshiped God in almost everything he did. In fact, the Bible says David was "a man after [God's] own heart" (1 Samuel 13:14).

Do you want to love and worship God that way? Today is a great day to start!

What's one way you can worship God as you're alone with Him right now?

_____

_____

_____

You can pray:

Dear God, I love the time we spend together! Thank You for always being there. In Jesus' name. Amen.

190 Can I Worship God Together with Other People?

Come near to God and he will come near to you. **James 4:8**

Have you ever wondered why people go to church? God is everywhere, and you can worship God on your own. So why do you need to go to church and meet with other people? Wouldn't it be better to just worship by yourself?

God does want you to worship by yourself. But God also wants you to worship with other Christians. Worshiping together honors God as our King and Lord. It shows that we belong to Him. God's Holy Spirit brings us together as brothers and sisters in Christ.

Worshiping God together also makes us stronger on the inside. We need each other. The Bible says, "Let us not give up meeting together . . . but let us encourage one another . . ." (Hebrews 10:25). Your Christian life is like a flaming branch. On its own that branch will quickly burn out. But put that flaming branch with others, and the fire will burn longer and brighter. Spending time with others who believe in Jesus will help your life burn long and bright for God. Besides, others who believe in Jesus can be the best friends you'll ever have!

WORSHIPING GOD

Why does God want you to worship with other Christians?

_____

_____

_____

You can pray:

Dear God, thank You for my brothers and sisters in Christ. Help us burn brightly together for You. In Jesus' name. Amen.

Have I Told God Everything?

God is spirit, and his worshipers must worship in spirit and in truth. **John 4:24**

Candace mixed the cookie dough together in a big bowl. She added flour, sugar and eggs. She added all the other ingredients that make cookies so yummy. But she forgot to do one important thing before she began. She forgot to clean the bowl!

Sometimes you and I try to worship God that way. We forget to clean the bowl! We do all the right things we should do in worship, but we forget to make sure our lives are clean before we begin. Just like cookie dough mixed in a dirty bowl, unclean worship is not very good.

How can you make sure your life is clean? God gives the answer in His Word. He says, "If we confess our sins, he is faithful and just and will forgive us our sins and purify us [make us clean] from all unrighteousness [sin]" (1 John 1:9).

Before you worship God, confess (agree with God about) the wrong things you've done. Thank Him for His forgiveness. Ask Him to help you not do those things again. When you do that, God promises to forgive your sin and make your life clean again. You'll be ready to worship Him in all the right ways—and with a clean life!

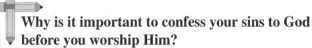

Why is it important to confess your sins to God before you worship Him?

_____

_____

_____

You can pray:

Dear God, I know I have done things that are sinful. Thank You for Your forgiveness. Help me live my life for You. In Jesus' name. Amen.

192 What Is the Right Attitude for Worship?

God is spirit, and his worshipers must worship in spirit and in truth. **John 4:24**

How do you behave when you're with a very important person like the principal of your school or the pastor of your church? You're probably very careful to show respect in what you say and do. If you show respect for important people, how much more should you show respect for God! He is most important of all!

Did you know that God invites you to meet with Him anytime? It's an incredible gift God gives you as His child. How should you come to God in worship? What should your attitude or way of thinking and acting be? The Bible says, "God is spirit, and his worshipers must worship in spirit and in truth" (John 4:24). Because God is a Spirit and you can't see Him, it's easy to forget that He is right there with you. But He is always there. He is real, and He is powerful. He deserves your reverence (honor and respect).

The Bible says, "The LORD is in his holy temple; the LORD is on his heavenly throne" (Psalm 11:4). The next time you pray to God, remember that you are approaching the King who rules all of creation. Honor Him in your thoughts and the words you say.

WORSHIPING GOD

How could you show honor to God?

_____

_____

_____

You can pray:

Dear God, help me to honor You every day, and to worship You with the right attitude. In Jesus' name. Amen.

Does God Want My Worship?

God is spirit, and his worshipers must worship in spirit and in truth. **John 4:24**

Someone has said, "Love makes the world go around." There's a lot of truth to that! Love is all around us, and it's the one thing that gives meaning to life. Think of the love between family members and friends. Think of the love we feel for pets or things we do and places we live. Each of these forms of love is different.

Above all these loves is a special love reserved only for God. Because God made you and knows all about you, your love for Him can be the deepest love you'll ever know. The way you show that love is through worship.

Does God really want your worship? Yes! God loves you as a perfect Father. He watches over you every second of your life. It's true that God can have anything He wants. He made all things and can do all things, but you are a special treasure to Him. He wants your love and worship more than anything in the world. That's why one of the Bible writers named King David wrote these words: "Come, let us bow down in worship, let us kneel before the LORD our Maker" (Psalm 95:6). God longs for your worship.

Why does God want your worship?

_____

_____

_____

You can pray:

Dear God, I do love You. Thank You for inviting me to worship You. In Jesus' name. Amen.

Can I Have a Conversation with God?

God is spirit, and his worshipers must worship in spirit and in truth. **John 4:24**

Having a conversation with someone means talking and listening. Conversations can be wonderful, especially when you talk with a good friend. The best friend you could ever talk to is God!

You can talk to God through prayer. You don't have to use special words. You don't even have to speak aloud–you can just think the words, and God will hear them. If you're too upset to talk, you can even cry to God. He will always hear you and understand. No matter what you say, He will never stop loving you. He knows all about you and always knows how to help.

You can listen to God through His Word and His Holy Spirit. As you read the Bible, you'll learn about things that happened long ago. God will use those stories to tell you what He wants you to do today. As you make decisions each day, God will use His Holy Spirit to guide you. He won't speak to you with a voice you can hear, but He will help you to know deep inside when you should do something and when you should not. Have you had a conversation with God lately? Ask God to help you be a good talker and listener today!

WORSHIPING GOD

Why is it important to both talk and listen to God?

_____

_____

_____

You can pray:

Dear God, help me to talk with You more and learn to listen as You talk to me. In Jesus' name. Amen.

How Do I Know the Truth?

God is spirit, and his worshipers must worship in spirit and in truth. **John 4:24**

If someone told you that all apples are red, would you believe him? Of course not! You can see for yourself that there are also yellow apples and green ones. But sometimes it's harder to know what's true and what isn't. How can you find out?

The first thing you must know is that all truth comes from God. The Bible says that God "does not lie" (Titus 1:2). Everything He has written in His Word is true. In fact, God is truth! The Lord Jesus Christ, God the Son, said, "I am the way and the truth and the life" (John 14:6).

The second thing you must know is that all lies come from God's enemy, Satan, the "father of lies" (John 8:44). Satan won't try to tell you that all apples are red, but he will try to make you believe God doesn't love you. He will try to lead you away from God and get you to sin.

You need to know God's truth. As you read God's Word, really think about what you're reading. Repeat in prayer to God what He has shown you. As God's truth begins to fill your mind, you'll have no more room for lies.

What is one truth you've learned today that you could pray back to God?

_____

_____

_____

You can pray:

Dear God, You are the truth. Thank You that I can trust You to never lie. In Jesus' name. Amen.

How Can God and I Have Fun Together?

God is spirit, and his worshipers must worship in spirit and in truth. **John 4:24**

What does God know about fun? Lots! God is a spirit and He doesn't do some of the things you do, but God does know about fun. Remember that He's the Creator! He's the one who made laughter, good times and fun! He wants you to enjoy life and the good things He has given you.

When you're alone and want a friend to play with, remember that God is right there with you. Talk to Him and ask Him to help you have fun right where you are. Then, find something to do and keep sharing that time with God. He loves just watching you grow and explore and learn new skills. He understands you, and He loves to hear you laugh.

When you spend time with friends, you can have even more fun when you let God join you. Yes, God is right there with you. But you let Him join you when you think about Him and talk about how wonderful He is. There's a special joy you can share with other Christians just by being together. Talking about God as you work or play makes your time together that much more special.

What will you do to have fun with God?

_____

_____

_____

You can pray:

Dear God, thank You that You know all about fun. Help me share my good times with You. In Jesus' name. Amen.

WORSHIPING GOD

How Do I Worship God?

Come, let us bow down in worship, let us kneel before the LORD our Maker; for he is our God . . . **Psalm 95:6-7**

WORSHIPING GOD

Have you ever wanted to do something, but you just didn't know how? Maybe worship is like that to you. You're not quite sure how to do it.

The most important thing to remember about worship is that it's not what you do but why you do it. Worship is showing God He is "worth it" to you. When you set aside a special time to worship God, the first thing you must do is be sure you're doing it for the right reasons.

The next thing you must do is confess your sins. Your obedience is more important than your worship to God. When you confess your sins, God will forgive you and gladly welcome your worship from a clean life.

After that, you can read or remember verses from God's Word, pray or sing praise songs or give to God in some other way. If you are worshiping with other Christians, there will be an order you follow so everyone worships together. When you're worshiping alone, you can really make the time personal and special. However you choose to worship, always be sure you are really worshiping God. Be sure you are letting Him know He is worth it to you.

Write three things you can do the next time you worship God.

_____

_____

_____

You can pray:

Dear God, help me show just how special You are to me. In Jesus' name. Amen.

198 What Is Praising God?

Come, let us bow down in worship, let us kneel before the LORD our Maker; for he is our God . . . **Psalm 95:6-7**

Have you ever wondered what it means to praise God? Praising God is telling how much you appreciate Him and the great things that He does. Praising God may sound difficult, but it's really one of the easiest things to do. You can praise God with prayers, songs, poems or even by drawing pictures. You could praise Him every moment of your life and still never run out of good things to say! The more you get to know God, the more you love Him and realize He is good in every way.

Even though praising God is easy, it's something we need to practice. One simple way you can start praising God more is to use the alphabet. Tell God one thing you love about Him, using each letter. You could say, "Thank You, God, for **a**lways being there for me. You are **b**eautiful in every way. I love the way You **c**are for me. You **d**o so many things for me each day." Then, continue with the rest of the letters.

The Bible says, "How good it is to sing praises to our God ..." (Psalm 147:1). Take time right now to find out!

Choose three letters and write what you love about God, using each letter.

_____

_____

_____

You can pray:

Dear God, I think You're amazing! Help me to think of new ways every day to praise You. In Jesus' name. Amen.

WORSHIPING GOD

Why Should I Praise God?

Come, let us bow down in worship, let us kneel before the LORD our Maker; for he is our God . . . **Psalm 95:6-7**

Have you ever done something without knowing why you were doing it? Praising God should never be that way. Praising God isn't just something you do because you should. It isn't something you do so that God will do something for you. Praising God is a way of worshiping Him. God commands us to praise Him. He is worth all of your praise. But, you should also praise God to show how much you love Him.

The Bible says, "Come, let us sing for joy to the Lord . . .

Come, let us bow down in worship, let us kneel before the LORD our Maker; for he is our God . . ." (Psalm 95:1, 6-7). Praise comes from a joyful heart. It's easy to be joyful when you think of who God is and all He has done for you. The Lord is the one who created you. He is God and He rules Heaven and Earth. He is the perfect one who suffered and died on the cross for your sins and then rose again. What a great God He is! When you praise God, remember who He is and give Him the worship He really deserves.

What are three reasons why you should praise God?

_____

_____

_____

You can pray:

Dear God, I praise You for being my God. Help me to always give You the praise You deserve. In Jesus' name. Amen.

260 What Can I Give to God?

Come, let us bow down in worship, let us kneel before the LORD our Maker; for he is our God . . . **Psalm 95:6-7**

Many people love the Christmas song about a little drummer boy. He was too poor to give a gift just right for the newborn King, but he did have one thing to give–his talent! The boy played his drum the best that he could. He knew that would please Jesus.

As God's child, what should you give? The Bible teaches that every good gift you have comes from God. Your money, clothes, home, family, friends–every good thing you have–comes from God. As a way to show God you love and trust Him, God wants you to give back some of what He gives.

You can give some of your money in the offering of your church. Instead of asking your parents for money, think of ways you can earn some money to give to God. You can also give time to God by helping at church or helping a neighbor. You can give your talents by singing or playing a musical instrument in a worship service or using some other skill for God.

There are so many ways you can give to God. Take time to thank Him for all He has given and then joyfully give back to God in worship!

WORSHIPING GOD

 Write two or three things that you will give to God.

_____

_____

_____

You can pray:

 Dear God, thank You for giving me so many good things. Help me to joyfully give back to You. In Jesus' name. Amen.

Does God Like Music? 261

Come, let us bow down in worship, let us kneel before the LORD our Maker; for he is our God . . . **Psalm 95:6-7**

WORSHIPING GOD

Did you know that the Bible is filled with songs? Whenever God's people wanted to praise Him and celebrate, they sang songs to Him. At other times, they sang sad songs as a way to express their feelings. Many of their songs are included in the Bible. In fact, a whole book of the Bible, the book of Psalms, is filled with such songs.

Does God like music? Yes! The Bible says, "Sing to [the Lord] a new song; play skillfully, and shout for joy" (Psalms 33:3). God wants His people to use their skills to worship Him with music.

Music was alive even before creation. When God created the world, "the morning stars sang together and all the angels shouted for joy" (Job 38:7). God uses beautiful words to describe a similar celebration in nature: " . . . the mountains and hills will burst into song . . . and all the trees of the field will clap their hands" (Isaiah 55:12). In Heaven the songs continue as God's people sing praises to Him.

God is the Creator of music and He loves songs that honor Him. When you sing songs that give praise to Jesus, you can be sure God is listening with joy.

Write your own short song of praise to God.

_____

_____

_____

You can pray:

Dear God, help me to honor You in the music I sing and listen to. Teach me to praise You in song. In Jesus' name. Amen.

How Can I Pray?

Come, let us bow down in worship, let us kneel before the LORD our Maker; for he is our God . . . **Psalm 95:6-7**

Do you sometimes not know what to say when you pray? You want to talk to God, but you don't know how! One thing to remember is to be yourself. Talk to God in your own words and not someone else's. You don't need big fancy words or rhyming prayers. God wants to hear what you have to say.

Earlier in this book, you learned how to use the word ACTS to help you know how to pray. Can you remember what each letter stands for? (Go back and read devotional #145 if you need help.) The A in Acts stands for _____. Tell God how you love, honor and respect Him. Praise God for who He is and what He does. The C stands for_____. Tell God about the wrong things you have done and agree with Him that they are sins. The T stands for_____. Express your gratitude to God for all the good things He does for you. The S stands for _____. Ask God to provide for your needs and for the needs of others.

God is your Heavenly Father. He wants you to talk to Him about everything that concerns you. He delights in meeting your needs.

WORSHIPING GOD

Why should you talk to God in your own words?

_____

_____

_____

You can pray:

Dear God, thank You that I can just talk to You as my Father and my best friend. In Jesus' name. Amen.

Is God Always Right Here?

Come, let us bow down in worship, let us kneel before the LORD our Maker; for he is our God . . . **Psalm 95:6-7**

WORSHIPING GOD

Where is God? Some say He's up in Heaven. Some people who know the Lord Jesus say He lives inside them. Some say God is very far away. All of those answers are right! God is omnipresent–He is everywhere at once.

If you know Jesus Christ as your Savior, you know God in a special way. The Bible teaches that God the Holy Spirit lives inside you! God has given you a special promise. In the Bible God says, "Never will I leave you . . . " (Hebrews 13:5). No matter what happens or what you do, God promises to always be with you.

Here's another promise to think about. The Bible also says, " . . . The Lord is my helper . . ." (Hebrews 13:6). Not only is God always with you, He is always there to help! He wants you to depend on Him to guide your life. He wants you to let Him help you with big things and small things. He is able to always give the help you need.

When you remember that God is always with you, it makes a big difference. You can know that He's always there to help, and you can worship Him wherever you go.

What will you do differently today because you know God is with you?

_____

_____

_____

You can pray:

Dear God, thank You that You will never leave me. Thank You for always being there to help. In Jesus' name. Amen.

264 Why Does God Sometimes Seem Far Away?

Come, let us bow down in worship, let us kneel before the LORD our Maker; for he is our God . . . **Psalm 95:6-7**

If God is always with you, why does He sometimes seem far away? One reason may be sin. When you sin, you hurt your relationship with God. You are still His child, but God wants you to confess your sin to Him and thank Him for His forgiveness.

Do you remember God's promise about confessing sin? The Bible says, "If we confess our sins, he is faithful and just and will forgive us our sins and purify us from all unrighteousness" (1 John 1:9). You need to agree with God that you have sinned and ask Him to help you do what is right. When you do

that, God promises to forgive your sin and make you clean. Then, your relationship with God will be close again.

God may also seem far away when you are discouraged or sick. You may not understand how God is working in your life. Even in times like these, you can know that God is still with you and is caring for you.

The next time God seems far away, remember His promise to be with you always (Matthew 28:20). Tell God how you feel and ask Him to help you to trust Him.

WORSHIPING GOD

What can you do when God seems far away?

_____

_____

_____

You can pray:

Dear God, thank You that You are always with me. In Jesus' name. Amen.

What Is the Body of Christ?

 But if we walk in the light, as he is in the light, we have fellowship with one another, and the blood of Jesus, his Son, purifies us from all sin. **1 John 1:7**

WORSHIPING GOD

When the Lord Jesus lived on Earth, He had a human body. He lived in that body and did many great things. Now that Jesus lives in Heaven, He does great things through a different kind of body called the Body of Christ.

A body can sometimes be a group of people. When we talk about the Body of Christ, we're not talking about Jesus' human body. We're talking about a group of people who represent Jesus Christ. These people are Christians–men, women, boys and girls who have trusted Jesus as Savior.

In the Bible, the Body of Christ is compared to a human body so we can understand it. In a human body, the head does the thinking and tells the other body parts what to do. In the Body of Christ, Jesus is the "head" or leader. He is the one who guides the people who make up the "parts" of His Body. These people do different things, but they are all part of one group.

If you're a Christian, you're in the Body of Christ! Have you ever thought of that? You belong to Jesus, your "head," and every other Christian is part of the Body with you.

 How should Christians in the Body of Christ treat each other?

_____

_____

_____

 You can pray:
Dear God, thank You that I'm part of Your Body. Help me to do what You say. In Jesus' name. Amen.

266 **A**m I in the Body of Christ?

But if we walk in the light, as he is in the light, we have fellowship with one another, and the blood of Jesus, his Son, purifies us from all sin. **1 John 1:7**

Now that you know what the Body of Christ is, you need to know if you're part of it!

The Bible teaches that "all have sinned" (Rom. 3:23). When you steal, tell a lie or do some other wrong thing, you sin. God is holy (sinless) and He must punish sin. That punishment is separation from God forever.

The only person who never sinned was Jesus Christ, God the Son. Because He loves you, He was willing to pay for your sin. He did it by letting Himself be hung on a cross, where He suffered, bled and died. His body was buried in a tomb, but three days later He came back to life. Today, He's alive in Heaven, and He wants you to join Him someday.

The only way you can be forgiven and know you are going to Heaven is to trust Jesus as your Savior. Tell God that you're sorry for your sin and believe Jesus died for you. Ask the Lord Jesus to come into your life and be your Savior. God promises to forgive your sin and help you live for Him. When you trust Jesus as your Savior, you become part of the Body of Christ.

What did Jesus do so that you could be part of the Body of Christ?

_____

_____

_____

You can pray:

Dear God, thank You that I can be part of the Body of Christ by trusting in Your Son as my Savior. In Jesus' name. Amen.

WORSHIPING GOD

Where Is the Body of Christ?

But if we walk in the light, as he is in the light, we have fellowship with one another, and the blood of Jesus, his Son, purifies us from all sin. **1 John 1:7**

WORSHIPING GOD

When you trust the Lord Jesus as your Savior, you become part the Body of Christ. Sometimes the Body of Christ is called the Church. All Christians (those who have trusted the Lord Jesus Christ as Savior) are also part of this Body. This large group of Christians lives all over the world. On Earth you will never meet most of these Christians, but you belong to the same group.

Each person in the Body of Christ needs to be part of a local church. Some Christians meet in buildings called churches. Others meet in homes or in other buildings. Where you meet isn't as important as what you do when you're together. The main reason to get together with others in the Body is to worship God. The Body also gets together to learn more about God and His Word, to encourage each other and to help each other become more and more like Jesus. God's plan is for you to be an active part of the local church.

Isn't it great to know there are Christians, not only where you live, but all around the world? What a wonderful privilege it is to be part of the Body of Christ!

Why do you need to be part of a local church?

_____

_____

_____

You can pray:

Dear God, thank You for Christians all over the world that make up the Body of Christ. In Jesus' name. Amen.

268 Is There a Right Way to Worship in the Body of Christ?

WORSHIPING GOD

> But if we walk in the light, as he is in the light, we have fellowship with one another, and the blood of Jesus, his Son, purifies us from all sin. **1 John 1:7**

In a family, people are joined together in a special relationship. The people in the family can be loud or quiet, careful or clumsy, loving or selfish. They can be different in so many ways and yet be part of one family.

The Body of Christ is like that. We all belong to the Lord Jesus Christ and yet we are different. One important way we are different is in our worship. Some Christians worship together in a loud and joyful way while others are quiet. Some like to move around while others like to be still. Some worship several hours while others have a shorter worship time. With so many differences, is there a right way to worship?

The answer is yes! Worship that pleases God comes from a person whose heart is right with Him. The Bible says we are to worship God "in spirit and in truth" (John 4:24). Whenever an obedient Christian gives honor and praise to God through the Lord Jesus, he is worshiping in the right way. The way someone else worships might look wrong to you, but God knows that person's heart attitude.

How can you worship God the right way?

_____

_____

_____

You can pray:

Dear God, help me learn to worship with others in the Body of Christ. I want to always honor You. In Jesus' name. Amen.

Can I Do Anything Special in the Body of Christ?

But if we walk in the light, as he is in the light, we have fellowship with one another, and the blood of Jesus, his Son, purifies us from all sin. **1 John 1:7**

When you trusted Jesus as your Savior, God gave you some skills called spiritual gifts. You read about them earlier in this devotional book. God wants you to use these gifts to serve Him and others in the Body of Christ.

If you have the gift of serving, you enjoy helping others. If you have the gift of giving you like to give your money, time or talents to help meet needs. The gift of mercy helps you comfort others who are hurting. If you enjoy studying God's Word and sharing what you've learned with others, you may have the gift of teaching. If you like to organize projects and get others involved, you may have the gift of leading.

Each of these gifts is important. What if everyone in the Body of Christ had the gift of leading? What if no one had the gift of giving or mercy? God is very wise to give different gifts to different people. He wants all of us to use our gifts. If you don't know what your spiritual gifts are, ask God to show you. As you begin serving God, you'll soon find what God has gifted you to do.

What special thing can you do to help the Body of Christ?

_____

_____

_____

You can pray:

Dear God, thank You for giving me spiritual gifts to serve You. Help me find out what they are. In Jesus' name. Amen.

WORSHIPING GOD

216 How Can I Use My Gifts?

But if we walk in the light, as he is in the light, we have fellowship with one another, and the blood of Jesus, his Son, purifies us from all sin. **1 John 1:7**

Do you know what your spiritual gifts are? If you're a new Christian, you probably don't! But you can find out. The best way to find out is by serving God. Your spiritual gifts are often things you enjoy and do well. Let's think about some of the spiritual gifts and how they might be useful in your church.

If you have the gift of serving, maybe you help set up chairs for a meeting or clean up when it is over. If you have the gift of giving, you enjoy bringing your offering to church–especially when there is a special project. If you have the gift of mercy, you may want to visit someone who is sick, just to sit and keep him company. If you have the gift of teaching you might decide to teach a Sunday school class. If you have the gift of leading, you enjoy being in charge of projects like organizing a special get-together for your class.

Whatever way you choose to use your spiritual gifts, be sure you use them with love. As you use your gifts to help others, you'll be serving God well and having a great time while doing it.

WORSHIPING GOD

Write how you could use one of your spiritual gifts in your church.

_____

_____

_____

You can pray:

Dear God, help me to find the best ways I can use my gifts to serve You. In Jesus' name. Amen.

What Is Fellowship?

 But if we walk in the light, as he is in the light, we have fellowship with one another, and the blood of Jesus, his Son, purifies us from all sin. **1 John 1:7**

WORSHIPING GOD

The Bible says that as Christians we can have fellowship with God and one another. Do you know what fellowship is and how you can have it?

Fellowship is a lot like friendship. It means caring about someone and talking with him. It means spending time together because you want to. Like friendship, fellowship comes from having something in common. What do Christians have in common? The Lord Jesus Christ. Because we know Jesus, we can all have a special love for God and each other.

Making friends can be hard because others may not always accept you. However, as a Christian you are already accepted because Christ accepts you! His love in you and other Christians allows you to have fellowship with God and one another. It's like having friends wherever you go. God is a friend who will never leave you, and other Christians can also be your closest friends.

As you worship God today, think about your fellowship with Him. The God who made you wants to have a special friendship with you. He loves you more than anyone ever could! He's multiplied His love by giving you fellowship with other Christians.

 Why do you think fellowship with God and other Christians is important?

_____

_____

_____

You can pray:

 Dear God, thank You for the fellowship I can have with You and with my brothers and sisters in Christ. In Jesus' name. Amen.

212 Why Do I Need Fellowship?

But if we walk in the light, as he is in the light, we have fellowship with one another, and the blood of Jesus, his Son, purifies us from all sin. **1 John 1:7**

As a Christian, God has given you many good gifts. He's given you so many good things that it's easy to miss out on some. One gift we sometimes forget is fellowship. We don't realize what a wonderful gift it is!

The Bible says, "As iron sharpens iron, so one man sharpens another" (Proverbs 27:17). When we fellowship with other Christians, they make us stronger and better. If we're not careful, many things in life can turn us away from God. We need fellowship with other Christians to keep us strong in Him.

Friends who aren't Christians can sometimes lead you astray. The Bible says, " . . . Bad company corrupts good character" (1 Corinthians 15:33). People who aren't Christians may not do many bad things, but because they don't believe in Jesus Christ, they look at the world in a different way. They depend on money, things and other people to make them happy. As a Christian you know that the Lord Jesus is the true source of happiness.

God knows you need fellowship to be strong as a Christian. Good fellowship with other Christians begins in fellowship with Him. Take time today just to enjoy your friendship with God. Worship Him!

WORSHIPING GOD

Why do you need fellowship?

_____

_____

_____

You can pray:

Dear God, thank You for Your gift of fellowship! Help me to enjoy my fellowship with You and other Christians. In Jesus' name. Amen.

THE MEMORY ZONE

Here are some great Bible verses about what you've learned so far. Put a check mark in the box as you memorize each one!

☐ **Psalm 34:3** "Glorify the LORD with me; let us exalt his name together."

☐ **James 3:9-10** "With the tongue we praise our LORD and Father, and with it we curse men, who have been made in God's likeness. Out of the same mouth come praise and cursing. My brothers, this should not be."

☐ **1 Corinthians 10:31** "So whether you eat or drink or whatever you do, do it all for the glory of God."

☐ **Hebrews 10:25** "Let us not give up meeting together, as some are in the habit of doing, but let us encourage one another–and all the more as you see the Day approaching."

☐ **Psalm 11:4** "The LORD is in his holy temple; the LORD is on his heavenly throne. He observes the sons of men; his eyes examine them."

☐ **Psalm 33:1-3** "Sing joyfully to the LORD, you righteous; it is fitting for the upright to praise him. Sing to him a new song; play skillfully, and shout for joy."

☐ **Proverbs 27:17** "As iron sharpens iron, so one man sharpens another."

☐ **Revelation 7:12** " . . . Praise and glory and wisdom and thanks and honor and power and strength be to our God for ever and ever. Amen!"

This is the end of the section of "Worshiping God" devotionals.

It is time to do the next activity page that came to you in the mail. Remember to add your prayer request so your mailbox friend can pray for you. When you finish the whole page, fold it on the lines so the Mailbox Club address shows. Put a small piece of tape on the bottom to keep it folded. Add a stamp and mail your activity page.

Your work will be marked and sent back to you, along with a personal note. The activity sheet for the next set of lessons will be sent to you, too.

Enjoy getting to know God better with your next group of devotionals!

Obeying GOD

213 Who Should I Obey?

I will hasten and not delay to obey your commands. **Psalm 119:60**

Chad was watching TV. His mom came into the room, stopped a minute, and said, "I don't want you to watch that program, Son." Chad changed the channel. Did he obey? Yes! However, as soon as Mom left the room, he switched back to see the rest of the program. Ooops! The Bible says, "Children, obey your parents in everything, for this pleases the Lord" (Colossians 3:20).

Emily listened as her coach explained a new rule. "That is just so dumb," Emily muttered. Later, she chose to break the rule. Is this a good idea? The Bible says, "Obey your leaders and submit to their authority" (Hebrews 13:17). Leaders include teachers and coaches. Leaders may be camp counselors, the police—even the president. You have lots and lots of leaders.

The greatest Leader we have is God Himself. He asks us to obey Him. Then, He gives us the power to do what He says. In Psalm 119:34 David wrote, "Give me understanding, and I will keep your law and obey it with all my heart." When you obey the leaders God gives you, you are obeying one of God's commands. Will you choose to do it today?

OBEYING GOD

List some of the people God wants you to obey.

_____

_____

_____

You can pray:

Dear God, I want to obey Your commands. Help me listen to my parents and my other leaders, and help me do what they say. In Jesus' name. Amen

Why Should I Obey God?

I will hasten and not delay to obey your commands.
Psalm 119:60

OBEYING GOD

It is easy to make a l-o-n-g list of what God wants you to do: **Be nice to people!** Pray! Tell the truth! Tell others about Jesus! Obey your parents!

What a list! Can you add other things? The hard part is to hasten (or hurry) and not delay (wait) to do those things. God wants you to pay attention to what the Bible says. Then, choose to obey cheerfully.

When you fail to obey God, you cannot expect Him to answer your prayers. You cause unhappiness for yourself and probably for other people. Most of all, you disappoint the God who loves you and sent Jesus to be your Savior.

Why should you obey God? In the Bible Jesus says, "If you love me, you will obey what I command" (John 14:15). The main reason you should obey God is because you love Him. Tell God you want to obey Him. Ask God to give you the power to obey Him. What will happen when you obey God's commands? The Bible says, " . . . you will be blessed if you do them" (John 13:17). Obeying God will bring you joy in your life here on Earth. Obeying God will bring you rewards in Heaven.

What are some of God's commands that are hard for you to obey?

_____

_____

_____

You can pray:

Dear God, I need Your strength to obey all of Your commands today. Help me choose to obey You and do what is right. In Jesus' name. Amen.

215 How Do I Obey God's Commands?

I will hasten and not delay to obey your commands. **Psalm 119:60**

Chris heard about a really great job. It would help him earn the money he needs for a new racing bike. However, he was disappointed to learn that he would have to work every Sunday morning when he normally goes to church. Now Chris will have to make a choice. He loves God and really wants to obey Him.

If you love God, you'll want to obey Him, too. First you need to know what God's commands are. As you read His Word each day, try to understand what He is saying to you. You may even want to memorize Bible verses so that you will remember His commands. Also,

you need to listen carefully whenever someone is teaching from the Bible. When you discover a command in God's Word, ask Him to help you obey it right away. Your love for God will be seen in your quick obedience to His commands.

In his quiet time, Chris discovered Hebrews 10:25 where God tells Christians, "Let us not give up meeting together." Chris realized that he needed to put God first. He decided not to take the job so that he could be in God's house on Sunday mornings. Chris was quick to obey God's command.

OBEYING GOD

How can you obey God's commands?

_____

_____

_____

You can pray:

Dear God, I love You and want to obey Your commands. Please show me what You want me to do, and help me to obey quickly. In Jesus' name. Amen.

Is It My Fault?

I will hasten and not delay to obey your commands.
Psalm 119:60.

OBEYING GOD

"But, Mom," Steve pleaded, "I've got to head for the park now. They've probably already started choosing teams. If I don't get there soon, I'll be left out."

Mom looked at Steve. She didn't say anything. She didn't have to. Steve's Mom never changed her mind about room cleaning. Not ever! Steve was accountable for this job. That meant it had to be done. Sometimes he tried to shift the blame for not doing a job by saying something like, "I didn't do it because my teacher gave us too much homework."

Homework or not, Steve needed to do his jobs.

You are accountable for some jobs, too. Being accountable means you are responsible for your thoughts and actions. When you get lazy or you choose to disobey and leave a job undone, whose fault is it? It is your fault! Most important, the Bible says that each of us will have to answer to God (Romans 14:12). God tells you in the Bible what He wants you to do. He expects you to obey Him. He gives you the power to do what is right. Don't blame others when you fail to do what you're supposed to do. You are accountable!

If you remember Psalm 119:60, how will it help you?

_____

_____

_____

You can pray:

Dear God, help me to remember that I'm accountable to You. Give me the strength to obey You quickly and with a right attitude. In Jesus' name. Amen.

217 What Happens If I Don't Obey God?

I will hasten and not delay to obey your commands. **Psalm 119:60**

Jonah loved God. God told Jonah to go to Ninevah. Very bad people lived in Ninevah, but God still loved them. Jonah was to tell them how they could have their sins forgiven.

Jonah knew God's command. Did he "hasten and not delay to obey"? No! He hurried and ran the other way. By disobeying God, Jonah caused problems for other people. He also got into big trouble. He was swallowed by a big fish. God kept him inside that fish for three days. Jonah sure had time to think about what a bad plan it was to disobey God.

Disobeying God is a bad plan for you, too. When you choose to do something wrong, you grieve the Holy Spirit. Because you love God, you shouldn't want to grieve His Spirit. Also, disobeying God makes you feel sad inside. You do not feel like talking to God or reading the Bible. You may get into trouble. Plus, you miss the real happiness that comes from choosing to obey God.

Jonah was sorry he did not obey God. When you choose to disobey, not always will another person know, but God will know. God knows everything. You will know, too, and, like Jonah, you will be sorry.

OBEYING GOD

Why is it such a bad idea to disobey God?

_____

_____

_____

You can pray:

Dear God, don't let me be like Jonah. I want to obey You. Thank You for loving me and for helping me do the right things. In Jesus' name. Amen.

What Happens If I Do Obey God?

I will hasten and not delay to obey your commands.
Psalm 119:60

OBEYING GOD

Just think! In Heaven, we will get to meet David. We learn quite a lot about him in the Bible. He was a shepherd. He played the harp. He killed the giant, Goliath. He was a king. God inspired him to write many of the Psalms in the Bible.

David really loved God and chose to obey Him. In Psalm 119:10 David says, "I seek you [God] with all my heart; do not let me stray from your commands." What a great prayer!

When you choose to obey God, He says your life will be longer and happier.

Also, you will get to know God and worship Him better. Other people will notice you are honest, kind and loving, and that you work hard. They will notice that you're full of joy! They will want to know why you are so different. Obeying God makes it possible for you to tell people that Jesus, your Savior, has changed your life.

So many people worry. Obeying God gives you peace in your heart. David had peace in his heart, even when he faced that giant. Why? Because he did not delay to obey God's commands. Will you choose to obey God, today and everyday?

Why are Psalm 119:60 and Psalm 119:10 good verses to remember?

_____

_____

_____

You can pray:

Dear God, I want to be like David and seek You with all my heart. Don't let me stray from Your commands. In Jesus' name. Amen.

219 When I Obey God, Will Good Things Always Happen?

I will hasten and not delay to obey your commands. **Psalm 119:60**

Isn't it nice when people say good things about you? Imagine God saying something good about you! Here is what God said about a man named Job: "... This man was blameless and upright" (Job 1:1). Job was a man who obeyed God with all his heart.

Since Job loved God and chose to obey Him, did that mean good things always happened to Job? No! His animals were stolen. His servants were killed. His ten children died in a storm. Wow! Job lost everything. He didn't know why God let all those bad things happen. But God gave Job the strength to get through those problems..

When you choose to obey God, even in the hard times, others see the special strength God gives you. Problems could turn you away from God. Instead, God uses problems to help you trust Him more and more. God promises He will never leave you (Hebrews 13:5). Remembering that will help you when bad things happen.

It would be great if everything would always be wonderful for those who choose to obey God. But things won't always be great—they weren't for Job. Job learned that God would get him through very bad days. You need to learn that, too.

What can you do when bad things happen?

_____

_____

_____

You can pray:

Dear God, help me to choose to obey You even when bad things happen. I do trust You, God. Thank You for promising to help me. In Jesus' name. Amen.

OBEYING GOD

Why Does God Oppose Pride?

. . . God opposes the proud but gives grace to the humble. **James 4:6**

Kevin couldn't resist. He raced around the block, the metal on his new bike sparkling. Knowing people were watching, he jumped the curb and pedaled faster. He heard Josh call, "Hey, Kev! Wait up! Let me see your bike," but Kevin stuck his nose in the air and rode right by. Kevin was proud of his new high-powered wheels. He circled and rode past Josh a second time. "Josh will never have a bike this great," he thought. "Plus, I'm the best rider!"

Do you like people to notice you? "Look what I did!" "Watch me!" "See what I have!" "I'm so-o-o good!" God opposes you when you have those proud thoughts. Why? Because you call attention to yourself and not to your God. You take all the credit for what God has helped you to do, or to get. God hates pride!

Pride is thinking too highly of yourself. It's right to be pleased when you get good grades, score the winning point or have something new. Thank God for it, but don't be proud. Proud people expect others to praise them. They act bossy and even rude. Jesus did not have a "notice me" attitude. Neither should you.

Why is it wrong to brag about something you own or something you can do?

_____

_____

_____

You can pray:

Dear God, forgive me for the times I've acted proudly. Thank You for what You have given me and for what You help me to do. In Jesus' name. Amen.

221

What Does It Mean to Be Humble?

. . . God opposes the proud but gives grace to the humble.
James 4:6

It's hard to believe! Jesus was with His disciples. Read what happened: "so he [Jesus] got up from the meal . . . and wrapped a towel around his waist. After that, he poured water into a basin and began to wash his disciples' feet, drying them with the towel . . ." (John 13: 4-5).

Jesus, God the Son, washing feet! People wore sandals. Roads were very dusty. When anyone came to visit, a servant had to wash feet. Was this a great job? No! Did servants like to do it? No! Did someone ask Jesus to wash feet? No!

Jesus chose to do this job to show He was not too proud to be a servant. Jesus had a humble heart. A humble person cares more about others than he cares about himself. He does not have a problem with pride. To be humble, like Jesus, you must be willing to help someone who has a need. Even if no one says "Thanks!" or "Great job!" Even if no one notices you. It's hard! We want people to praise us and give us prizes.

God will help you. Look for ways to serve others. Don't expect everyone to pay attention to you. Follow the example of Jesus.

Who can you serve today, and what can you do for them?

_____

_____

_____

You can pray:

Dear God, help me learn how to serve You with a humble heart. Help me to be a humble servant to someone today. In Jesus' name. Amen.

OBEYING GOD

Am I Proud or Humble?

 . . . God opposes the proud but gives grace to the humble. **James 4:6**

OBEYING GOD

Would you like to have a name like Nebuchadnezzar? (Neb-you-kad-NEZ-ur) Imagine learning to spell it. Whew!

He was a king. He made a huge gold statue of himself. Everyone had to bow down and worship his statue. King Nebuchadnezzar was proud. Pride is a serious sin. The Bible says, "When pride comes, then comes disgrace, but with humility comes wisdom" (Proverbs 11:2).

Proud King Nebuchadnezzar was disgraced. For seven years, he became like an animal. He crawled on the ground and ate grass (Daniel 4:33). Really! God tells us about Nebuchadnezzar to show us He hates pride.

If you brag about what you can do or what you have, you have a pride problem. God wants you to be humble, not proud. God made you. Without God, you cannot do any good thing. Give God the credit for all you have and all you can do. Look for ways to help people. Be happy when others win a game. By choosing to be humble, you may get to tell others about your wonderful Savior.

Humbly honoring God will fill your life with blessings. Pride can destroy you. Look what happened to Nebuchadnezzar.

 When people compliment you, how can you humbly answer them?

_____

_____

_____

You can pray:

 Dear God, I want to quietly help others even if no one notices me. When people say something nice about me, help me to give You the credit. In Jesus' name. Amen.

223 What Is a Lazy Person?

Whatever you do, work at it with all your heart, as working for the Lord, not for men. **Colossians 3:23**

Are you lazy? A lazy person waits and waits to start doing his work. This makes other people angry or sad. Do you do this?

A lazy person sits and sits, thinking about this and that. He should be listening to the teacher or studying a lesson. Do you do this?

A lazy person hurries through his work. He does such a bad job that he has to do it over. Do you do this?

Lazy Christians do not work to learn more about God. They do not memorize Bible verses. They do not read the Bible and pray. What about you?

Lazy people are not willing to work hard or to get jobs done on time. They think only about themselves and what they want. They forget about people who are counting on them. Worst of all, they forget about God. The Bible says, "Lazy hands make a man poor . . ." (Proverbs 10:4).

Don't be lazy! Work with all your heart. Because you belong to God, He will help you with whatever you do. He wants you to choose to do each of your jobs right away. This will please other people. Best of all, this will please God.

OBEYING GOD

What are three things you know you should do this week?

_____

_____

_____

You can pray:

Dear God, I don't want to be lazy. Help me to do my very best on each of my jobs. I choose to work for You. In Jesus' name. Amen.

What Is a Diligent Person? **224**

 Whatever you do, work at it with all your heart, as working for the Lord, not for men. **Colossians 3:23**

OBEYING GOD

Your parents probably tell you things like, "Do your homework! Clean your room! Practice the piano!" Can you add to that list? It is tempting to say, "Not now!" or "I don't feel like it!" A diligent person starts working right away. A diligent person works hard to finish a job and do it well.

Proverbs 13:4 says, "The sluggard [lazy person] craves and gets nothing, but the desires of the diligent are fully satisfied." Sluggards want many things. They do not get them because they do not work for them. Diligent people often get what they want because they work hard.

Diligent people get busy clearing the dishes off the table instead of sitting and pouting about it. Diligent people get up on time instead of being too late to even make their bed. Diligent people take care of their clothes instead of throwing them on the floor. It doesn't take very long to do these jobs. Be diligent!

Choose to work to please God, not just other people. Do not complain about what you have to do. Do the very best you can because God wants you to. When you're tempted to be lazy, remember Colossians 3:23. Then, smile and get started.

 What are some jobs God helped you to do diligently this week?

_____

_____

You can pray:

 Dear God, I want to be a diligent person. When I am tempted to be lazy, help me remember Colossians 3:23. In Jesus' name. Amen.

225 What Will Happen If I Am Diligent?

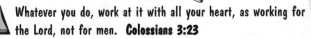

Whatever you do, work at it with all your heart, as working for the Lord, not for men. **Colossians 3:23**

God tells lazy people they should watch ants. Really! No one says to ants, "Do this!" or "Go there!" Ants just do what they are supposed to do. Because they work hard all summer, they have the food needed for winter. No one says to ants, "Great job!" or "Let me pay you!" Ants work and work even though no one pays attention to them. The Bible says, "Go to the ant, you sluggard [lazy person]; consider its ways and be wise!" (Proverbs 6:6).

If you are diligent, you may not get any money for your hard work. People may not even notice. God will know! Remember that whatever you do, you are working for the Lord. God is pleased when you do your work with all your heart. He will see that your needs are met.

You can become a better Christian by being diligent. Learn new Bible verses. Review verses you already know. Read God's Word every day. Take time to pray. You should not wait for someone to tell you to do this. Just be diligent and do it.

Diligent people see jobs that need to be done and they do them. Remember that's what ants do!

OBEYING GOD

Why does God tell us to study the ants?

_____

_____

_____

You can pray:

Dear God, help me to be diligent in everything I do today. Help me to work with all of my heart to please You. In Jesus' name. Amen.

Why Is It Important to Make Right Choices?

226

. . . choose for yourselves this day whom you will serve . . . as for me and my household, we will serve the LORD.

Joshua 24:15

OBEYING GOD

Julie's teacher asked, "How many brothers and sisters do you have?"

Julie said, "Three," but in her mind she added "sort of." Julie and her older brother have the same dad. Her mom never married their dad. Then, there is Andy. Julie's mom never married Andy's dad either. Later, Julie's mom got married and had a child named Brenda. Now her mom and Brenda's dad are divorced.

Julie's mom has filled her life with wrong choices. Julie is determined to ask God to show her which man to marry. Julie wants to fill her life with right choices so she can serve the Lord.

Making right choices means obeying God's Word. You have to make choices many times each day: Will I obey my mom? Will I read my Bible? Will I work hard in school? Will I tell the truth? Wrong choices make you feel sad and sometimes scared. Wrong choices disappoint God.

Make right choices day by day. This will help you make right choices for very important things later in life, like "Who will I marry?" The wrong choice–all wrong choices–will cause problems for you, and for many other people. Julie could tell you that is true.

Why is it so important to choose the right person to marry?

_____

_____

You can pray:

Dear God, I need Your help to make right choices today, and for the big decisions I'll have to make later. In Jesus' name. Amen.

How Can I Keep from Making the Wrong Choices?

... choose for yourselves this day whom you will serve ... as for me and my household, we will serve the LORD. **Joshua 24:15**

Suppose, when you needed to make a choice, you could say, "Should I watch this TV program?" If God liked your choice, a special light would turn green–Go! If not, the light would be red–Stop!

This would be so-o-o great. "Should I invite Sean to my house?" –Green! "Should I visit this web sight?" –Red! "Should I eat spinach?" –Red . . . well, maybe green!

Some choices are very important: Who should I choose for friends? How will I act when others make fun of me? Paying attention to God's Word and deciding to obey it every time will help you make right choices.

When you don't know what God wants you to do, ask a godly Christian to help you. A godly person reads and obeys the Bible, prays and goes to church. He talks about the Lord Jesus Christ. He lives to please God.

There is no "right choice" light, but God does give you the Holy Spirit to live inside you. The Spirit guides your thoughts and helps you make right choices. When God shows you what to do, be sure you obey. Knowing what to do and choosing not to do it would be a very bad choice.

OBEYING GOD

What are three things you can do to help you make right choices?

_____

_____

_____

You can pray:
Dear God, help me to obey Your Word and listen to the Holy Spirit so I won't make bad choices. In Jesus' name. Amen.

What If I Make the Wrong Choice? 228

> . . . choose for yourselves this day whom you will serve . . .
> as for me and my household, we will serve the LORD.
> **Joshua 24:15**

O B E Y I N G   G O D

Sometimes wrong choices are mistakes. Sometimes wrong choices are on purpose. King David made a wrong choice on purpose. He wanted to marry Bathsheba. She was already married. David told the commander of his army to put her husband up front on the battlefield so he would be killed. Then, David married Bathsheba. Perhaps David thought he could get away with choosing to sin.

Nathan, a prophet of God, knew what David had done. He showed David the terribleness of his sin. David confessed his sin to God. God forgave David, but He also punished him. David and Bathsheba's first baby died.

When you choose to do wrong, don't think, *So what? I'll confess my sin to God. He will forgive me.* Bad things happen because of sin. When you choose to disobey your parents or teacher, you may have to stay in your room or miss an important game. Sin ruins your chance to talk to people about Jesus because they will not trust what you say.

Don't think you can sin on purpose and get away with it. It didn't work for David, and it will not work for you. Confess your sins to God and do what's right.

What happens if you choose to do wrong?

_____

_____

_____

You can pray:
Dear God, thank You for reminding me that wrong choices will cause trouble in my life. Help me to make right choices. In Jesus' name. Amen.

229 What Is Godly Counsel?

Pay attention and listen to the sayings of the wise . . .
Proverbs 22:17

Joash was seven years old when he became the King. When he was given the crown, " . . . the people clapped their hands and shouted, 'Long live the king!'" (2 Kings 11:12). How could little Joash know what to say and do to lead so many people? What a lot of pressure! He needed help from wise people who loved God.

You are not the king of a country, but you, too, have lots of pressure. How do you know what to say? How do you know what to do? Like Joash, you need godly counsel.

Godly counsel–help in knowing what to do–comes from people in your life who know God's Word better than you do. In Proverbs 22:17, God says, **"Pay attention and listen to the sayings of the wise."** To know people who love the Lord Jesus Christ is a great gift from God. God may give you parents, teachers, pastors, Sunday school teachers and older Christians to teach you. There are books written by godly people that can help you know what to do.

Because Joash listened to godly counsel, he became a wise king. Will you listen to those who can help you become wise?

OBEYING GOD

Who are some people who could give you godly counsel?

_____

_____

_____

You can pray:

Dear God help me to listen to godly counsel so I can become a wise person. In Jesus' name. Amen.

Why Is Good Counsel Important?

Pay attention and listen to the sayings of the wise . . .
Proverbs 22:17

O B E Y I N G   G O D

God chose Moses to be a leader. People knew that God spoke to Moses. Therefore, when they had arguments or questions, people came to him for good counsel. Day after day, from morning until evening, people lined up to talk to him. Moses was getting tired.

Jethro, his father-in-law, told Moses this was too much for him to do alone. Jethro said, "I will give you some advice" (Exodus 18:19). He told Moses to assign other godly men to help him. Moses listened to Jethro's good counsel and followed his advice. With other men now helping him, Moses' job had become easier.

It is wise to listen to what good counselors say. They can stop you from making mistakes. They can explain things in the Bible you don't understand. They can help you make right decisions like choosing good friends or joining the right club.

Even as you become wiser, there will still be things for you to learn. Moses was a leader, but he needed good counsel. Proverbs 9:9 says, "Instruct a wise man and he will be wiser still ..." Keep studying God's Word. Obey what it says. Then, someday you will be able to give good counsel to many people.

What are some things you could learn from a good counselor?

_____

_____

You can pray:

Dear God, I praise You for people who can give me good counsel. Help me to listen to them and to Your Word. In Jesus' name. Amen.

231 How Can I Tell Bad Counsel from Good Counsel?

Pay attention and listen to the sayings of the wise . . .
Proverbs 22:17

"Come on," Jed yelled. "Follow the leader." As he jumped on his bike, Randy followed and tried to trace Jed's path. Down the sidewalk. Across the street. Down one driveway and up the next.

Both boys stopped at a busy intersection to catch their breath. That was as far as either boy was allowed to ride. But Jed started walking his bike across the highway saying, "Let's keep going!" Randy wanted to follow, but he knew it was a bad idea because God tells us in Ephesians 6:1 to obey our parents.

Like a bad idea from a friend, bad counsel does not feel right.

God's Holy Spirit lives inside you to help you know if the counsel someone gives you is right or wrong. The Spirit reminds you of things you have heard from God's Word. Good counsel always agrees with God's Word. The more of God's Word you learn, the easier it will be for you to tell bad counsel from good counsel.

The right thing to do may not always be the most fun. Randy knew that. He may have wanted to follow Jed, but he decided to go home. Will you ask God to help you know and do what is right?

OBEYING GOD

How does the Holy Spirit help you decide if counsel is good or bad?

_____

_____

_____

You can pray:

Dear God, please help me decide if people are giving me bad or good counsel. Then help me to choose to do what is right. In Jesus' name. Amen.

Why Do People Complain?

232

Be joyful always; pray continually; give thanks in all circumstances, for this is God's will for you in Christ Jesus. **1 Thessalonians 5:16-18**

OBEYING GOD

Do you ever say things like, "This is a dumb assignment; I don't see why we have to do it." "You never choose me. It's my turn." "Are we having that for dinner again? I hate it!" "Do this! Do that! Why do I have to do so much work?" "How come he gets to go, but I don't?"

Complain! Complain! Complain! When you complain, you forget God is in control. You forget God loves you. You forget God promised to give you whatever you need. Complaining shows you are self-

ish. Complaining makes you unhappy, and other people do not want to be around you. It is impossible to complain and please God at the same time. Why? Because God says, "Be joyful always" and "give thanks in all circumstances."

Each time you are tempted to complain about food, homework assignments, clothes, jobs or anything else, stop and see if you can say something good instead. Be happy you have something to eat. Be thankful if you are well and can go to school, do your work or play a game. Ask God to help you say words that show you really believe God is good.

Write something you've complained about that turned out to be good.

_____

_____

_____

You can pray:

Dear God, please help me to stop complaining, and to be thankful instead. In Jesus' name. Amen.

233 What Does God Think about Complaining?

Be joyful always; pray continually; give thanks in all circumstances, for this is God's will for you in Christ Jesus.
1 Thessalonians 5:16-18

When Moses led God's people, they had many reasons to be thankful. God split the Red Sea and let His people cross it on dry ground. Thank You, God! God sent wonderful food called manna down from Heaven each day. Thank You, God! Moses hit a rock with a stick, and God sent enough water pouring out for the whole thirsty crowd. Thank You, God!

Thank You, God! That's what those people should have said over and over and over. Do you know what they did instead? They complained saying, "We need more water! We're tired of manna! We need a new leader."

They even complained about God. Because of this sin, God sent snakes to punish them–many snakes full of poison that bit people! Many people died. Moses prayed and God answered by making a way for them to be forgiven for their sin of complaining. (Numbers 21:5-9)

The Bible says, "Do everything without complaining or arguing" (Philippians 2:14). Notice it says, everything. When you complain, you forget God promised to give you whatever you need. God is in control and He loves you. Be joyful, give thanks and stop complaining!

OBEYING GOD

Why do you think that complaining is a sin?

_____

_____

_____

You can pray:
Dear God, help me to be thankful and to stop complaining. In Jesus' name. Amen.

How Can I Be Thankful?

Be joyful always; pray continually; give thanks in all circumstances, for this is God's will for you in Christ Jesus. **1 Thessalonians 5:16-18**

OBEYING GOD

"I hate my clothes!" Rachel shouted. "What's wrong with them?" Stacy asked. "I think you always look nice." Rachel frowned at her friend. "They're all so old!" she exclaimed. "I never have anything new. I just get my sister's old clothes when she grows out of them. I know my parents don't have a lot of money, but I want new clothes like everybody else!"

Like Rachel, when you complain about something, you act like God doesn't know what He is doing. Don't think that way! Stop for a moment and think about God. Remember that God is love, and He loves you! God is wise, and He knows what is best for you! God is powerful, and He can help you!

Give thanks to God for all the great things He has done for you. The Bible says, "always giving thanks to God the Father for everything . . ." (Ephesians 5:20). Sing a song to praise Him instead of complaining. Say the words "I will" and then quote 1 Thessalonians 5:16-18. Do this whenever you feel like complaining about your clothes, your family, the weather, schoolwork or whatever. You can be thankful if you will choose to be.

How can you remember to be thankful instead of complaining?

_____

_____

_____

You can pray:

Dear God, help me, today, to be thankful instead of complaining. In Jesus' name. Amen.

What Is Gossip?

Do not let any unwholesome talk come out of your mouths, but only what is helpful for building up others . . . **Ephesians 4:29**

Rachel carried her lunch to the table where Kirsten was sitting. As soon as she sat down, she lowered her voice and whispered, "Did you hear that Marcia got a very bad grade on her math test?" Kirsten whispered back, "She did? I thought she was smart."

Rachel said, "She's lazy. Look! She's coming this way! Her hair is a mess today." Kirsten added, "And she's wearing that awful pink sweater."

Does this sound like talk that would please God? Are Rachel and Kirsten saying words that would build up Marcia? No!

This is what Ephesians 4:29 calls "unwholesome talk." This is gossip.

Gossip should never come out of your mouth. Gossip is saying unkind (and often untrue) things about other people. Gossip is sin. You can try to stop others when you hear them gossip. For example, if Rachel told you about Jenny's bad test grade you could say, "What could we do to help her with the next test?" When someone says unkind words about another person, you could say, "It isn't right to talk that way." Then, change the subject. Do everything you can to stop gossip.

OBEYING GOD

Why do you think God calls gossip a sin?

_____

_____

_____

You can pray:

Dear God, please help me not to gossip about other people. Help me always to use words that build up others. In Jesus' name. Amen.

What Does Gossip Do?

 Do not let any unwholesome talk come out of your mouths, but only what is helpful for building up others . . . **Ephesians 4:29**

O B E Y I N G G O D

Dave and Tim were best friends until last summer. Dave made the soccer team. Tim didn't. Tim was angry, hurt and jealous. So Tim said some words to other people he never should have said.

Tim told Dustin, "The only reason Dave made the soccer team is because his dad is friends with the coach." He told Sarah, "Dave will ruin the soccer team. He's too fat to run fast." Soon, Dave heard what Tim was saying about him. Now he was hurt and angry. Dave and Tim were no longer friends. The Bible says in Proverbs 16:28, " . . . gossip separates close friends."

People who gossip tell your secrets. Tim told Dave that he felt so bad about not making the team that he cried. Should Dave tell others about that? No! Proverbs 11:13 says, "A gossip betrays a confidence, but a trustworthy man keeps a secret."

God hears the words you say when you gossip. He knows the harm you have done. One day God will ask, "Why did you say that?" God says in Matthew 12:36, "But I tell you that men will have to give an account . . . for every careless word they have spoken." Remember that, and you will not gossip.

 How might gossip hurt your friendships?

_____

_____

_____

You can pray:

 Dear God, help me to be careful about the words I say and to remember that You are always listening. In Jesus' name. Amen.

237 How Can I Build up Others?

Do not let any unwholesome talk come out of your mouths, but only what is helpful for building up others . . . **Ephesians 4:29**

Do you know what your name means? A man in the Bible had a name with a very special meaning. His name was Barnabas, and his name meant "son of encouragement." Isn't that a great name? The Bible tells us that Barnabas did just what his name says–he built up other people by encouraging them.

We first meet Barnabas in the New Testament, right after Saul (later called Paul) became a Christian. People were afraid of Saul. In Acts 9:26-27 we learn that Barnabas took Saul to other believers, told them Saul was now a Christian and that they didn't need to be afraid of him. Barnabas encouraged Paul when they traveled together. Barnabas encouraged people to listen to God's Word and believe it. Barnabas encouraged people to live for the Lord.

Are you an encourager like Barnabas? You can be! Encourage people by saying things like: "You did a great job!" "Thanks for working so hard!" "I like being on your team!" "God loves you and so do I." "I'm glad I know you!" "You are a great friend!"

The Lord Jesus Christ living in Barnabas helped him to build up others. He can do the same for you!

OBEYING GOD

What will you say to build up someone today?

_____

_____

_____

You can pray:

Dear God, help me to build up others by encouraging them. In Jesus' name. Amen.

What Does It Mean to Misuse God's Name?

You shall not misuse the name of the LORD your God, for the LORD will not hold anyone guiltless who misuses his name. **Exodus 20:7**

OBEYING GOD

Storm clouds fill the sky. It is getting darker and darker. The wind is really blowing. You watch out the window. All of a sudden, you see a twisting funnel-shaped cloud. You yell, "Oh God, it's a tornado!"

However, in saying "Oh God," you are not even thinking about the true and living God. You are not talking to the one who has the power to make storms and to stop them. You are misusing God's name.

Maybe you are watching a TV program. A family is having a big argument. In anger, one person spits out the words "Jesus Christ." The words are not said with love or respect. The words are not used to help those listening think of our wonderful Savior. This person is misusing the name of the Lord.

When you misuse the name of the Lord, you say "God" and "Lord" and "Jesus Christ" as empty words, even angry words. God is real! God the Son, the Lord Jesus Christ, suffered and died for us. Now Jesus is alive! It is very very wrong to use names of God as just words. You should feel sad whenever you hear someone do this.

Why is it wrong to misuse God's Name?

_____

_____

_____

You can pray:

Dear God, Your name is wonderful. Help me to honor Your name and to never misuse it. In Jesus' name. Amen.

239 Why Should I Be Careful about My Words?

You shall not misuse the name of the LORD your God, for the LORD will not hold anyone guiltless who misuses his name.
Exodus 20:7

The Bible has much to say about speaking. Read the verses on this page carefully. Read them more than once.

" . . . a harsh word stirs up anger" (Proverbs 15:1).

"Reckless words pierce like a sword, but the tongue of the wise brings healing" (Proverbs 12:18).

"Out of the same mouth come praise and cursing . . . this should not be" (James 3:10).

"He who guards his lips guards his life, but he who speaks rashly will come to ruin" (Proverbs 13:3).

"If anyone considers himself religious and yet does not keep a tight rein on his tongue, he deceives himself and his religion is worthless" (James 1:26).

Words are powerful. Your mouth can praise God or misuse His name. What you say can help people or hurt them. The words you use can tell people how they can become a Christian. People listen to what you say. When you, as a Christian, misuse God's name, people will not forget it. They may never believe you when you try to tell them that the Lord Jesus wants to be their Savior. It may not seem fair, but people remember the bad things you say longer than the good things, so be careful with your words!

Why are your words important to God?

_____

_____

_____

You can pray:
Dear God, help me remember that my words can hurt people or help them. Help me speak only the words that please You. In Jesus' name. Amen.

How Can I Have "Wise" Lips?

240

You shall not misuse the name of the LORD your God, for the LORD will not hold anyone guiltless who misuses his name. **Exodus 20:7**

Mandy likes to talk a lot! She talks about what she did yesterday and what she wants to do tomorrow. She talks about people and places. She talks about sports, about homework, her computer, TV programs, church, vacations, things she likes and things she doesn't like.

Do people who talk so much have "wise" lips? Proverbs 10:19 says, " . . . he who holds his tongue is wise." To "hold your tongue" means to be quiet. Why would God say to "hold your tongue"? Because every time you speak it is possible you will say something un-

true, unkind or unimportant. Also, when you talk so much, people may stop listening. The Bible says, " . . . let your words be few" (Ecclesiastes 5:2).

Queen Esther wanted to speak to the king. She had a plan to save God's people from being killed (Esther 4-5). She had to think and pray so she would say exactly the right words. She had "wise" lips. How can you have "wise" lips? The Bible says, "Set a guard over my mouth, O LORD . . ." (Psalm 141:3).

Be careful what you say. Use words to help people. Use God's name in a right way. Remember this: Pray more! Listen more! Talk less!

How can listening, instead of talking, help you to have "wise" lips?

_____

_____

You can pray:

Dear God, help me to know when to talk and when to be quiet. I want to have "wise" lips. In Jesus' name. Amen.

241 What Does It Mean to Be Loyal?

A faithful man will be richly blessed . . . **Proverbs 28:20**

Naomi, her husband and two sons left their home in Bethlehem and traveled to Moab. While living there, Naomi's husband died. Her sons got married, choosing Ruth and Orpah. Then, both sons died. What a sad time it must have been.

Naomi decided she would return to Bethlehem. Ruth and Orpah started out with her. Naomi told the two women to go back to their homes. (Ruth 1:6-14)

Orpah went home, but Ruth said to Naomi, " . . . Where you go I will go, and where you stay I will stay. Your people will be my people and your God my God"

(Ruth 1:16). Ruth was loyal to Naomi and to her God.

Loyalty is being faithful to those who deserve your love and support. Christians are to be loyal to God first of all. Also, be loyal to family and friends, except when those people choose to disobey God over and over.

When you are loyal to a person, you stand up for him when someone is mean to him. You say good things about him. You help him when he is in trouble. That's what Ruth did. Because of her faithful loyalty, she was blessed richly. Will you follow the wonderful example of Ruth?

OBEYING GOD

How can you show loyalty to a friend this week?

_____

_____

_____

You can pray:
Dear God, please help me to be loyal to my family and friends. Mostly, help me to be loyal to You. In Jesus' name. Amen.

How Can I Be Loyal to God?

A faithful man will be richly blessed . . .
Proverbs 28:20

OBEYING GOD

Jason was a Christian. He wanted to be loyal to God. Matt sat right behind him at school. He poked Jason with a pencil, sneered at him and whispered, "Don't get mad, Jason. If you're a Christian, you'll forgive me!" Then, he poked him again and laughed.

What would you do if someone like Matt teased you because you are a Christian? It takes strength greater than your own to stay loyal to God. God can give " . . . grace to help us in our time of need" (Hebrews 4:16).

Loyal Christians read the Bible and pray each day. They go to church faithfully. It is easier to stay loyal to God when you spend time with other Christians. Christian friends help each other live for God. The real test of your loyalty to God is your obedience to Him.

It will be hard for you to be loyal to God if you have close friends who do not love and serve God. That's why Jason did not choose Matt for a close friend. But Jason and his friends pray for Matt. That pleases God. Be loyal to God and obey Him with all of your heart.

 How can you show God you are loyal to Him?

_____

_____

_____

You can pray:

Dear God, thank You for loving me. Even when it is hard, I want to be loyal to You. In Jesus' name. Amen.

243 Why Is It Important to Be Faithful?

A faithful man will be richly blessed . . .   **Proverbs 28:20**

When you know you should do something, but you don't feel like doing it, what do you say to yourself? "I'm too-o-o tired!" or "I want to do something else" or "This is the right thing to do, and God will help me do it!"

When you tell yourself something like that last thought, you are learning to be faithful. Faithfulness means staying true to God in your thoughts, words and actions. What does Proverbs 28:20 say? Being faithful to God brings His blessing–joy–to your life!

When you say you are a Christian, but you are not faithful, people don't trust you. They don't want to be like you. They don't want to hear the important things you should be telling them about God.

When you are faithful, people can see God has made a difference in your life. You use your money wisely. You use your time to help other people. You study the Bible and go to church. You use your talents (the things you do well) to serve God.

There is great joy in choosing to obey God. When you trust God to help you be faithful, you will be blessed richly. God says so!

Why is it hard, sometimes, to be faithful?

_____

_____

_____

OBEYING GOD

You can pray:
Dear God, help me to faithfully use my money, time and talents to serve You. I want to be someone others can depend on. In Jesus' name. Amen.

THE MEMORY ZONE

Here are some great Bible verses about what you've learned so far. Put a check mark in the box as you memorize each one!

☐ **Psalm 119:34** "Give me understanding, and I will keep your law and obey it with all my heart."

☐ **Hebrews 13:17** "Obey your leaders and submit to their authority. They keep watch over you as men who must give an account. Obey them so that their work will be a joy, not a burden, for that would be of no advantage to you."

☐ **James 1:22** "Do not merely listen to the word, and so deceive yourselves. Do what it says."

☐ **Proverbs 11:2** "When pride comes, then comes disgrace, but with humility comes wisdom."

☐ **Philippians 2:14-15** "Do everything without complaining or arguing, so that you may become blameless and pure, children of God without fault in a crooked and depraved generation, in which you shine like stars in the universe."

☐ **Psalm 119:9** "How can a young man keep his way pure? By living according to your word."

☐ **Philippians 4:8** " . . . whatever is true, whatever is noble, whatever is right, whatever is pure, whatever is lovely, whatever is admirable–if anything is excellent or praiseworthy–think about such things."

☐ **Psalm 141:3** "Set a guard over my mouth, O LORD; keep watch over the door of my lips."

This is the end of the section of "Obeying God" devotionals.

It is time to do the next activity page that came to you in the mail. Remember to add your prayer request so your mailbox friend can pray for you. When you finish the whole page, fold it on the lines so the Mailbox Club address shows. Put a small piece of tape on the bottom to keep it folded. Add a stamp and mail your activity page.

Your work will be marked and sent back to you, along with a personal note. The activity sheet for the next set of lessons will be sent to you, too.

Enjoy getting to know God better with your next group of devotionals!

Living
for
GOD

244 What Does God Say about Respecting Life?

I praise you because I am fearfully and wonderfully made . . .
Psalm 139:14

L I V I N G F O R G O D

Has anyone ever told you, "You look just like your dad" or "You have your mother's smile"? Why is that? You were born with certain qualities that make you like your parents.

Just as there are family likenesses, God, the Creator, made all people in His likeness. The Bible says, "God created man in his own image . . ." (Genesis 1:27). How are you made in God's image? You have a personality. You can think about things. You can feel emotions like joy and sadness. You can make choices. God also made you with a soul that will live forever. These are a few of the wonderful ways God has made you. God created the entire universe but only man was made in His image.

All life is important, or valuable, to God, but, because you are made in God's image, you have a special value to Him. No animal or plant is made in His image like you. In the Bible God commands, "You shall not murder" (Exodus 20:13). Each person's life is important to God. No one has the right to take another person's life. God wants you to honor Him by respecting and protecting life.

 Why does God want you to respect life?

_____

_____

_____

You can pray:

Dear God, thank You for making me in Your image. Help me to respect my life and the lives of those around me. In Jesus' name. Amen.

How Did People in the Bible Respect Life?

245

I praise you because I am fearfully and wonderfully made . . . **Psalm 139:14**

"Kill all the baby boys born to the Israelites!" ordered angry Pharaoh, the king of Egypt (Exodus 1:22). Two Israelite nurses hurried from Pharaoh's presence. They understood his order, but they wanted to obey God.

The Israelites were slaves in Egypt. Pharaoh was afraid they would join his enemies and fight against him. That's why he wanted the boys killed. Pharaoh had no respect for human life, but the two nurses did. They protected the lives of the baby boys.

All human life is important to God. When does life begin? Life starts when God begins to form a baby inside the mother's body. God values unborn babies. The Bible says God forms every detail of their bodies even before they are born into this world (Psalm 139:13).

When a doctor performs an abortion (killing a baby before or while he is being born), he is killing a life God created. Only God has the right to give life and to take it away. Leaders of many countries have made laws that allow unborn babies to be killed. Pray that the leaders of all countries will obey God. Pray that they will want to respect and protect human life.

Write a thank you prayer to God for the life He has given you.

_____

_____

You can pray:

Dear God, thank You for creating me. Please help me to protect and respect human life. In Jesus' name. Amen.

246 How Can I Respect Life?

I praise you because I am fearfully and wonderfully made . . .
Psalm 139:14

Do you enjoy playing video games? Some of them are lots of fun, but there are some video games that are violent. They encourage you to "kill" others to win the game. You might think that it's not so bad—it's only a game. However, the more you play those kinds of games, the less troubled you become by the violence.

Violence is on TV, in our movies, in our music—even in cartoons! Some people listen to a lot of music that talks about killing. Soon, they are thinking about hurting others or even themselves. Some people watch movies that show people killing or being killed. Then, they go and try to copy what they've seen. Some kids have taken guns to school to hurt and kill others.

God hates this violence. He says, "You shall not murder" (Exodus 20:13). Taking someone's life—or even your own life—is sin. No one has the right to take away life. God wants you to respect life, including your own.

Be careful what you listen to and what you watch. Don't fill you mind with thoughts of killing. Turn off the violent TV shows or video games. Listen to music that celebrates life. You honor God when you honor life.

LIVING FOR GOD

What are three things you can do to show your respect for life?

_____

_____

_____

You can pray:
Dear God, help me to say "no" to violent games, TV shows and music. Help me to honor You by honoring life. In Jesus' name. Amen.

I praise you because I am fearfully and wonderfully made
... **Psalm 139:14**

L
I
V
I
N
G

F
O
R

G
O
D

Jason threw paper wads at the girls sitting in the bus seats ahead of him. The bus driver told him to stop, but as soon as he wasn't looking, Jason started causing trouble again. Keshia's teacher told her not to push in line in front of others. Keshia rudely talked back to her teacher. Jason and Keshia weren't showing respect for those in authority over them.

Do you show respect to those in authority over you? Or do you talk back to them or disobey them? The Bible says, "Everyone must submit himself to [willingly obey] the governing authorities . . ." (Romans 13:1). God's plan is for you to respect your leaders by speaking kindly to them and obeying. God puts people in authority over you for your good. They are there to help you keep the rules so you will be safe. They help you make right choices so that everyone can get along.

Those who are rude or do not obey authority are punished. When you are rude or disobey, you cause problems for yourself and others. If you've been rude or disobedient, confess that sin to God. Ask Him to help you respect those in authority over you.

List several people you need to be more respectful to.

_____

_____

_____

You can pray:

Dear God, please forgive me for the times I've been rude or disobeyed those in authority. Help me to show respect to them. In Jesus' name. Amen.

248 How Did David Respect Authority?

I praise you because I am fearfully and wonderfully made . . .
Psalm 139:14

God promised a young man named David that someday he would be king of Israel. Until then, he would have to patiently respect the authority over him—King Saul.

One day, the women praised David as being a better soldier than Saul. Saul was jealous. Later, as David played his harp, hate and jealousy took control of Saul's mind. He threw his spear at David, but God saved David's life. From that time on Saul chased David. He wanted to kill him!

David knew that God had planned for him to be king. He could have turned against Saul. But David respected Saul's authority over him. Once Saul entered a cave. He didn't know that David and his soldiers were hiding in the back. David's men wanted to kill Saul, but David refused. He cut a piece of cloth from Saul's robe to show that he could have killed him. Later, David felt guilty about cutting the king's robe. He respected the king's authority even though Saul was disobeying God.

Like David, you can show respect for authority. Be patient and wait for God to work out His plan. When the time was right, God honored David. He was made king of Israel. God will honor you, too, as you respect those in authority.

LIVING FOR GOD

How was David able to respect King Saul?

_____

_____

_____

You can pray:

Dear God, help me to respect authority even when it's hard. In Jesus' name. Amen.

How Can I Respect Authority?

I praise you because I am fearfully and wonderfully made . . . **Psalm 139:14**

LIVING FOR GOD

In the Bible, God gave ten commandments, or rules. His commandments show you how to respect authority. The most important person who has authority over you is God. His first commandment says, "You shall have no other gods before me" (Exodus 20:3). Nothing should be more important than God. He deserves first place. Give God first place by spending time with Him each day in prayer and Bible reading. Give Him the first day of the week by going to church on Sunday.

Even God's name deserves respect. In another commandment God says, "You shall not misuse the name of the LORD your God" (Exodus 20:7). Using God's name as a curse word is disrespectful. Remember that God is holy. Use His name with respect.

God has placed different people in authority in your life. Probably the first ones you think of are your mom or dad. One of God's commandments says, "Honor your father and your mother . . ." (Exodus 20:12). One of the best ways to honor your parents is to obey them with a right attitude. God has put Himself and other people in authority over your life. Ask Him to help you respect them.

Name two ways you can honor your parents.

_____

_____

_____

You can pray:

Dear God, thank You for my parents. Help me to respect them by obeying with a right attitude. In Jesus' name. Amen.

250 What Does It Mean to Covet?

But godliness with contentment is great gain. **1 Timothy 6:6**

"**Give me your vine-yard!**" King Ahab demanded. (A vineyard is a garden where grapes are grown.) The vineyard belonged to a man named Naboth. It had been owned by his father and grandfather.

"**No,**" **Naboth replied,** "**I will not give you my vineyard.**" King Ahab was furious. He stomped back to his palace, lay on his bed, faced the wall and refused to eat any food. He pouted because he couldn't get his own way. King Ahab coveted Naboth's vineyard. Coveting is a strong desire to have something that doesn't belong to you. The king coveted Naboth's vineyard so much, he later had Naboth put to death! Coveting can lead to terrible things.

But, God knew what was in King Ahab's heart. After Naboth was put to death, King Ahab went to the vineyard to claim it as his own. God sent his prophet, Elijah, to meet him there. Elijah told the king that God was going to punish him for his terrible actions.

The Bible says, " . . . **Watch out!** Be on your guard against all kinds of greed [coveting] . . ." (Luke 12:15). God is warning you not to want what isn't yours. Rather, be thankful to God for what you have. Put God first and you will have all that you need.

What should you do when you are tempted to covet?

_____

_____

_____

You can pray:
Dear God, show me ways that I am coveting. Help me to be satisfied with what You have given me. In Jesus' name. Amen.

What Does God Say about Contentment?

> But godliness with contentment is great gain.
> 1 Timothy 6:6

"Mom, may I have money to buy ___?" How would you fill in the blank? A toy? A video game? Candy? Maybe you've seen children at a store begging and whining for something. Maybe you've done it, too.

Here are some steps from the Bible to help you be content:

•*Be prayerful.* Ask God first if you should buy or ask for something. God will help you know what is right: " . . . in everything, by prayer and petition, with thanksgiving, present your requests to God" (Philippians 4:6).

•*Be patient.* God will give you what you need, when you need it: "And the peace of God, which transcends [is greater than] all understanding, will guard your hearts and your minds in Christ Jesus" (Philippians 4:7).

•*Be content.* If God says no, remember that His answer is best for you: " . . . be content whatever the circumstances" (Philippians 4:11).

•*Be trusting.* God will provide for your needs: "And my God will meet all your needs according to his glorious riches in Christ Jesus" (Philippians 4:19).

Being content with what you have will give you great joy and peace in life. Paul, the writer of Philippians in the Bible, learned to be content in everything. You can too!

Which of the four steps do you find the most difficult? Why?

_____
_____
_____

You can pray:

Dear God, thank You for meeting all my needs. In Your strength I will be content. In Jesus' name. Amen.

252 How Can I Be Content?

But godliness with contentment is great gain. **1 Timothy 6:6**

One of the richest men in the world was asked, "How much money does it take to be happy?" His answer was, "A few more dollars." He was saying he never had enough. He always wanted more.

Many Christians often have the same problem of wanting more. The Bible says, " . . . be content with what you have, because God has said, 'Never will I leave you . . .'" (Hebrews 13:5). Contentment is being satisfied with what you have. When you are not content, you are really saying that God is not taking care of you.

If you've trusted in Jesus as your Savior, He promises He will never, never leave you. He will be with you at home, at school—wherever you are. He will meet your needs. With Jesus you can be content just the way you are—just how you look, just where you live, and with just what you have.

Whenever you are not content, stop and thank God for what you already have. Thank Him that He is with you and will meet all of your needs. Our verse says, "godliness [being like Jesus] with contentment is great gain." When you have Jesus, you have all you need—and more! Are you content today?

LIVING FOR GOD

List three things that you can thank God for.

_____

_____

_____

You can pray:

Dear God, thank You for giving Jesus to be with me all the time. Help me to be content in Him. In Jesus' name. Amen.

What Does God Say about Greediness and Stealing?

But godliness with contentment is great gain.
1 Timothy 6:6

253

LIVING FOR GOD

Markia loved strawberries. One night her mom served strawberries for dessert. When the bowl was passed to her, Markia filled her dish with strawberries. She left only a few for her brother and sister. Markia was being greedy. She wasn't content to take a few and share the rest. She wanted it all for herself.

Greed is a strong desire to have all that you can get. When you are greedy you are thinking only of yourself. The Bible says, "A greedy man brings trouble to his family . . ." (Proverbs 15:27).

Keith was in a store when he saw some apples in a basket by the door. He waited till the store owner was busy, and then he walked over to the basket. Keith took an apple and put it inside his shirt. He walked out without paying for the apple. Keith was stealing.

God's eighth Commandment says, "You shall not steal" (Exodus 20:15). Stealing is taking something that doesn't belong to you. You should use your hands to work and earn money to buy what you need. You're not to take it from someone else. Greediness and stealing are selfish desires that will keep you from being content.

What should you do when you are tempted to be greedy or to steal?

_____

_____

You can pray:

Dear God, thank You for reminding me not to steal or be greedy. Help me to be content with what I have. In Jesus' name. Amen.

254 What Happened When Achan Was Greedy?

But godliness with contentment is great gain. 1 Timothy 6:6

"Hurrah! Victory is ours! God has given us victory over Jericho." God helped the army of Israel defeat the large city of Jericho. But when they went to fight the much smaller city of Ai, Israel lost the battle. Joshua, the leader, came with deep sadness before the Lord. God told Joshua the problem. "Israel has sinned" (Joshua 7:11). Someone had stolen treasure from Jericho.

God had given clear instructions. All treasure taken from Jericho was to be given to the Lord's house. Anyone keeping treasure for himself would bring God's punishment. During the battle of Jericho, a man named Achan became greedy. He took some valuable things and buried them in his tent. God showed Joshua that Achan was the guilty one. Achan admitted what he had done. Achan, his family and all that he owned were destroyed–all because of greed. (Joshua 7)

If you allow greed in your life, you may have to face a terrible punishment. Think of how many other people may also be affected by your greed. You will be setting a bad example for others to follow. Some may even decide not to receive Jesus as their Savior because of what they see in you.

L
I
V
I
N
G

F
O
R

G
O
D

How might your greed affect other people?

_____

_____

_____

You can pray:
Dear God, help me to be a godly example to others by being content with what I have and not being greedy. In Jesus' name. Amen.

How Can I Avoid Being Greedy?

But godliness with contentment is great gain.
1 Timothy 6:6

LIVING FOR GOD

Greed is a strong desire to have something for yourself. The opposite of being greedy is to be content–to be satisfied with what God has given you. Only God can help you to be content. Thank God for forgiving your sin and giving you all the good things you have. When you are content, you'll want to give instead of always getting things for yourself.

You can give God your time by praying and reading your Bible. You can give part of your allowance to God in your church offering. You can give your talents and abilities to serve God. Maybe you can sing a song in the worship service or draw a picture to decorate the church. Giving to God is a great way to keep from being greedy.

God can also help you to give to others instead of being greedy. You can share your toys. You can allow others to get in line in front of you. You can give others first choice at dessert.

Ask God to show you how you can help meet the needs of others. Let God help you to be content. Give to God and others, and you won't have time to be greedy!

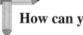

How can you guard against being greedy?

_____

_____

_____

You can pray:

Dear God, help me to be content, and to give to You and to others so I can guard against being greedy. In Jesus' name. Amen.

. . . Everyone should be quick to listen, slow to speak and slow to become angry. **James 1:19**

"Wait" is one of the hardest words to obey. But, God uses waiting to teach you patience. Patience is being able to wait calmly, even through hard or boring times. God sometimes allows hard things to happen to His children to help them learn to be patient. It can be a hard lesson to learn!

The Bible says, "Consider it pure joy, my brothers, whenever you face trials [hard times] of many kinds, because you know that the testing of your faith develops perseverance [patience]" (James 1:2-3). Hard times in your life will test your faith in God. You might want to say to God, "Help me get better now!" or "Help me get a new bike soon!" Will you be patient and keep living for God even if He says, "Wait"?

As a Christian, you can wait patiently on the Lord knowing your life is in God's control. "Wait for the LORD; be strong and take heart and wait for the LORD" (Psalm 27:14). When you show patience by waiting on the Lord, you will grow stronger. Next time you face a hard time, let God use it to teach you to be patient.

LIVING FOR GOD

Write how God has been teaching you to be patient.

_____

_____

_____

You can pray:

Dear God, thank You for the hard times in my life. Help me to patiently wait for You to work and to trust Your plan. In Jesus' name. Amen.

How Did God Reward Job's Patience?

... Everyone should be quick to listen, slow to speak and slow to become angry. **James 1:19**

LIVING FOR GOD

Job was a rich man. He had 7000 sheep, 3000 camels, 500 oxen and 500 donkeys. Job and his wife had seven sons and three daughters.

Most importantly, Job had faith in God. Job's relationship with God was more important to him than anything. But God allowed hard times in Job's life. One day, all his oxen, donkeys and camels were stolen by enemies, and his sheep were killed in a fire. His children were eating in a house when a strong wind came and the house fell, killing them all. Job's sadness was more than you can imagine, yet Job did not sin by blaming God (Job 1:14, 18-19).

Next, God allowed Job to get painful sores all over his body (Job 1:7). Job's wife told him to "curse God and die" (Job 2:9). Life couldn't get much worse. Yet Job did not sin in what he said. Job lost everything except his faith in God. His friends and family discouraged him, but Job was patient. He believed that God was in control.

The Bible says that God finally rewarded Job's patience. He gave back to Job twice what he owned. He also gave Job more children. God had given him even more than he had before (Job 42:12).

How did Job remain faithful to God through all of his hard times?

_____

_____

_____

You can pray:

Dear Lord, help me to be patient in hard times, and may I always be faithful to You. In Jesus' name. Amen.

How Can I Be Patient?

... Everyone should be quick to listen, slow to speak and slow to become angry. **James 1:19**

"I wish I had my own dog," Tom thought. He daydreamed about playing catch in the yard and wrestling in the grass with his dog. He had asked his parents, but they said they couldn't afford to keep a dog. Tom didn't complain. He just kept praying and hoping. Finally, after a long time, Tom's parents agreed that he could get a dog. Tom's patience was rewarded!

Sometimes God or your parents may say "no" or "wait" when you ask for something like a dog, bike or game. At times like these you must "be still before the LORD and wait patiently for him" (Psalm 37:7). Don't fuss and complain. Keep praying and trusting God to do what is best.

Maybe you are asking God for something much more serious like healing for a friend who is dying or help in a serious family problem. Being still and waiting patiently for God is difficult. Remember that God knows the future. Part of being patient is knowing God will do what is best for you. You may have to wait for years. Patience is trusting God to do what is best in His time.

LIVING FOR GOD

How has God rewarded your patience?

_____

_____

_____

You can pray:

Dear God, help me to wait patiently and trust You to answer my prayers in Your perfect time. In Jesus' name. Amen.

What Does God Say about Anger?

 . . . Everyone should be quick to listen, slow to speak and slow to become angry. **James 1:19**

LIVING FOR GOD

What kinds of things make you angry? Is it when your little brother wrecks your room or your sister wears your clothes? Maybe it's when your parents say "no" to something you want to do.

Anger can cause many problems. Anger can make you say or do things that you will feel badly about later. It can cause you guilt and shame. It can ruin your friendships. People don't like to be with an angry person. It can even ruin your health! It is normal to feel angry sometimes, but anger that is uncontrolled is sin.

God's desire is for you to live at peace–with Him, with yourself and with others. That isn't always easy to do!

A good rule to follow is this: ". . . Do not let the sun go down while you are still angry" (Ephesians 4:26). In other words, don't let anger control your life. If you've been letting anger control you, admit it to God and ask His forgiveness. If you are angry at another person, talk to that person. Try to work out the problem. You might even have to apologize. Remember our Bible verse, "Everyone should be quick to listen, slow to speak, and slow to become angry" (James 1:19).

 How can anger hurt your life?

_____

_____

_____

 You can pray:

Dear God, please help me to be patient with others and slow to become angry. In Jesus' name. Amen.

Is It Ever Right to Be Angry?

. . . Everyone should be quick to listen, slow to speak and slow to become angry. **James 1:19**

Parents had brought their children to the Lord Jesus so He could hold them and pray for them. When the disciples saw the children coming, they tried to keep them away. Jesus became angry with the disciples. He commanded them to let the children come to Him (Mark 10:13-16).

Another time, Jesus entered the temple (place of worship). He found people there who were buying and selling animals, exchanging money and cheating others. They had used God's holy temple for their own greedy plans. Jesus pushed them out and turned over their tables. He shouted, "My house will be called a house of prayer for all nations but you have made it a den of robbers" (Mark 11:17).

In both of these situations, Jesus was angry at sin. You, too, should be angry at sin. Be angry if someone offers you drugs. You should be angry when you hear God's name used as a swear word. Being angry doesn't mean that you sin. God's Word tells us, "In your anger do not sin . . ." (Ephesians 4:26). We are to be angry at sin, but not to let that anger control us. Ask God to give you a right attitude, especially when it comes to anger.

LIVING FOR GOD

Why should you be angry at sin?

_____

_____

_____

You can pray:

Dear God, thank You for teaching me about the right kind of anger. Help me not to let my anger turn into sin. In Jesus' name. Amen.

How Can I Have Self-Control?

. . . Everyone should be quick to listen, slow to speak and slow to become angry. **James 1:19**

LIVING FOR GOD

Self-control means letting God work through you to control your thoughts, feelings and actions rather than letting those things control you. Jesus showed us the way to live a self-controlled life. As a child, the Lord Jesus had self-control to obey His parents. (Luke 2:41-51) As a man, Jesus showed self-control by refusing to sin when tempted by Satan. (Luke 4:1-13) Even when He was dying, Jesus showed self-control when He forgave those who crucified Him. (Luke 23:34)

Self-control is part of the fruit of the Spirit that you learned about earlier in this devotional book (read #82 again). Through the power of the Holy Spirit you can have self-control. Allow the Holy Spirit within you to control what you think, say and do. Stay away from people and places that tempt you to lose your self-control.

Each morning give God control of yourself. You might say, "God, I give you my mouth to speak the truth. I give you my hands to help others. I give you my mind to think pure thoughts. I give you my eyes to read your Word." Developing self-control takes hard work. Trust and allow the Holy Spirit to work in you.

In what areas of your life is it hardest for you to have self-control?

_____

_____

_____

You can pray:

Dear God, help me to give You every part of my life to be controlled by the Holy Spirit. In Jesus' name. Amen.

What Does God Say about Kindness?

Would other people describe you as being kind? Kindness is treating others with love and respect. Kindness is love in action. Think about how kind Jesus was when He lived on the Earth. Even though people didn't deserve it, He treated them with kindness. He was kind to the poor, to the sick, to children and to elderly people. He was kind to His friends, and to His enemies. He even showed kindness to people that others hated.

The greatest demonstration of Jesus' love and kindness was when He died on the cross for your sins and mine. He willingly suffered, bled and died a cruel death so that we could be forgiven. He was even kind to those who put Him to death.

Because Jesus has shown such kindness to us, as His children, we should show the same kindness to others. Show kindness at home by helping around the house without being asked. Show kindness at school by being friends with someone that no one else seems to like. Show kindness in your neighborhood by helping an elderly person to clean up the yard or take out the trash. Look for ways to show God's kindness to others.

LIVING FOR GOD

 How can you show kindess to someone this week?

_____

_____

_____

You can pray:

 Dear God, help me to show Your love and kindness to others. In Jesus' name. Amen.

How Was Abram Kind to Lot?

 Be kind and compassionate to one another, forgiving each other, just as in Christ God forgave you. **Ephesians 4:32**

LIVING FOR GOD

Abram was a wealthy man. God had told him to leave his home and go to a new country to live. God promised Abram that his family would become a great nation and have a land to call home. (Genesis 12:1-2)

Traveling with Abram and his wife, Sarai, was his nephew, Lot. Abram and Lot both had many animals and servants. When they arrived in the new country, they found that the land did not have enough food and water for all the animals. Their servants argued about this problem. (Genesis 12:5, 13:7)

Abram told Lot that they would have to separate so that their herds would have enough food and water. God had already given the land to Abram, but Abram made a kind, generous offer to Lot. He allowed Lot to have first choice. Lot chose the best land, with clean wells and rich soil. Abram took what was left. He could have kept the best land, but he decided to show kindness, by giving the best land to Lot. (Genesis 13:8-11)

Abram shows us a great example of being kind to family members. It's not always easy, but God can help you to do it!

 How can you show kindness to a member of your family?

_____

_____

_____

You can pray:

 Dear Lord, thank You for my family. Help me to show kindness to each member, even when it's hard. In Jesus' name. Amen.

How Can I Be Kind to Others?

Be kind and compassionate to one another, forgiving each other, just as in Christ God forgave you. **Ephesians 4:32**

Showing kindness to others involves your thoughts, words and actions. Do you think of others before yourself? Think of the letters, **J-O-Y**: **J**esus first, **O**thers second and **Y**ourself last. That's what it means to, " . . . consider others better than yourselves" (Philippians 2:3).

Our words are also important in showing kindness. People may say, "Words will never hurt me," but words do hurt. Some children remember the mean names they were called for a whole lifetime. Think before you speak. If you don't have anything good to say, don't say anything at all. Look for something kind to say.

Finally, showing kindness to others involves actions. Look for ways you can help others. Help a classmate who is not doing well in school. Help a neighbor rake the leaves. Help your mom by watching your little brother or sister. Help a sick friend by making him a card.

Showing kindness can help you show others you are a Christian. You may be able to tell them about the great kindness the Lord Jesus has shown to you. As you show kindness to others you are showing the love of Jesus to them.

LIVING FOR GOD

List three ways you will be kind to others this week.

_____

_____

_____

You can pray:

Dear God, help me show Your kindness to others in my thoughts, words and actions. In Jesus' name. Amen.

What Does God Say about Forgiving Others?

 Be kind and compassionate to one another, forgiving each other, just as in Christ God forgave you. **Ephesians 4:32**

LIVING FOR GOD

Forgiveness means letting go of my anger and desire to get even with someone who has hurt me. True forgiveness comes from God. Ever since sin entered the world through the first people, Adam and Eve, individuals have needed God's forgiveness. Jesus Christ, God the Son, died on the cross to make the way for us to be forgiven for our sins. Those who trust in Jesus as their Savior are forgiven–made clean from their sins. If you have trusted the Lord Jesus as your Savior, you can thank Him that He has forgiven you.

Once you have received God's forgiveness, He wants you to forgive others who hurt you. Our verse says, "Be kind and compassionate to one another, forgiving each other, just as in Christ God forgave you" (Ephesians 4:32). You need to forgive others because God has forgiven you. Maybe someone has said or done something mean to you. Don't hold on to your anger toward that person. Think of all the sinful things God has forgiven in your life. Then, choose to forgive the one who's hurt you. Even if that person never apologizes for what he did, you can forgive others because God has forgiven you.

 Why should you be willing to forgive others?

_____

_____

_____

You can pray:

 Dear God, thank You for Your forgiveness. Help me forgive others as You have forgiven me. In Jesus' name. Amen.

266 How Did Joseph Treat His Brothers?

Be kind and compassionate to one another, forgiving each other, just as in Christ God forgave you. **Ephesians 4:32**

If anyone had a good reason to hate his brothers it was Joseph. We learned earlier in this book about how Joseph's brothers threw him into a pit, made plans to kill him and finally sold him into slavery. With God's help and blessing, Joseph became the second most powerful leader in Egypt. When a terrible famine (lack of food) came to the land, people came from miles around to buy food in Egypt.

One day as Joseph was giving out the food, he saw his ten older brothers standing before him. He knew them but they didn't recognize him because he now looked and spoke like an Egyptian. Joseph could have taken revenge on his brothers, but he didn't. Joseph forgave them. He even thanked God for sending him to Egypt. Joseph realized that God had used his brothers to work out His perfect plan. Joseph forgave completely. He invited his father, brothers and their families to come live in Egypt where he could take care of them. (Genesis 50:16-21)

Like Joseph, you need to learn to forgive others as God has forgiven you. Only God can give you the strength inside to forgive.

LIVING FOR GOD

How is Joseph's forgiveness of his brothers like God's forgiveness of you?

_____

_____

_____

You can pray:

Dear God, thank You for teaching me about Joseph. Help me to forgive completely. In Jesus' name. Amen.

How Can I Forgive Those Who Hurt Me?

Be kind and compassionate to one another, forgiving each other, just as in Christ God forgave you. **Ephesians 4:32**

LIVING FOR GOD

Courtney cried quietly, alone in her room. The older kids on the school bus had been teasing her again. Courtney was hurt and angry.

Eldon was shocked. He had heard his parents argue late at night, but he never expected his dad to pack a suitcase and leave. Now Eldon felt it was his fault. Eldon was hurt and angry.

Every person has had hurt feelings. Sometimes the hurt is physical like being hit or kicked. Often with the hurt comes anger toward the person who caused the hurt. Remembering God's forgiveness can help you forgive those who hurt you. It is only by His strength that you can truly forgive.

Pray for the person who has hurt you. Ask God to change him. Think of something kind you can do for him. This may be hard. God doesn't say, "Just be kind to your friends." You are to be kind to friends and enemies.

Remember the forgiveness Jesus had for those who nailed him to the cross and watched Him die. He said, "Father, forgive them, for they do not know what they are doing" (Luke 23:34). Ask God to help you forgive in the same way.

How can you forgive those who hurt you?

_____

_____

_____

You can pray:

Dear God, I have been hurt by others. With Your help I now forgive them (say their names to God). In Jesus' name. Amen.

What Does God Say about Being Honest?

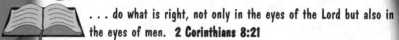

... do what is right, not only in the eyes of the Lord but also in the eyes of men. **2 Corinthians 8:21**

Have you ever heard the phrase, "Honesty is the best policy?" Although it is not in the Bible, it is a good phrase to remember when you are faced with a choice.

God reminds believers to " . . . **do what is right**, not only in the eyes of the Lord but also in the eyes of men" (2 Corinthians 8:21).

There are times when you can make an honest (right) choice or you can make a dishonest (wrong) choice. There are people who may tell you it's okay to be dishonest as long as you don't get caught. The truth is you do get caught–every time. God knows all your actions and even your thoughts! The Lord Jesus Christ sees all you do.

You are also to do right "in the eyes of men." Be honest. Others are watching you. If you are dishonest, others may not believe you when you witness to them about Jesus.

Honesty is so important to God that He even wants your thoughts to be honest. The Bible says, "Finally, brothers, whatever is true (honest) . . . think about such things" (Philippians 4:8). Remember that God is watching, and others are watching, too. Think and act honestly.

How can others tell that you're an honest person?

_____

_____

_____

You can pray:

Dear God, help me to think and live honestly so that my life will glorify You. In Jesus' name. Amen.

LIVING FOR GOD

What Happened When Jacob Was Dishonest?

. . . do what is right, not only in the eyes of the Lord but also in the eyes of men. **2 Corinthians 8:21**

The Bible tells about two men, Esau and Jacob, who were twins, but different. Esau, born first, liked to hunt and be outside. Jacob worked near their home and liked to cook.

One day, their father, Isaac, wanted to give Esau a special blessing. Jacob decided to trick his father into giving him the blessing instead. With the help of his mother, Rebekah, they prepared a meal. Then, Rebekah tied goat skins on Jacob's neck and hands. Dishonest Jacob carried the meal into his father's tent. He gave his father the food, pretending to be his brother.

Isaac was probably over 100 years old. He could not see well. Isaac reached out and touched his son's hands–they were hairy like Esau's hands. "This must be Esau," thought Isaac. Isaac ate the food and blessed his son. Jacob had tricked his father!

When Esau arrived, he was furious at what Jacob had done. "I will kill my brother Jacob," Esau said (Genesis 27:41).

Jacob had to go away for many years. Later, Jacob's wife's father was dishonest to him many times. Often what you do to others will eventually be done to you. What sad things happened in this family, all because of dishonesty.

How might your dishonesty affect other members of your family?

_____

_____

You can pray:

Dear Lord, help me to be honest with my family and my friends. In Jesus' name. Amen.

LIVING FOR GOD

270 How Can I Be Honest in All Things?

. . . do what is right, not only in the eyes of the Lord but also in the eyes of men. **2 Corinthians 8:21**

Daryl and his brother, David, loved to play games. Since Daryl was older, he would keep the score for their games. David wasn't very good with math, so he was happy to let Daryl keep score. One afternoon when Daryl was losing, he thought about adding extra points to his score. David wouldn't know. What should he do? Does it really matter? It was just a game.

Ashley went to the grocery store to buy some items for her mom. She paid for the groceries, but when the cashier gave her the change, Ashley noticed that he had given her twenty-five cents too much. What should Ashley do? Does it really matter? It was only twenty-five cents.

Yes, it does matter to God. He wants your words, thoughts and actions to be honest. Remember that God knows all you do. He knows if you change the score of the game or if you keep the extra change. Even small things matter to Him.

When others see your honesty in small ways, often they will trust you with bigger jobs and responsibilities. Think honestly and then act honestly. God will be pleased when you do.

LIVING FOR GOD

Why is it important to be honest, even in small things?

_____

_____

_____

You can pray:

Dear God, please help me to be honest for You, even in small things. In Jesus' name. Amen.

What Does God Say about Being Afraid?

When I am afraid, I will trust in you. **Psalm 56:3**

LIVING FOR GOD

King David knew what it was to feel afraid. He had many scary experiences in his life. As a shepherd boy, he had to protect his sheep from wild animals. As a young man, David fought against a giant, who had been terrorizing all of Israel.

Later as an adult, David led his army into many battles, and his life was often threatened. However, in all of these scary experiences, David knew what to do about his fear.

In Psalm 23:4, David wrote, "...I will fear no evil, for you [God] are with me." In another Psalm David wrote, "When I am afraid, I will trust in you [God]" (Psalm 56:3). David often reminded himself that wherever he went, God was there. God was always with him.

It's natural to feel afraid sometimes. However, if you have trusted Jesus as your Savior, you can be sure that God is with you all the time. He has promised in His Word, "Never will I leave you . . ." (Hebrews 13:5). He is with you every moment of every day, everywhere you go. When you are afraid, do what David did. Remember that God is with you, and put your trust in Him.

What did David do when he felt afraid?

_____

_____

_____

You can pray:

Dear God, thank You that You are with me all the time. Help me to trust You when I am afraid. In Jesus' name. Amen.

272 What Did Jesus' Disciples Do When They Were Afraid?

When I am afraid, I will trust in you. **Psalm 56:3**

"Row for your life! The waves are going to sink us!" Jesus' disciples were terrified. They never imagined their day with Jesus would end in such fear.

The Lord Jesus Christ had been teaching along the shore of the Sea of Galilee. When evening came, He and His disciples got into a small boat to cross to the other side of the lake. As they started out, Jesus was soon asleep in the boat.

Then, a strong storm began to blow. The waves came over the sides of the boat, and the disciples tried to keep it from sinking. Fearing for their lives, the disciples woke Jesus and cried, "Teacher, don't you care if we drown?" (Mark 4:38). Jesus got up and spoke to the wind and waves. "Quiet! Be still!" He commanded them (Mark 4:39). Immediately the wind and the waves stopped. All was still.

Jesus said to his disciples, "Why are you so afraid? Do you still have no faith?" (Mark 4:40). The disciples were beginning to see that Jesus, God the Son, had great power over all things. Jesus wanted them to learn that they could trust Him when they were afraid. That's a lesson Jesus wants you to learn, too!

LIVING FOR GOD

Write about a time you were afraid and Jesus helped you have courage.

_____

_____

_____

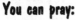

You can pray:

Dear God, thank You for being with me. Help me to trust You when I am afraid. In Jesus' name. Amen.

What Should I Do When I Am Afraid?

 When I am afraid, I will trust in you. **Psalm 56:3**

LIVING FOR GOD

What makes you afraid? Perhaps it is things like darkness or storms. Maybe you're afraid of being home alone or having to give a report in front of the class. Sometimes serious problems make you afraid like illness or your parents getting divorced.

Whether it's caused by something small or something great, fear can be a terrible problem. Being afraid can even affect your body, making you ill. Fear is a natural thing that God has built into your body to help you escape from danger. But, when fear takes control of you, it becomes a problem.

God's solution for fear is trust in Him. Nothing that happens is ever a surprise to God. He is in control of all things. Here is a special promise from God that you can remember when you are afraid: "Be strong and courageous. Do not be terrified; do not be discouraged, for the LORD your God will be with you wherever you go" (Joshua 1:9). God is with you, no matter what. Tell Him about the thing that is making you afraid. Say this verse to yourself and believe what it says. Trust in God when you are afraid. He will never let you down!

 What will you do the next time you are afraid?

_____

_____

_____

You can pray:

 Dear God, when I am afraid, help me to remember that You are with me. Help me to trust in You. In Jesus' name. Amen.

This is the end of the section of "Living for God" devotionals.

It is time to do the next activity page that came to you in the mail. Remember to add your prayer request so your mailbox friend can pray for you. When you finish the whole page, fold it on the lines so the Mailbox Club address shows. Put a small piece of tape on the bottom to keep it folded. Add a stamp and mail your activity page.

Your work will be marked and sent back to you, along with a personal note. The activity sheet for the next set of lessons will be sent to you, too.

Enjoy getting to know God better with your next group of devotionals!

Trusting
GOD

274 What Is God's Providence?

And we know that in all things God works for the good of those who love him . . . **Romans 8:28**

Have you ever put a picture puzzle together? When you spread out all the pieces, it's quite a mess! However, each piece has a special place. When all the pieces are in the right place, you see a beautiful picture!

God has a plan for your life that has many pieces to it. There are many good things that God has planned for you. He also allows hard things to happen in your life. Like a great puzzle, God is putting all of these things together in His special way. This is called God's providence (PROV-uh-dense). Providence means that God al-ways cares for His people and controls all that happens in their lives. The Bible says, "And we know that in all things God works for the good of those who love him . . ." (Romans 8:28).

At times you may not understand the reason something happens to you, but nothing is ever a surprise to God. You can praise God for His providence even when you can't see how the puzzle will turn out. Each day look for ways that God is at work. God always knows and does what is best. Thank Him today for His providence.

How have you seen God's care and control in your life?

_____

_____

_____

You can pray:

Dear God, thank You for Your providence. Help me to trust You in all that happens in my life. In Jesus' name. Amen.

Does God Have a Purpose for My Life? 275

And we know that in all things God works for the good of those who love him . . . **Romans 8:28**

"Why am I here?" Many people have asked that question. Is there a reason that God put you on this Earth? The answer is, "Yes!" God does everything for a reason. People keep life going on our planet, but there's so much more than just living.

In His perfect plan, God made you special. There's no one else like you, even if you have a twin! Your personality, the way you think about things, what makes you laugh or cry—all make you different from others. God purposely made you this way. You are one-of-a-kind!

God also has a purpose (plan) for what He wants you to become. He wants your life to glorify (honor) Him. In the Bible God says, "'For I know the plans I have for you,' declares the LORD, 'plans to prosper you and not to harm you, plans to give you hope and a future'" (Jeremiah 29:11). God has good plans for your life. In His providence, He allows only what is best. Even when hard things happen, remember that God has a purpose—a plan—that He is working out for your good and His glory.

Write three things about you that make you different from your friend.

_____

_____

_____

You can pray:

Dear God, thank You for making me special. Thank You that You have a good purpose for my life. I trust You to work out Your plan for me. In Jesus' name. Amen.

276 What Was God's Purpose for Joseph?

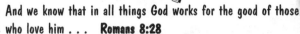
And we know that in all things God works for the good of those who love him . . . **Romans 8:28**

The Bible tells about a young man named Joseph. He grew up with ten older brothers! Joseph's father loved him most of all. He even gave Joseph a beautiful robe. But Joseph's brothers were jealous.

One day, the brothers were in a field taking care of their father's sheep when they saw Joseph coming. They took his beautiful robe and threw Joseph into a deep hole in the ground. Later, they sold Joseph as a slave. Joseph went through many more hard times. He even had to go to prison in Egypt for something he didn't do.

While Joseph was in prison, the king had a strange dream. God gave Joseph wisdom to understand the dream. The king rewarded Joseph by giving him an important job. God told Joseph to save lots of grain because soon there would be no food to eat. Joseph obeyed and many people were saved from starving.

God had good plans for Joseph's life, even though it was sometimes hard. God's purpose was for Joseph to learn to trust and obey Him. Joseph's hard times prepared him for the important work that God had for him to do. Joseph followed God's plan and his life glorified God.

TRUSTING GOD

Write down two ways you see God's providence in Joseph's life.

_____

_____

_____

You can pray:

Dear God, thank You for the good plans You had for Joseph. Please help me to trust and obey You like he did. In Jesus' name. Amen.

How Did Joseph Respond to Hard Times?

And we know that in all things God works for the good of those who love him . . . **Romans 8:28**

TRUSTING GOD

Imagine being hated by your family. Imagine being sold as a slave. Imagine being put into prison for something you didn't do. Those hard things happened to Joseph in the Bible.

How did he respond? Did he get angry with God? Did he want to get even with his brothers? No! Even though it was hard, Joseph trusted and obeyed God. He worked hard and did the best that he could. After much suffering, Joseph became an important man in Egypt.

One day his brothers came to buy grain. They didn't recognize Joseph, but he recognized them. Joseph had the power to punish them. However, instead of punishing them, Joseph forgave his brothers! He said, "You intended [planned] to harm me, but God intended it for good . . ." (Genesis 50:20). Joseph took care of his family the rest of his life.

Joseph saw that everything that had happened was part of God's plan. God had cared for him and worked out His purpose. Although people may have evil plans, God's good plans can never be ruined. Joseph responded to his hard times with forgiveness and trust in God's providence. How do you respond to your hard times?

How should you respond to hard times in your life?

_____

_____

_____

You can pray:

Dear God, thank You for taking the bad things in my life and making them turn out for good. Help me to forgive and to trust in You. In Jesus' name. Amen.

278

What Was God's Purpose for Esther?

And we know that in all things God works for the good of those who love him . . . **Romans 8:28**

Esther was good at keeping secrets. She was a young girl, who lived a long time ago in Persia. The Bible tells how she was chosen to be the queen. Queen Esther had a secret that not even the king knew. Her uncle, Mordecai, had warned her not to tell that she was Jewish.

A proud man named Haman worked for the king. He liked to have people bow down to honor him. Mordecai refused to bow to anyone but God. Haman was angry. He learned that Mordecai was Jewish. Haman made a terrible law. On a certain day, all of the Jewish people would be killed.

Mordecai told Esther about the law. He wanted her to get help from the king, but, Esther was afraid. If she went to the king without being invited, he could have her killed. Esther told Mordecai she couldn't do it. Mordecai sent a message back to her telling her that God may have made her queen for such a time as this.

God had a special purpose in allowing Esther to become queen. She was in just the right place to save the Jewish people. Would Esther trust God's plan for her? Would you?

TRUSTING GOD

What would you do if you were Esther?

_____

_____

_____

You can pray:
Dear God, thank You that You have a special place for me. Help me to have courage to trust Your plan. In Jesus' name. Amen.

How Did Esther Respond to Hard Times?

279

And we know that in all things God works for the good of those who love him . . . **Romans 8:28**

TRUSTING GOD

Esther was having a hard time. She wanted to help her people, but she was afraid to go to the king. Esther knew the true and living God. She believed that God let her be the queen for a special reason. Esther trusted God's plan for her.

She sent this message to Mordecai: "Go, gather together all the Jews . . . and fast for three days" (Esther 4:16). To fast means to go without eating. Usually when people fasted in the Bible, they used that time to pray. After three days, Esther would go to the king to plead for her people. She knew that she could trust God's plan for her, even if it meant that she would die.

After three days of fasting, Esther went before the powerful king. To her relief, the king welcomed her! She told him Haman's evil plan. The king had Haman put to death. The old law couldn't be changed, but a new law was made. The Jewish people could defend themselves from their enemies. God used Esther to save the Jewish people.

How did Esther respond to hard times? She did the two best things anyone could do—she prayed and she trusted God! Will you remember to pray and trust God when you have hard times?

Write down a hard time in your life when you need to pray and trust God.

_____

_____

_____

You can pray:

Dear God, thank You that I can pray and trust You in any situation. Help me to remember that whenever I have a hard time. In Jesus' name. Amen.

280 What Is God's Purpose for Me?

And we know that in all things God works for the good of those who love him . . . **Romans 8:28**

You may not live in a palace like Joseph or Esther. Maybe you live in an apartment in a crowded city. Maybe you live with a stepparent and lots of brothers and sisters. Wherever you live or whatever your family is like, God has a purpose for you.

Ricardo trusted Jesus as his Savior when he was eight years old. He lived in a scary neighborhood. There were gangs and drugs and guns. Ricardo knew that joining a gang would not honor God.

Sometimes Ricardo wondered, "Does God have a purpose for me?" To find the answer he read the Bible, prayed and trusted

God. He looked for ways to honor God. Whenever he had a chance, Ricardo told his friends about Jesus. Some of them trusted Jesus, too. Ricardo also went to church. He sang in the choir. He also helped with an after-school program for the children.

What was God's purpose for Ricardo? To honor God and be a shining light in his neighborhood! That is God's purpose for you as well. God has given you ways to serve Him. He has told you about many of them in His Word, the Bible. Ask Him to show you each day what you can do to honor Him.

TRUSTING GOD

Write down three ways that you can honor God in your neighborhood.

_____

_____

_____

You can pray:

Dear God, thank You that I can be a shining light in my neighborhood. Help me to look for ways I can honor You. In Jesus' name. Amen.

How Should I Respond to Hard Times? 281

And we know that in all things God works for the good of those who love him . . . **Romans 8:28**

TRUSTING GOD

"It's not fair!" "Why do bad things always happen to me?" Have you ever said or thought things like this? We all go through hard times in our lives. Illness or divorce in your family can be hard experiences to go through. Maybe your family has no place to live because your parents don't have a job. Maybe others make fun of you because you're a Christian.

It's tempting to respond to hard times by getting angry with God. You might think, "If God really loved me, He wouldn't let this bad thing happen." That's not true. God always loves and cares for you! He is always working out His plan for your life. God uses hard times to help you trust Him more. In this way, others will see Jesus at work in you, and your life will honor God.

When hard times come, remember that God is sovereign—He is in control! He knows about everything that happens to you, and He allows only what is best. Tell God how you feel. Ask Him to help you trust Him. Ask Him to give you quietness on the inside. Then, patiently wait for God to work things out for your good.

 Write what you believe God's purpose is for your life.

_____

_____

_____

You can pray:

Dear God, thank You that You have a purpose for me. Help me to trust You and to wait for You to work out Your plan. In Jesus' name. Amen.

Why Is There Suffering in the World?

And the God of all grace, . . . after you have suffered a little while, will himself restore you and make you strong, firm and steadfast. **1 Peter 5:10**

Why can't things just be good all the time? Why does there have to be suffering? God wants you to grow strong to be like Him. That means He sometimes allows you to suffer.

Suffering means to hurt in your body or your feelings. Some people suffer from sickness and pain. Other people suffer because of sadness, anger or hurt feelings. There was no suffering in the world until the first people, Adam and Eve, sinned. Part of the result of that sin is that suffering would be in the world. Now everyone has times of suffering.

Sometimes God allows suffering to help you grow to be more like Him. Suffering can help you become more patient as you wait for God to work. Suffering can help you learn to have courage as you trust God to take care of you.

God never lets you suffer alone. He is always there to help you. One day God will take away all suffering from His children. Until then, trust Him to be with you. Let Him help you to be calm on the inside even while you are suffering. Let God use suffering in your life to help you grow strong.

TRUSTING GOD

Write about something that may be causing you to suffer, then tell God about it.

You can pray:

Dear God, thank You that You are good and wise. Thank You that You are with me in my suffering. Help me to trust You. In Jesus' name. Amen.

How Can I Find Comfort in Suffering?

And the God of all grace, . . . after you have suffered a little while, will himself restore you and make you strong, firm and steadfast. **1 Peter 5:10**

TRUSTING GOD

The Bible tells about a man who suffered more than most people. His name was Job. His children were killed in a storm. He lost his house and all that he owned. He also had a painful sickness. Some people said that God was punishing him, but Job knew that God cared. He told God about his problems and how he felt inside.

You need to do what Job did when you are suffering. You might feel angry. Maybe you think God doesn't care. But, God does care. Tell Him about your suffering. Ask God to help you be patient and brave.

One way God comforts His children is through His Word. If you have a Bible, read some verses in the book of Psalms. God's Word says that through patience and comfort of the Bible, we can have hope (Romans 15:4).

As you talk to God and read His Word, He may give you an answer to your problem. However, He may choose to comfort you in a different way. He may just remind you that He loves you and has a plan for your life. Be like Job and trust that God is at work, even in your suffering. Let God comfort you.

Write down two ways that God can comfort you when you are suffering.

_____

_____

_____

You can pray:

Dear God, thank You for comforting me when I suffer. Thank You for Your Word that gives me hope. Help me to trust Your plan for me. In Jesus' name. Amen.

284 What Does It Mean to Be Persecuted?

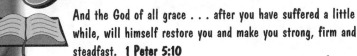

And the God of all grace . . . after you have suffered a little while, will himself restore you and make you strong, firm and steadfast. **1 Peter 5:10**

Did you know that some people suffer because they believe in Jesus? Suffering for what you believe is called persecution. Family members or friends may not understand why you've trusted Jesus Christ as your Savior. They might make fun of you or be mean to you in other ways. Your enemy, Satan, wants you to be discouraged or get angry with God when you are persecuted. He wants to stop you from telling other people about Jesus.

God's Word says, "If you suffer as a Christian, do not be ashamed, but praise [honor] God . . ." (1 Peter 4:16). How can you honor God when you are persecuted? The Bible tells about a man named Stephen. He believed in Jesus as his Savior. He told others about Jesus. Some people hated Stephen and wanted to get rid of him. They threw stones at him until he died. But as Stephen was dying, he had courage and joy. He prayed and knew Jesus was waiting to welcome him to Heaven. Stephen honored God, even in his death (Acts 7:57-60).

You may never be persecuted like Stephen. However, if you are persecuted in some way, ask God to give you courage to honor Him.

TRUSTING GOD

What should you do if you are persecuted for believing in Jesus?

_____

_____

_____

You can pray:

Dear Lord, thank You that You are with me, even when I am persecuted. Help me to honor You with my words and my attitude. In Jesus' name. Amen.

What Should I Do When I Am Persecuted?

And the God of all grace . . . after you have suffered a little while, will himself restore you and make you strong, firm and steadfast. **1 Peter 5:10**

TRUSTING GOD

Latisha sat in the school lunchroom staring at her sandwich. She wanted to thank God for her lunch before she ate, but the other kids were watching. Yesterday, she prayed before she ate her lunch. They laughed and made fun of her. It made her feel awful. Latisha was being persecuted for being a Christian.

Why does God allow His people to be persecuted? Sometimes it's because persecution helps us learn to trust Him more. Also, God may want to use your example to encourage others who are suffering.

What should you do when you are persecuted? First, remember that God is in control of all that happens. He will never allow more than you can handle with His help. Second, think about how Jesus Christ, God's Son, was persecuted for you. He allowed men to beat Him and nail Him to a cross so that your sin could be forgiven. Third, follow the example of others like Stephen. Pray and think about promises in God's Word. One good promise to remember is the one written at the top of this page. After a little while, God will make you secure and stronger. Trust Him and keep doing what's right.

How could you honor God if you were in Latisha's situation?

_____

_____

_____

You can pray:
Dear God, help me to honor You, even when I am persecuted. Help me to remember the promises in Your Word and do what is right. In Jesus' name. Amen.

286 What If My Family Doesn't Believe in Jesus?

And the God of all grace . . . after you have suffered a little while, will himself restore you and make you strong, firm and steadfast. **1 Peter 5:10**

You might think that everyone wants to believe in Jesus, but not everyone does. Maybe you're the only one in your family who has. Perhaps your parents are angry that you've become a Christian. Maybe your brothers and sisters make fun of you. It's hard when your family doesn't understand.

Pray for your family every day. Ask God to help them see that they need to trust Christ, too. If you behave in a kind and obedient way, your family will see God's love in you. God can give you strength to be kind even when they are not.

Also, you can ask God to help you tell your family about the Lord Jesus. Let God give you the right words to say at the right time. You can't make your family believe, but God may use your words, spoken in a gentle way, to help them understand. If you go to a church that teaches about Jesus, invite your family to go with you. They may say "no," but don't give up. Keep on praying. Keep on being kind. Keep on telling them about Jesus. One day, they might believe. You'll be so glad you didn't give up!

TRUSTING GOD

List your family members who need to believe in Jesus.

_____

_____

_____

You can pray:

Dear Lord, thank You for my family. Help me to be kind and obedient and to tell them about You. In Jesus' name. Amen.

Can God Help Me When My Family Has to Move?

Cast all your anxiety on him because he cares for you.
1 Peter 5:7

TRUSTING GOD

Maria watched tearfully as the last pieces of furniture were loaded into a big truck. Her family was moving to a new city. Maria was going to miss her friends. She worried about finding new friends. What would her new school be like?

Maybe your family is moving and you have some of the same questions Maria had. Saying good-bye to friends can be hard. It can be hard getting used to new things and new places, but God can help you! The Bible says, "Cast [give] all your anxiety [troubles] on him [Jesus] because he cares for you" (1 Peter 5:7). You can tell the Lord Jesus about the things that trouble you. You can know that He will take care of you.

Remember that God is in control of all that happens. He has planned every step in your life. He knows about the new place you are going—He's already there! He will be there with you in your new neighborhood and your new school. Ask God to help you to trust Him to take care of things. Ask Him to lead you to new friends. Thank Him that He is with you wherever you go.

How can God help you when you have to move to a new place?

_____

_____

_____

You can pray:

Dear Lord, thank You that You are with me and will take care of me wherever I go. In Jesus' name. Amen.

288 How Can I Get Along with My Brothers and Sisters?

 Cast all your anxiety on him because he cares for you.
1 Peter 5:7

Sometimes the people you live with are the hardest ones to love! Maybe your brother or sister is different from you. Perhaps you are neat and they are messy. Maybe you get better grades or they are better at sports. Perhaps they get to do things you're not allowed to do. It's easy to get angry and fight, especially if you share a bedroom! It's often hard to get along with people who are different from you. You need to give that trouble to Jesus.

You didn't choose your brothers and sisters–but God did! He planned each member of your family. He knows what each of you is like. Try to think of good things about your brother or sister. What talents or abilities does each have? What talents or abilities do you have? How can you help each other? Maybe you can help your brother with a subject in school that is hard for him. Perhaps your sister can help you learn to do something well. Thank God for the family He's given you. Ask Him to help you appreciate your brothers and sisters instead of fighting with them.

TRUSTING GOD

Write three things you appreciate about your brother or sister.

_____

_____

_____

You can pray:

 Dear Lord, thank You for my brothers and sisters. Help me to appreciate my family and to get along with each one. In Jesus' name. Amen.

Will God Be with Me Even in the Hospital?

Cast all your anxiety on him because he cares for you.
1 Peter 5:7

TRUSTING GOD

When your body doesn't feel good, trusting God can be hard. If you are very sick, you may need to go to the hospital. You might feel afraid, but remember that God always knows where you are. He is right there with you. God is the one who made your body. He knows more about it than even the best doctor. He will allow only what is best for you. He can give the doctor wisdom to find out what is wrong and how to help.

When you must go to the hospital, give that trouble to Jesus. Pray for your doctor—that God will help him to know what to do for you. Ask God to help you be brave. You can say along with one of the Bible writers, "When I am afraid, I will trust in you [God]" (Psalm 56:3).

Maybe you'll get to share with your doctor or nurse how God is helping you to be brave. You may even be able to encourage someone else who is scared. Whether you're in the hospital just a few days or for a long time, God will be there. You can trust Him to help and care for you!

Why can you trust God even in the hospital?

_____

_____

_____

You can pray:

Dear Lord, thank You that You know all about my body. Help me to be brave even if I have to go into the hospital. In Jesus' name. Amen.

290 Is It Okay to Miss Someone Who Dies?

Cast all your anxiety on him because he cares for you.
1 Peter 5:7

Jeremy's grandpa died. He would miss him so much. Tears came to Jeremy's eyes as he thought about all the fun times he'd had with grandpa.

When someone you love dies, it's normal to feel sad. It's okay to cry. God knows how you feel. You will miss that person, and you may wonder why he had to die. God has planned all of our days. He knew when we would be born. He knows when each person will die.

The Bible says, "Precious in the sight of the LORD is the death of his saints" (Psalm 116:15). A saint is a person who knows Jesus as his Savior. When that person dies, he goes to be with the Lord Jesus. If you know Jesus as your Savior, you'll see that person again in Heaven someday. You can know he is happy and peaceful in Heaven. Maybe you're not sure if the person who died knew Jesus. You'll have to trust that God knows. God always does what is fair and right. Talk to God about how you feel. God is your Heavenly Father. He can comfort you when you are sad. Isn't it good to know you can give this trouble to Jesus?

TRUSTING GOD

Write something good you remember about someone who has died.

_____

_____

_____

You can pray:

Dear Lord, I'm glad You know how I feel when someone I love has died. Help me to remember the good things about that person. In Jesus' name. Amen.

Why Do My Mom and Dad Always Yell at Me?

Cast all your anxiety on him because he cares for you.
1 Peter 5:7

Jenna's mom had a bad temper and yelled a lot. Jenna knew her mom worked hard and worried about having enough money to pay their bills. Jenna knew it wasn't her fault when her mom yelled, but it made her feel bad. Sometimes it made her angry.

Maybe you have a mom or dad who yells at you a lot. Perhaps your parent even uses bad language. It's not your fault. It's normal for you to feel bad and maybe even angry. But God can help you love your parents even when they yell.

Choose a time when things are calm and talk to your parents about the problem. Tell them how their yelling makes you feel. They might not realize that they are hurting you this way. Be sure that you are obeying your parents when they give you a chore to do. You might want to ask if there's something else you can do that will make it easier for them.

Most of all, pray for your parents. Perhaps they need to trust Jesus as their Savior so that He can change them on the inside. Remember that God knows about your family. Give your family troubles to the Lord Jesus. You can trust Him to help you.

How could you show your parents you love them?

_____

_____

_____

You can pray:

Dear God, thank You for my parents. Help me to be patient with them. Help me to show them love and kindness. In Jesus' name. Amen.

Will God Be with Me If My Parents Get Divorced?

Cast all your anxiety on him because he cares for you.
1 Peter 5:7

Having divorced parents is a big trouble for many children! It's scary to think that your family won't be together. It's sad when one of your parents goes to live somewhere else. But God knows all about it. He can help you through any situation–even divorce. You can give this big trouble to the Lord Jesus.

One thing you need to know is that it's not your fault if your parents get divorced. There are many reasons why some parents decide they can't be married anymore. Divorce is an adult decision. You don't need to feel guilty.

If your parents divorce, ask God to help you have a right attitude. You need to be loving and kind to both parents. They will need your love in a special way during this painful time. Pray for your parents. If they don't know Jesus as their Savior, ask God to help them realize that they need Him. Ask God to bring healing to your family. Also, ask God to help you trust Him. God is with you no matter where you live. He knows what is happening in your family. He is your Heavenly Father and He will always take care of you.

TRUSTING GOD

 How could you help your parents when they are getting divorced?

_____

_____

_____

You can pray:

 Dear God, thank You for always taking care of me. Help me to love my parents, no matter what. In Jesus' name. Amen.

Can God Help Me Get Along with My Stepmom and Her Kids?

293

Cast all your anxiety on him because he cares for you.
1 Peter 5:7

TRUSTING GOD

Juan was so sad when his parents divorced. Juan and his sisters lived with their father. Two years later, Juan's father married a lady who had two children. Now Juan had a stepmother and two stepbrothers. Juan didn't like it when his stepmother gave him a job to do. He wanted to yell, "You're not my mother!" Juan worried that maybe his dad liked his new sons more than he liked Juan.

Do you live with a stepfamily? Maybe you sometimes feel like Juan. It's normal to feel angry that someone is taking the place of your parent. It's hard to get used to having new brothers and sisters.

Remember that God is in control and He knows everything. He knows all about your new family. He has allowed your stepparent to be in charge of you. Ask God to help you to grow in love and respect for your stepparent. Ask Him to help you get along with stepbrothers or stepsisters. God has allowed them in your family. Find out what they like to do. Maybe you would enjoy doing those things together. Give this trouble to the Lord Jesus. He can help you learn to love your stepfamily.

Write something you like about your stepparent or stepbrothers or sisters.

_____

_____

_____

You can pray:

Dear God, put Your love in my heart for my new family. Help me to obey my stepparent and to get along with stepbrothers and stepsisters. In Jesus' name. Amen.

294 Should I Tell If Someone Touches Me in Wrong Ways?

Cast all your anxiety on him because he cares for you. 1 Peter 5:7

God made your body in a wonderful way. He made you to enjoy certain kinds of touch. Maybe you enjoy holding your dad's hand when you walk or hugging your mom before you go to bed.

Some parts of your body are to be kept private. God made them to bring you special joy when you are married. Until then, God wants you to be careful not to allow anyone to touch the private parts of your body in a wrong way.

If someone touches you this way, you need to tell an adult. The person touching you may say it's a secret, but you need to tell. Tell God about this trouble. Ask Him to give you courage to talk to an adult. Perhaps you can tell your parent, your teacher, the pastor of your church or some other adult you trust. You may feel ashamed, but it's not your fault. The person touching you is the one who is wrong.

If you've trusted Jesus as your Savior, God says your body is a temple–the place where His Spirit lives (1 Corinthians 6:19-20). He wants you to honor Him with your body. Don't let anyone treat it in a wrong way.

What should you do if someone touches you in wrong ways?

_____

_____

_____

You can pray:

Dear God, thank You for making my body special. Give me courage to tell if someone touches me in a wrong way. In Jesus' name. Amen.

Does God Care When There's Violence in My Family?

295

TRUSTING GOD

Cast all your anxiety on him because he cares for you.
1 Peter 5:7

Elisa's dad drank a lot and became angry. He hit her mom, and sometimes he hit her. Elisa didn't want anyone to know. She wore blouses with long sleeves to cover her bruises. Elisa thought about telling someone. However, she was afraid of making her dad angrier.

Elisa had believed in the Lord Jesus Christ as her Savior. She began to cast her troubles on Jesus. She told Him about her father. She knew Jesus cared for her. God gave Elisa courage to tell her teacher about her father. The teacher told Elisa that it wasn't her fault that her father hurt her. The teacher found help for Elisa's family.

If you live in a family like Elisa's, you might think that nobody cares about you, but God cares. Remember what you learned from Joseph's story (#277)? Even though people do evil things to you, God can turn them to good (Romans 8:28). He wants you to cast your troubles on Him. He can give you courage to tell an adult about what is happening to you. If you live in this kind of home, don't try to keep it to yourself. Tell someone and let that person help you.

Write what you can do if someone in your home is hurting you.

_____

_____

_____

You can pray:

Dear God, thank You for caring about me. Please give me courage to tell someone if I am being hurt in my home. In Jesus' name. Amen.

296 Will God Take Care of Me If My Family Doesn't Have a Home?

Cast all your anxiety on him because he cares for you. 1 Peter 5:7

Have you ever watched a bird build a nest? She uses twigs, grass or other things to make her nest safe and secure. God made you with that same need for a place of safety. However, there are children whose families don't have a house in which to live. Sometimes they live in shelters with other homeless families. Some live in their cars or even on the street. Does God know and care about where you live? Yes, He does!

Things don't always go well, even for Christian families. A parent may lose his job or get sick. There might not be enough money to pay for a home. God knows about everything that happens to His children. He is never surprised. He is always working out His perfect plan for you. This is another trouble you can cast on the Lord Jesus. He wants you to bring your needs to Him and trust Him.

If your family is homeless, you are still a family. Talk to your Heavenly Father. Tell Him about your needs and trust Him to help you. He may provide a job. He may send someone to help your family. Whatever He chooses to do will be right and good.

TRUSTING GOD

Write a prayer to God, thanking Him for caring for you and your family.

_____

_____

_____

You can pray:

Dear God, I'm glad You know all about me and my family. Thank You for caring for us every day. In Jesus' name. Amen.

What Is Faith? **297**

> "For I know the plans I have for you," declares the LORD, "plans to prosper you and not to harm you, plans to give you hope and a future." **Jeremiah 29:11**

T R U S T I N G G O D

Are you sitting down? Did you examine the chair first to see if it would hold you? No! You probably didn't even think about it. Now lift your feet off the floor. With all of your weight on the chair, you are now trusting the chair alone to hold you. You have faith in the chair.

The Bible says, "Without faith it is impossible to please [God]..." (Hebrews 11:6). Faith in God means believing without questioning what God says and acting on it. It means trusting Him completely. You put your faith in the Lord Jesus Christ when you believed in Him as your Savior. Now that you are a Christian, God wants you to continue to have faith in Him.

You need faith to handle the hard things that come into your life. You need faith to say "no" to sin. You need faith to trust God's plan for you. In Hebrews, chapter 11, the Bible lists a whole group of people who were heroes because of their faith in God. They were just like you and me. God tells us about them to encourage us to have faith. God is faithful to you–you can have faith in Him!

Finish this sentence: To me, faith in God means . . .

_____

_____

_____

You can pray:

Dear God, thank You that You are faithful to me. Help me to have faith in You for everything in my life. In Jesus' name. Amen.

298 Am I a Doubter?

"For I know the plans I have for you," declares the LORD, "plans to prosper you and not to harm you, plans to give you hope and a future." **Jeremiah 29:11**

Have you heard the words, "Seeing is believing?" Many people are doubters–they refuse to believe something until it is proven. Even Christians can be doubters. They have trouble trusting God and His Word.

In John 20:24-29, the Bible tells about a doubter named Thomas. He was a friend and follower of the Lord Jesus. Jesus had told his followers that He would die. He also told them He would come back to life again. After Jesus died, His followers were sad and afraid. Then, Jesus appeared to them–but Thomas wasn't there. When the others told him that Jesus was alive, Thomas doubted. He told them that unless he could see Him and touch the nail scars in His hands, he would not believe (John 20:25).

Later, Jesus appeared again. This time, Thomas was there. The Lord Jesus invited Thomas to touch His hands so he would no longer doubt. Thomas now believed. He fell to his knees and worshiped Jesus as his Lord. Jesus said, "Because you have seen me you believed. Blessed [happy] are they who have not seen and yet have believed" (John 20:29).

Someday you'll see Jesus in Heaven. Until then, don't be a doubter. Have faith in God–believe His Word.

TRUSTING GOD

Why is it wrong to be a doubter about God?

_____

_____

_____

You can pray:
Dear God, thank You that I can have faith in You and in Your Word. Help me not to doubt, but to believe You. In Jesus' name. Amen.

Why Should I Trust God?

TRUSTING GOD

"For I know the plans I have for you," declares the LORD, "plans to prosper you and not to harm you, plans to give you hope and a future." **Jeremiah 29:11**

Have you ever looked at an American dollar bill? These important words are printed on it: "In God we trust." The men and women who founded America knew that God is trustworthy. He deserves our trust–our faith. There aren't too many things in our world that are trustworthy. Things that you buy will eventually break or wear out. Even people that you love are not always deserving of your trust.

But God is always trustworthy. That's because God cannot lie–He always keeps His promises. And God also has power to do what He says He will do. When God tells you to cast your care on Him because He cares for you–you can trust Him. When God says, "I know the plans I have for you . . . plans to prosper [help] you and not to harm you, plans to give you hope and a future," you can trust Him.

God has always been faithful to do what He says. The Bible says, " . . . he [God] who promised is faithful" (Hebrews 10:23). No matter what happens, you can trust God. He knows all about your life and He is working out His plan. Don't worry. Don't doubt. Trust God, who is trustworthy!

Write two reasons that you can trust God.

_____

_____

_____

You can pray:

Dear God, thank You that You are trustworthy. Help me to trust You more each day. In Jesus' name. Amen.

300 How Can I Trust God?

"For I know the plans I have for you," declares the LORD, "plans to prosper you and not to harm you, plans to give you hope and a future." Jeremiah 29:11

A young man named David had a GIANT problem! The Bible tells about a giant named Goliath, who shouted threats at the army of Israel. He made fun of the true and living God. The Israelites were all afraid–even the king!

David was angry when he heard Goliath's evil words. He went to King Saul and said he would fight the giant. But, David was young. He was not a mighty soldier. How could he fight this huge enemy?

David knew he couldn't beat Goliath–but God could. David told the king that when he took care of his father's sheep, a lion and then a bear came to attack them. God helped David kill them. Then David said, "The LORD who delivered me from the paw of the lion and the paw of the bear will deliver me from the hand of [Goliath]" (1 Samuel 17:37).

When you have a problem, you can do what David did. Think about problems God has helped you with before. Think about how faithful and trustworthy God is. Then trust God to help you again. He did it for David! With God's help, David killed the giant. God will help you, too, if you'll trust Him.

TRUSTING GOD

Write one way God helped you with a big problem.

_____

_____

You can pray:

Dear God, thank You for the ways You've helped me before. Thank You that I can trust You with all kinds of problems, even giant ones. In Jesus' name. Amen.

If I Pray, Will God Make Problems Stop?

361

"For I know the plans I have for you," declares the LORD, "plans to prosper you and not to harm you, plans to give you hope and a future." **Jeremiah 29:11**

TRUSTING GOD

Often when people pray, God makes problems stop, but not always. A man in the Bible named Paul had a big problem. It might have been a painful physical problem. Whatever it was, Paul wanted to get rid of it. So he prayed–not once or twice, but three times! Each time, Paul asked God to take the problem away. (2 Corinthians 12:7-8)

God answered Paul's prayer, but not in the way you might think. God said to Paul, "My grace is sufficient [enough] for you, for my power is made perfect in weakness"(2 Corinthians 12:9). Because God's strength shows up best in our weak areas, His answer to Paul was "no." He allowed Paul's problem to continue. God wanted to show His grace in Paul's life by giving him the strength to go through the problem.

God may take away your problem when you pray, but sometimes God wants to give you grace to go through it. He wants your life to bring honor and praise to Him. At times, that may be done best through suffering. As others see how God gives you strength to trust Him, they will praise Him. Maybe they will be encouraged to trust Him, too.

Why doesn't God always take away your problems?

_____

_____

_____

You can pray:

Dear God, thank You that I can have Your strength to go through problems. Help me to trust You even through my suffering. In Jesus' name. Amen.

362 How Can I Thank God in Hard Times?

"For I know the plans I have for you," declares the LORD, "plans to prosper you and not to harm you, plans to give you hope and a future." Jeremiah 29:11

There has probably never been anyone who suffered as a Christian more than a follower of Jesus named Paul. In 2 Corinthians 11:23-33, Paul tells about many of his hard times. Often he was put in prison for telling people about Jesus. He was beaten many times. He suffered in shipwrecks and was stranded on the open sea. He was attacked by bandits. He was falsely accused of wrongdoing. His life was constantly in danger. Toward the end of his life, Paul was chained in a cold, damp prison dungeon. Eventually, he would be put to death for being a Christian.

Did Paul complain or feel sorry for himself? No, he thanked God! In his dark prison cell, Paul wrote these words, "Rejoice in the Lord always" (Philippians 4:4). How could Paul rejoice? He knew that God was in control. He trusted in God no matter what.

What about you? Are you thankful, even in hard times? Don't give in to grumbling and complaining or feeling sorry for yourself. Instead, be thankful. How? Remember all God has done for you. Thank Him that He is in control and He's there to help you.

TRUSTING GOD

Write a short poem, thanking God for helping you, even in hard times.

_____

_____

_____

You can pray:

Dear God, thank You that You're always with me to help me, even in hard times. In Jesus' name. Amen.

What Should I Do about People Who Hurt Me?

"For I know the plans I have for you," declares the LORD, "plans to prosper you and not to harm you, plans to give you hope and a future." **Jeremiah 29:11**

TRUSTING GOD

Have you ever wanted to get even with someone who hurt you? That is a normal response. But, angry feelings kept inside will grow into bitterness and hate. They may even cause you to become physically ill.

Instead of anger and hate, you are to forgive. Forgiveness means letting go of your anger and your desire to get even. The Bible says you're to forgive others "just as in Christ God forgave you" (Ephesians 4:32). Think of all God has forgiven in your life. Your sin against God is worse than anything anyone could do to you. If you're His child, He's forgiven you for all of your bad thoughts, words and actions. God forgives you because Jesus Christ, His perfect Son, took the punishment you deserved!

Forgiving others can be hard, but the Lord Jesus said that God will forgive you only as you are willing to forgive others (Matthew 6:14-15). You may not be able to forget the hurt, but you can choose to forgive the one who has hurt you. Are you keeping angry feelings inside toward someone? Confess it to God and ask Him to help you forgive.

Why is it important for you to forgive?

_____

_____

_____

You can pray:

Dear God, thank You for forgiving me for all my sin. Help me to be willing to forgive others who have hurt me. In Jesus' name. Amen.

304 What Does It Mean to Persevere?

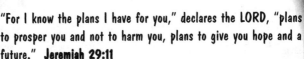

"For I know the plans I have for you," declares the LORD, "plans to prosper you and not to harm you, plans to give you hope and a future." Jeremiah 29:11

Are you a quitter? A quitter gives up when things are hard or uncomfortable. A quitter gets discouraged thinking a job will never be finished. Instead of quitting, God wants you to persevere.

Persevering means to keep going through a hard time without giving up. The Bible tells about a man named Nehemiah. God gave him a big job to do. The wall around the city of Jerusalem had been broken down by enemies. Nehemiah was in charge of getting the huge wall rebuilt. As Nehemiah began the work, many problems came along. Nehemiah faced fear and discour-agement, but Nehemiah perse-vered until the wall was fin-ished!

There will be hard times in your life when you'll be tempted to quit. You might feel sorry for yourself and think it's just too hard to be a Christian, but God can give you persever-ance. God has wonderful plans for you. He just wants you to trust Him as He works them out in your life. Don't get discouraged. Don't be a quitter. Keep on keeping on! God says, "Let us not become weary in doing good, for at the proper time we will reap a harvest [be rewarded] if we do not give up" (Galatians 6:9).

TRUSTING GOD

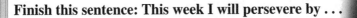

Finish this sentence: This week I will persevere by . . .

_____

_____

_____

You can pray:
Dear God, please help me to persevere, even through the hard times when I feel like quitting. In Jesus' name. Amen.

THE MEMORY ZONE

Here are some great Bible verses about what you've learned so far. Put a check mark in the box as you memorize each one!

☐ **Hebrews 11:6** "And without faith it is impossible to please God, because anyone who comes to him must believe that he exists and that he rewards those who earnestly seek him."

☐ **Joshua 1:9** " . . . Be strong and courageous. Do not be terrified; do not be discouraged, for the LORD your God will be with you wherever you go."

☐ **1 Peter 4:16,19** " . . . If you suffer as a Christian, do not be ashamed, but praise God that you bear that name . . . those who suffer according to God's will should commit themselves to their faithful Creator and continue to do good."

☐ **Philippians 4:4-5** "Rejoice in the Lord always. I will say it again: Rejoice! Let your gentleness be evident to all. The Lord is near."

☐ **1 Corinthians 6:19-20** "Do you not know that your body is a temple of the Holy Spirit, who is in you, whom you have received from God? You are not your own; you were bought at a price. Therefore honor God with your body."

☐ **Psalm 27:1** "The LORD is my light and my salvation–whom shall I fear? The LORD is the stronghold of my life–of whom shall I be afraid?"

☐ **Galatians 6:9** "Let us not become weary in doing good, for at the proper time we will reap a harvest if we do not give up."

☐ **1 Corinthians 15:58** " . . . stand firm. Let nothing move you. Always give yourself fully to the work of the Lord, because you know that your labor in the Lord is not in vain."

This is the end of the section of "Trusting God" devotionals.

It is time to do the next activity page that came to you in the mail. Remember to add your prayer request so your mailbox friend can pray for you. When you finish the whole page, fold it on the lines so the Mailbox Club address shows. Put a small piece of tape on the bottom to keep it folded. Add a stamp and mail your activity page.

Your work will be marked and sent back to you, along with a personal note. The activity sheet for the next set of lessons will be sent to you, too.

Enjoy getting to know God better with your next group of devotionals!

Taking a Stand

365 Are Some Things Absolutely Right or Wrong?

Be very careful, then, how you live—not as unwise but as wise, making the most of every opportunity, because the days are evil.
Ephesians 5:15-16

"I'm going to tell!" yelled Justin. Ricky knew he'd be in trouble if anyone found out what he had done. "Wait, Justin. If you don't tell, I'll give you my lunch money." If Justin took the money, he could buy a treat after school. He thought that maybe what Ricky did wasn't that bad.

Have you ever had to make a choice like the one Justin had to make? Maybe you told a lie because you thought it was just a "little" one. Or maybe you copied an answer from a friend's paper because you wanted to get a good grade. You might try to fool yourself into thinking your sin isn't so bad, or that you have a good reason to do wrong. The Bible tells us that some things, like showing God's love to others, are always right. Other things, like lying and stealing, are always wrong. God warns you to stay away from these wrong things because He knows they will hurt you. God loves you and wants the best for you. In His Word He says, "Do what is right and good in the LORD's sight, so that it may go well with you . . ." (Deuteronomy 6:18).

TAKING A STAND

Write one thing you know is right, and one thing you know is wrong.

_____

_____

_____

You can pray:

Dear God, thank You that You love me. Help me to say "no" to what is wrong, and to do what You have said is right. In Jesus' name. Amen.

Does God Accept People No Matter How They Live?

366

Be very careful, then, how you live—not as unwise but as wise, making the most of every opportunity, because the days are evil. **Ephesians 5:15-16**

TAKING A STAND

The Bible tells about two cities that you won't find on a map–Sodom and Gomorrah. The people who lived in these places did terrible things. God loved them, but He hated the wrong things they were doing. The people didn't care about God. They liked living in sin. They didn't want to change. God could not let them live in this sinful way anymore. The things they did were so bad that God had to destroy them. Even the cities were completely destroyed. That's why you won't find them on any map!

Did you know that God cares about the way you live? If you have never trusted Jesus as your Savior, you need to know that God loves you, but your sin is serious to Him. He may not destroy you because of your sin, but you will be separated from Him forever if your sin is not forgiven.

If you are a Christian, you should want to live God's way. When you choose to obey the Lord and say no to sin, you please God. The Bible calls this living as a wise person. Do you know someone whose life doesn't please the Lord? Pray for him and be an example by the wise way you live.

Why does God care about the way you live?

_____

_____

_____

You can pray:

Dear God, thank You for helping me live a life that will please You. Please help me to be wise and obey Your Word. In Jesus' name. Amen.

How Can I Make Choices That Honor God?

Be very careful, then, how you live—not as unwise but as wise, making the most of every opportunity, because the days are evil.
Ephesians 5:15-16

367

TAKING A STAND

The Bible tells about King Reheboam, the king of Israel, who made a BIG mistake! His friends had told him to do some awful things–and he did them! Now the people of Israel were angry. Things would never be the same again. If only he had listened to the godly men who had tried to tell him what was right, but now it was too late. He had made a bad choice.

Have you ever let someone talk you into doing something wrong? Afterwards, were you glad you had listened to them, or did you wish you had done the right thing instead? Many times you know right away what is right and what is wrong, but sometimes the choice is not so easy.

How can you make choices that honor God? First, pray and ask God to help you know what is right. Second, read your Bible. Look for things that will help you understand the right thing to do. Third, ask people who love God what they would do if they had to make your choice. Fourth, when you know the right thing to do, DO IT!

Write the names of three people who can help you make wise choices.

_____

_____

_____

You can pray:

Dear God, thank You for giving me all I need to make wise choices. When I know what is right, help me to do it. In Jesus' name. Amen.

Do My Reactions to Others Matter to God? 368

Be very careful, then, how you live—not as unwise but as wise, making the most of every opportunity, because the days are evil. **Ephesians 5:15-16**

TAKING A STAND

What food do you like the best? What games do you like to play? Usually, the things we like best are the things we are used to. It can be hard to get used to things that are different. Sometimes, people are mean to each other just because they are different. They may have a different skin color, speak a different language or have a different personality than you. Perhaps they just don't enjoy the things you enjoy.

God says being mean to others is sin. He loves everyone. Every person is important to God. It does not matter what they're like, where they live or how they look. God says you should not make up your mind about what people are like just by looking at them. The Bible says, " . . . Man looks at the outward appearance, but the LORD looks at the heart" (1 Samuel 16:7).

Do you know people who are different than you are? As a Christian it is your job to show them God's love. Get to know them. Soon you will find out that you have more in common than you thought. You will begin to forget that they are different at all.

How can you show kindness to someone who is different than you are?

_____

_____

_____

You can pray:

Dear God, thank You that You love everyone. Help me to show Your love to people who are different. In Jesus' name. Amen.

How Can I Be Respectful, yet Still Stand True to God?

Be very careful, then, how you live—not as unwise but as wise, making the most of every opportunity, because the days are evil.
Ephesians 5:15-16

The Bible tells about a man named Daniel who loved God. He obeyed the people in charge and they trusted him. There were some men who wanted to get rid of Daniel. These men talked the king into writing a new law saying that people could only pray to the king. Anyone breaking the law would be thrown to the lions to be eaten alive.

Daniel heard about the law, but he did not argue or complain. He just did what he knew was right. He prayed to the one true God. The king's men had him thrown to the lions. When the king heard what happened to Daniel, he wished he had never made the law. He told Daniel that he hoped God would keep him safe. The next day, the king came to see if Daniel had been eaten, but he had not! God had shut the mouths of the lions, and Daniel was safe. (Daniel 6:1-23)

You please God by obeying the people in charge of you. But if you are told to do something that would cause you to disobey God, ask Him for the courage to do what's right. Like Daniel, you can be respectful, yet still take a stand for God!

TAKING A STAND

What should you do when someone in charge tells you to do something wrong?

_____

_____

_____

You can pray:

Dear God, thank You for the people You put in charge of me. Help me to be respectful to them as I obey You. In Jesus' name. Amen.

Why Should I Obey God When Others Don't?

Be very careful, then, how you live—not as unwise but as wise, making the most of every opportunity, because the days are evil. **Ephesians 5:15-16**

TAKING A STAND

Why should you bother doing what's right when other people seem to get away with doing wrong? A long time ago a man named Asaph was unhappy. Many people were getting away with the wrong things they were doing. He told God how angry he was. He asked God to help him understand.

God helped Asaph, and he began to see things God's way. He learned that God wanted him to do right even when others were getting away with doing wrong. He knew that God wanted him to be different.

You should be different than the people who don't belong to God. His Holy Spirit will help you have the power to obey even when it is hard. God has promised you good things in your life when you do right. He has also promised you a reward in Heaven.

Keep doing what you know is right even though other people might be doing wrong. It may seem like some people are getting away with doing wrong, but someday God will make everything right. Ask God to help you see things His way. The Bible says, "Let us not become weary in doing good . . ." (Galatians 6:9).

Why is it important for you to do right, even if others are doing wrong?

_____

_____

_____

You can pray:

Dear God, thank You for giving me the power to obey. Please help me to do right no matter what other people do. In Jesus' name. Amen.

How Can I Obey God and Not Judge Others?

Be very careful, then, how you live—not as unwise but as wise, making the most of every opportunity, because the days are evil.
Ephesians 5:15-16

Have you ever tried to learn a new game that had a lot of rules? Forgetting a rule might make you lose the game. Some people think that being a Christian is like that. They think that to make God happy, they have to learn a lot of rules.

In Bible times, people called Pharisees, the religious leaders, did just that. They made up a lot of rules and said that the only way to make God happy was to obey all the rules on their list. Many of the Pharisees were busy judging others. They forgot God's most important rule–to show His love to others.

In the Bible, God has given you rules or commands to obey. You are responsible for your own behavior in obeying God by keeping His rules. You may not agree with someone else's choices, but you are not responsible for what other people do. Let God judge (decide) if that person's actions are right or wrong. Your job is to show him God's love and help him do what is right. Be wise. Don't be like the Pharisees who loved finding fault in others and judging them.

TAKING A STAND

How should you respond when you think others are doing wrong?

_____

_____

_____

You can pray:

Dear God, thank You for loving me. Help me not to judge others even when I think they are doing wrong, but to love them. In Jesus' name. Amen.

Did God Really Mean to Make Everyone Different? **312**

 Be very careful, then, how you live—not as unwise but as wise, making the most of every opportunity, because the days are evil. **Ephesians 5:15-16**

TAKING A STAND

What would happen if God made everyone the same? It would be confusing and boring! God has made each person unique. Even twins who look exactly alike have things about them that are different. God made people different so we could each do an important job that is just right for us. The Bible says He gave each person his or her own special gifts. "We have different gifts, according to the grace given us" (Romans 12:6).

God compares our differences to the different parts of the body. If the eye wanted to do the same job as the ear, we would not be able to see. If the foot wanted to do the same job as the heart, we would not be able to walk. Each part of the body is important.

You are special and important, too. God has given you gifts and abilities that He can use in a special way. He did that on purpose. He wants you to be able to do the work He has for you. He has given you just the right body, talents and family to be able to serve Him. Thank Him for the way He has made you.

 Write three gifts or abilities that God has given you.

_____

_____

_____

You can pray:

 Dear God thank You for making me special. Help me to appreciate the way You have made each person different. In Jesus' name. Amen.

313

How Can I Love People I Don't Agree With?

Be very careful, then, how you live—not as unwise but as wise, making the most of every opportunity, because the days are evil.
Ephesians 5:15-16

When Jesus lived on Earth, many of the religious leaders didn't like the men and women He spent time with. Jesus went to dinner with people who had stolen and lied. He was friendly with people who broke God's rules.

Did Jesus know that they had done so many wrong things? Yes! Jesus was God the Son. He knew all about the wrong things these people had done. He never said that their sinful ways were right. He explained that anyone who sins is someone who needs God. He showed them His love so they would know the way to have their sins forgiven.

Do you know people who do things or believe things you know are wrong? Do not join them in doing wrong. Tell them that God loves them. Show them kindness. Let them see Jesus living in you.

When Jesus was on Earth, He saw the sins of the world. He did not agree with the wrong things people were doing, but He still showed them God's love when He died and rose again. He can give you the power to show His love to others, no matter what they choose to do. "Love is patient, love is kind . . ."
(1 Corinthians 13:4).

Finish this sentence: I should love others I don't agree with because . . .

_____

_____

_____

You can pray:

Dear God, thank You that Jesus loves me even though I have done wrong things. Help me to show Your love to others. In Jesus' name. Amen.

How Does Satan Lie about God? 314

... he [the devil] is a liar and the father of lies.
John 8:44

Did you know the very first lie was told to the first people God ever created? It happened when Satan, God's enemy, tricked Adam and Eve into disobeying God. He made them believe a lie.

Did you know that Satan, the devil, will try to trick you, too? He will make you doubt that God is in control. He wants you to think that God doesn't care because He allows things like sickness, hurt and war. The truth is that all sickness, hurt and war started because of sin and Satan. God is a good and loving God. The Bible says, " . . . he is good; his love endures forever" (Psalm 106:1).

Satan might try to make you believe that he is stronger than God. The truth is that God has already won the battle with Satan. When Jesus came alive again after dying on the cross for our sins, He showed that Satan did not have any power over Him. If you have trusted Jesus as your Savior, Satan has no power over you either. The Bible says, " . . . the one [Jesus] who is in you is greater than the one [Satan] who is in the world" (1 John 4:4).

Satan is called the father of lies. When you are afraid or worried, don't listen to Satan's lies. Instead, talk to God. Ask Him to help you see the truth.

Why shouldn't you fear Satan or his lies?

_____

_____

_____

You can pray:
Dear God, I know You are stronger than Satan. I know You never lie. Help me to trust Your Word and not to believe Satan's lies. In Jesus' name. Amen.

315 How Does Satan Lie about Jesus?

. . . he [the devil] is a liar and the father of lies. **John 8:44**

Many people believe that Jesus Christ was a good man and a great teacher, but they don't believe that He is God's Son and their Savior. They've believed one of Satan's lies. Satan wants you to believe that the Lord Jesus was just a man. He does not want you to trust Jesus as your Savior.

But, Jesus was more than just a man; He was God in a human body. "The Word [Jesus] became flesh and made His dwelling among us . . ." (John 1:14). Jesus never did anything wrong. He was perfect. "God made him who had no sin to be sin for us . . ." (2 Corinthians 5:21). No other man has ever been perfect, no matter how great he may have been.

Because Jesus Christ was perfect, He could die to pay the price for your sins. Because He was God, He could come back to life. "God has raised this Jesus to life . . ." (Acts 2:32). No other great man has ever raised himself from the dead.

Remember, Satan is a liar. Listen to God's truth. "Jesus answered, 'I am the way and the truth and the life. No one comes to the Father except through me'" (John 14:6).

TAKING A STAND

Name two ways that Jesus is different from any other man that ever lived.

_____

_____

_____

You can pray:

Dear God, thank You for sending Your Son to die for me. Thank You for raising Him to life. In Jesus' name. Amen.

How Does Satan Lie about Our Relationship to God?

 ... he [the devil] is a liar and the father of lies.
John 8:44

God created man to have a close, loving relationship with Him. God gave Adam and Eve, the first man and woman, a beautiful home with plenty of food and lots to do (Genesis 2:15). Every day God came to their garden home to spend a special time with them (Genesis 3:8).

But there was someone who wanted to spoil this special relationship. That was Satan. Satan lied to Eve and convinced her to disobey God. He made her believe that God might not know what was best and that it wouldn't hurt to disobey.

When Adam and Eve disobeyed God they were filled with fear and shame. God couldn't let them stay in their beautiful home anymore. The special times they had with God were ruined. (Genesis 2:1-8, 23)

Satan wants to spoil your relationship with God, too. He wants to convince you that your loving Heavenly Father doesn't really care about you. He doesn't want you to trust that God is in control. He wants you to disobey God. Don't listen to Satan's lies. Spend time with God each day. Trust Him and obey His commands. Ask Him to make you wise and strong so you can say "no" to Satan's tricks.

 What can you do to build your relationship with God?

_____

_____

_____

You can pray:

 Dear God, thank You that You want to spend time with me. Please help me get to know You better. In Jesus' name. Amen.

317 What Is New Age Teaching?

. . . he [the devil] is a liar and the father of lies. **John 8:44**

Have you ever heard the words, "New Age"? You may have heard these words in school, on television or you may have read about them in a book. New Age is a way of thinking and believing that goes against what the Bible teaches. It's not really new–it's full of Satan's old ideas.

One New Age belief is that people are good and not sinners. God's Word says, "for all have sinned . . ." (Romans 3:23). Another New Age belief is reincarnation. This means that people die and come back to Earth many times in different forms. But God says, " . . . man is destined to die once, and after that to face judgment" (Hebrews 9:27). New Age also teaches that you are god. New Age believers say, "You can do anything–you are your greatest power." However, in the Bible, God tells us He is the one true and living God. Jesus Christ, God the Son, says, " . . . apart from Me you can do nothing" (John 15:5).

There are many other false New Age ideas. Satan often makes them sound like truth. Always check to see if an idea agrees with what the Bible says. If it disagrees, it is wrong. Don't be fooled!

Why do you think Satan wants people to believe New Age teaching?

_____

_____

_____

You can pray:

Dear God, thank You for telling me the truth in Your Word. Help me to recognize Satan's lies and not to be fooled. In Jesus' name. Amen.

Can I Be Good without God?

> . . . he [the devil] is a liar and the father of lies.
> **John 8:44**

TAKING A STAND

"Why did I do that?" "I can't believe I did something so terrible!" Have you ever said words like these after doing something wrong? Sometimes, even when we want to be good, we aren't.

God's faithful servant, Paul, asked himself the same kind of questions. In Romans chapter 7 he wrote, "I know that nothing good lives in me . . . I have the desire to do what is good, but I cannot carry it out" (Romans 7:18). Paul said that many times he didn't do what he knew was right, and all too often he did do what he knew was wrong. He knew that he could not be good in his own strength.

Just like Paul, you cannot be good without God. There's good news. If you're a child of God, you have His Holy Spirit living inside of you. He can give you the power to do what's right and to stay away from what's wrong. Tell God that you know you need His power to be good. Ask Him to help you know what's right through His Holy Spirit. Obey His Spirit when it's time to make a choice between right and wrong.

 Write something you need God's help to stop doing.

_____

_____

_____

You can pray:

Dear God, I know I need Your help to obey. Please give me the strength to do what is right. In Jesus' name. Amen.

319 Why Can't I Save Myself?

... he [the devil] is a liar and the father of lies. **John 8:44**

One night a young man came to talk to the Lord Jesus. He wanted to know how to be saved. Perhaps he expected Jesus to tell him that he was already doing all of the right things. He knew the Scriptures, spent a lot of time in prayer and did his best to be a good person. Jesus' answer surprised him. Jesus let the young man know that all of these things were good, but none of them would save him. The disciples were surprised, too. The Bible says, "...they were greatly astonished and asked, 'Who then can be saved?'" (Matthew 19:25).

God tells us in His Word that no one can save himself. You were born with a sinful nature already inside of you. Only Jesus can give you the gift of salvation because He never sinned. "God made him who had no sin to be sin for us . . ." (2 Corinthians 5:21). Because Jesus took the punishment for your sins, you can be saved. The gift of salvation is possible only because of God's love and grace. "For it is by grace you have been saved, through faith–and this not from yourselves, it is the gift of God" (Ephesians 2:8).

How can you be saved from your sins?

_____

_____

_____

You can pray:

Dear God, thank You for doing what I couldn't do. Thank You for saving me from my sins. In Jesus' name. Amen.

Are God's Promises Really for Me?

> . . . he [the devil] is a liar and the father of lies.
> **John 8:44**

Has anyone ever made you a promise and then let you down? There's one person who will never break His promises to you–God. The Bible says, " . . . he has given us his very great and precious promises . . ." (2 Peter 1:4). For example, God has promised to give eternal life to all who will believe in His Son, Jesus Christ. He has promised to care for His children. He has promised to always hear and answer prayers. He has promised to be with you always if you are His child.

Satan, the father of lies, will try to make you believe that **God has not kept His promises.** He might even try to trick you into believing that God's promises aren't really for you. He wants you to think that God has forgotten about you. Don't believe Satan's lies. God's Word says, " . . . he [God] who promised is faithful" (Hebrews 10:23).

Sometimes God may answer your prayers in a different way or at a different time than you expected. These are times when Satan might try to fool you. Remember God loves you. He wants the best for you. He will keep His promises at just the right time.

List three of God's promises to you.

_____

_____

_____

You can pray:

Dear God, thank You for keeping Your promises. Please help me to keep mine, too. In Jesus' name. Amen.

How Does Satan Lie about the Bible?

They exchanged the truth of God for a lie, and worshiped and served created things rather than the Creator . . . **Romans 1:25**

Satan does not want you to read your Bible. He knows it will build your faith and help you stay away from sin. The Bible says, "I have hidden your word in my heart that I might not sin against you" (Psalm 119:11).

To keep you from reading your Bible, Satan will lie to you. He might try to make you believe that God's Word is full of mistakes. God is perfect. He cannot make mistakes. His Holy Spirit spoke to men who wrote exactly what God wanted written. The Bible says, ". . . men spoke from God as they were carried along by the Holy Spirit" (2 Peter 1:21).

Satan might try to make you think the Bible is just a good book. God says, "All Scripture is God-breathed" (2 Timothy 3:16). Every Word God has written is true because God cannot lie.

Also, Satan may try to make you believe that reading your Bible is not important. Don't let him trick you. Take time to read your Bible every day. God says to study His Word carefully so that you'll know what it says and means. When you do this, you'll be able to stand against Satan's lies about the Bible.

TAKING A STAND

How do we know the Bible is God's Word?

_____

_____

_____

You can pray:

Dear God, thank You for the Bible. Help me to read it every day. In Jesus' name. Amen.

What Does Satan Want Me to Believe about Creation?

322

They exchanged the truth of God for a lie, and worshiped and served created things rather than the Creator . . .
Romans 1:25

TAKING A STAND

Pretend that your family is building a house. Instead of carefully planning what your house will look like, you take all of the boards, nails and paint and throw them up in the air. Will the pieces fall together to make a beautiful home? Of course not! There has to be a plan. There also has to be someone to carry out the plan.

A house can't be built without a builder. The Earth was not created without a Creator. "In the beginning God created the heavens and the earth" (Genesis 1:1). Satan has tried to make people believe that the Earth was created by accident after a big explosion.

Satan also lies and says that God didn't create people. He says that, over a long time, people evolved [changed] from animals. God says that's not true. "The LORD God formed the man from the dust of the ground and breathed into his nostrils the breath of life, and the man became a living being" (Genesis 2:7).

Why does Satan want you to believe you're an accident? He doesn't want you to know that you're special and that you have a loving Heavenly Father who made you in His image.

Do you believe God created the world? Why?

_____

_____

_____

You can pray:

Dear God, thank You for all the things You have created. Thank You for making me just the way You wanted me to be. In Jesus' name. Amen.

323 What Is the Occult?

Did you know you're in a battle? The Bible says that Christians are in a spiritual war. "For our struggle is not against flesh and blood, but against . . . the spiritual forces of evil . . ." (Ephesians 6:12). There are many people that Satan has drawn into occult practices. These practices like witchcraft, voodoo, astrology and fortune telling are against God and His Word.

Many people use occult practices as their religion. They worship the Earth, the sun and moon or even Satan himself. The Bible says, "They exchanged the truth of God for a lie, and worshiped and served created things rather than the Creator . . ." (Romans 1:25).

Others get involved because they think it's fun. They read their horoscope or go to fortune-tellers. They hope to find supernatural knowledge and power, but this knowledge and power doesn't come from God. It comes from Satan, who wants to trick people into serving and worshiping him. These things may look like fun, but they will lead you away from God.

Satan does not want good things for you. He doesn't want you to believe God's truth. God says to stay away from occult practices. Trust Him to help you win your spiritual battles.

TAKING A STAND

Why should you stay away from occult practices?

_____

_____

_____

You can pray:

Dear God, thank You that You are stronger than Satan. Help me to stay away from occult practices. In Jesus' name. Amen.

Can People Really See into the Future?

They exchanged the truth of God for a lie, and worshiped and served created things rather than the Creator . . .
Romans 1:25

What's going to happen in the future? To find out, some people ask a fortune-teller, sometimes called a psychic. Psychics claim to know the future. Most of them just make guesses. Sometimes their guesses are right and sometimes they are not.

Some psychics are not just good guessers, though. There are some who are listening to Satan and his demons. God's Word tells about a time when a man named Paul met a fortune-teller. She was a slave and was making a lot of money for her masters by telling fortunes. She wasn't just making guesses. She was controlled by a demon. The Bible says Paul, who was preaching God's Word, commanded the demon to leave her. When it left, the girl could no longer see into the future. Satan's power over her was broken. (Acts 16:16-19)

When you listen to a psychic, you have "exchanged the truth of God for a lie." Satan wants to keep you from trusting God for your future. You may think psychics are just for fun, but listening to them and taking their advice can be very dangerous. Don't be fooled by Satan's lies! Trust God and His Word for your future.

Why should you not listen to a psychic?

_____

_____

_____

You can pray:

Dear God, thank You that You know the future. Help me to trust You alone and not be fooled by Satan's tricks. In Jesus' name. Amen.

TAKING A STAND

325 Why Do Some People Believe in Astrology?

They exchanged the truth of God for a lie, and worshiped and served created things rather than the Creator . . . **Romans 1:25**

Have you ever heard of the zodiac? It is a chart divided into sections or signs. Each sign shows the positions of the stars and planets for particular years. Astrologists (people who study the zodiac) use these signs to write horoscopes. Horoscopes tell people what they should and shouldn't do according to their signs and make predictions of what will happen to people. Many individuals read their horoscopes each day. They believe the stars and planets cause them to act a certain way. They depend on astrology to show them the future.

Your enemy, Satan, would love for you to depend on your horo-scope instead of God. He wants you to think that astrology can answer your questions about the future. However, God didn't make the stars and planets to answer your questions about life and the future. The answers to those questions can be found in the Bible. God gave you His Holy Spirit to help you understand His Word. He helps you grow in wisdom as you learn about Him and trust Him with your future.

Learn about God's creation. Praise Him for the wonderful things He has made. Be sure to worship the Creator and not His creation.

TAKING A STAND

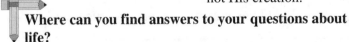

Where can you find answers to your questions about life?

_____

_____

You can pray:

Dear God, thank You for Your beautiful creation. Help me to remember to trust You for my future. In Jesus' name. Amen.

What's Wrong with Playing Occult Games? 326

They exchanged the truth of God for a lie, and worshiped and served created things rather than the Creator . . .
Romans 1:25

TAKING A STAND

Have you ever had someone tease you and then seem surprised when your feelings were hurt? Maybe they said, "I was just kidding around." They thought what they were doing was fun, but it really turned out to be hurtful. There are some games like that– games like Dungeons and Dragons and Ouiji boards. They look like fun, but they could really be hurtful. Satan can use these games to take control of you and cause you to think and do things that are against God.

Some people think games that ask you to pretend you have supernatural powers, cast spells or look into the future are harmless fun. That's just what Satan wants them to think. Satan can make things look good when they are really harmful. God's Word says to stay away from occult practices– things that involve demons, witchcraft and fortune telling.

God loves you and wants the best for you. Satan only wants to hurt and destroy. Obey God's Word. Refuse to play games that could be tricks from the devil. Don't let Satan fool you into disobeying God. "Finally, be strong in the Lord and in His mighty power . . . take your stand against the devil's schemes [tricks]" (Ephesians 6:10-11).

Why should you stay away from occult games?

_____

_____

_____

You can pray:
Dear God, thank You for loving me and showing me the truth in Your Word. Help me not to be fooled by Satan's tricks. In Jesus' name. Amen.

327 Where Does True Power Come From?

> They exchanged the truth of God for a lie, and worshiped and served created things rather than the Creator . . . **Romans 1:25**

TAKING A STAND

You've probably seen characters in cartoons or comic books that have supernatural power. They can do amazing things and no one can stop them! Have you ever wished you had power like that? Some people believe you can have power by building up your body or taking special vitamins. Others think that you already have supernatural power within you–you just need to bring it out! What is the truth? Where does true power come from?

True power comes from God. When you became a Christian, God's Holy Spirit came to live in you. Only God can give you real power. Having God's power doesn't mean having a super strong body. God's power is inner strength that makes you able to stand up for Him and live your life in a way that's pleasing to Him.

God gives you the power of His Holy Spirit to help you win over sin and Satan. You can grow strong in God's power by reading God's Word and praying every day. Ask His Holy Spirit to give you the power you need to stand for Him. Choose to obey God and do what's right. Thank God for the victory His power gives you.

What can you do to grow strong in God's power?

_____

_____

_____

You can pray:
Dear God, thank You for sending Your Holy Spirit to live in me. Help me to depend on Your power to win against sin and Satan. In Jesus' name. Amen.

How Can I Become Wise? 328

My grace is sufficient for you, for my power is made perfect in weakness. **2 Corinthians 12:9**

TAKING A STAND

If you could have any one thing in the world that you wanted, what would it be? Money? Friends? God told a king named Solomon that He would give him anything he asked for. Solomon asked God for wisdom. King Solomon knew that wisdom came from God and was very valuable (1 Kings 3:5, 7-12).

Wisdom is knowing what is right in God's eyes and then doing it. Did you know that God promised to give you wisdom if you ask for it? "If any of you lacks wisdom, he should ask God . . . and it will be given to him" (James 1:5).

Maybe you don't feel very wise. Sometimes you might make mistakes even though you try very hard. The good news is that you don't have to become wise in your own strength. God says that His power will give you the strength you need. "My grace is sufficient for you, for my power is made perfect in weakness" (2 Corinthians 12:9). If you really want God's help to be wise, ask Him to give you wisdom. Read His Word and obey it. Ask Him to help you make wise choices. God will keep His promise.

How can you be wise?

_____

_____

_____

You can pray:

Dear God, please give me wisdom. Help me to please You in all I do. In Jesus' name. Amen.

329 Where Can I Find Answers to Things I Don't Understand?

My grace is sufficient for you, for my power is made perfect in weakness. **2 Corinthians 12:9**

King David lived a very unusual life. Sometimes he must have wondered why God chose to give him so many adventures. There must have been many things David didn't understand. Some of David's questions were probably never answered while he lived.

Are there things you don't understand? You can find many answers in the Bible. God can give you understanding when you pray, too. God also may have given you wise, godly adults to help you when you don't understand something. However, sometimes you will have questions that will not be answered until the day you are with God in Heaven.

When there is something you don't understand, search God's Word and ask Him to help you. If you still don't understand why things are a certain way, decide to trust Him anyway. Don't rely only on what you understand, but admit that God's mind is greater than yours. Remember that He loves you. He has promised that when you trust Him, He will guide your paths. The Bible says, "Trust in the LORD with all your heart and lean not on your own understanding; in all your ways acknowledge him, and he will make your paths straight" (Proverbs 3:5-6).

TAKING A STAND

Write something about your life that you don't understand.

_____

_____

_____

You can pray:
Dear God, help me to trust You when I don't understand why things happen. In Jesus' name. Amen.

Does God Talk to Me?

My grace is sufficient for you, for my power is made perfect in weakness. **2 Corinthians 12:9**

How do you know if someone is talking to you? Normally you can see that person looking at you and hear his or her voice. When God talks to you, you can't see His face, and you won't hear His voice, but He does talk to you.

God can talk to you through His Word. When you read your Bible, you are seeing God's Words written down. God wants you to pay attention to His written Word just as well as you would if He spoke to you aloud.

God can talk to you through His Holy Spirit. When you pray and think about God's Word, His Holy Spirit can bring Scripture and godly thoughts into your mind. When you wonder if something is right or wrong, His Spirit can give you an understanding to know the truth.

God can also talk to you through other Christians. Sometimes God uses people to help you understand what He has to say to you. Listen to godly people and ask God to help you see if what they are saying agrees with the truth in His Word. God does talk to you. Do you listen?

 Write three ways God can talk to you.

_____

_____

_____

You can pray:

 Dear God, please help me to listen and obey when You talk to me. In Jesus' name. Amen.

Does God Have Grace for Everyone?

My grace is sufficient for you, for my power is made perfect in weakness. **2 Corinthians 12:9**

It was terrible. He was sure no one had ever done anything as awful as he had done. Surely, God would never forgive him. He was so ashamed.

This must be how Peter, one of Jesus' followers felt. On the night that the Lord Jesus was arrested, Peter told three different people that he didn't even know Him. Peter was so afraid! Did he deserve to be forgiven? No, but he was! Jesus Christ died on the cross to take the punishment for Peter's sins and the sins of the whole world. This was God's grace–His undeserved kindness toward sinful people.

God's grace is for you, too. There is nothing you can do to earn God's forgiveness. God promises to forgive you when you trust in Jesus as your Savior. But, God's grace doesn't end there. God's grace continues throughout your life. It is by God's grace that you have health and life. It is by His grace that you can pray and witness for Him. God also forgives you by His grace when you confess your sins each day to Him. Aren't you glad for God's wonderful grace in your life? Have you thanked God for His grace today?

TAKING A STAND

What is grace?

_____

_____

_____

You can pray:

Dear God, thank You for Your grace. Thank You that You forgave me even though I didn't deserve it. In Jesus' name. Amen.

When Does God's Grace End?

My grace is sufficient for you, for my power is made perfect in weakness. **2 Corinthians 12:9**

TAKING A STAND

The Lord Jesus told the story of a young man who asked his father to give him the money that would be his when his father died. Even though it made the father sad, he gave his son what he asked for.

The young man moved to a big city and spent his money on everything he wanted. Soon he ran out of money. He had nowhere to live and nothing to eat. He finally realized how wrong he had been. He hoped that if he begged, his father might give him a job as a servant. He decided to go home.

Before he even reached his house, his father ran to hug him. He was so glad his son had come home. He had never stopped loving him. The father was eager to show his love and kindness to his son, who didn't deserve it. He welcomed his son back into the family and had a big party to celebrate his return. (Luke 15:11-32)

This story is a wonderful picture of God's grace for you. God will never stop loving you no matter what you do. He will always forgive you when you confess your sins to Him. His grace never ends!

 Write a short prayer, thanking God for His grace.

_____

_____

_____

You can pray:

 Dear God, thank You that You always forgive. Help me to show You my love by obeying You. In Jesus' name. Amen.

333 How Can I Experience God's Grace?

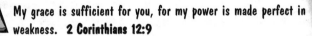

My grace is sufficient for you, for my power is made perfect in weakness. **2 Corinthians 12:9**

One day a man named Saul traveled toward a city to arrest Christians. He hated them and wanted to stop them from telling others about Jesus. As he traveled, a bright light suddenly flashed around him, causing him to fall to the ground. Then he heard a voice saying, "Saul, Saul, why do you persecute me?" It was the Lord Jesus speaking to him! Saul was never the same again. He realized that Jesus truly is God the Son. He learned that he could be forgiven because of God's grace–His undeserved kindness.

Have you ever experienced God's grace? God loves you even though you don't deserve His love. God's Word says, "But God demonstrates his own love for us in this: While we were still sinners, Christ died for us" (Romans 5:8). God wants to forgive your sin and make you part of His family, not because you deserve it, but because of His grace. "For it is by grace you have been saved, through faith–and this is not from yourselves, it is the gift of God . . ." (Ephesians 2:8). You experience God's grace by trusting in God's Son, the Lord Jesus to save you from your sin. Have you experieced God's grace?

TAKING A STAND

How can you experience God's grace?

_____

_____

_____

You can pray:

Dear God, thank You for loving me and for showing Your grace through the Lord Jesus Christ. In Jesus' name. Amen.

How Can I Live by God's Grace? 334

My grace is sufficient for you, for my power is made perfect in weakness. **2 Corinthians 12:9**

TAKING A STAND

We have learned how God shows His grace to us by forgiving our sins and how we can experience His grace in our lives. But, how can we live each day by God's grace?

First, you can be thankful for God's grace which saved you from the punishment for your sins. When was the last time you said "thank You" to God for the Lord Jesus, who died for your sins and rose again?

Second, you can depend on God to give you grace to live for Him each day. Everything that you do is by God's grace. Can others tell by what you do and say that you are depending on God?

Third, you can be kind to others and forgive them when they hurt you. The Bible says, "Be kind and compassionate to one another, forgiving each other, just as in Christ God forgave you" (Ephesians 4:32). Because God has shown His grace to you by forgiving you for your sins, you should show His grace to others by forgiving them when they do something against you.

Ask God to help you be thankful for His grace, depend on His grace and show His grace to others today!

How can you live by God's grace?

_____

_____

_____

You can pray:

Dear God, thank You for the grace You have given to me. Help me to live by Your grace each day. In Jesus' name. Amen.

This is the end of the section of "Taking a Stand" devotionals.

It is time to do the next activity page that came to you in the mail. Remember to add your prayer request so your mailbox friend can pray for you. When you finish the whole page, fold it on the lines so the Mailbox Club address shows. Put a small piece of tape on the bottom to keep it folded. Add a stamp and mail your activity page.

Your work will be marked and sent back to you, along with a personal note. The activity sheet for the next set of lessons will be sent to you, too.

Enjoy getting to know God better with your next group of devotionals!

What I
Believe

God Is Three in One!

 Great is the LORD, and most worthy of praise. **Psalm 48:1**

Sometimes you may think no one understands you, how you feel, why you do what you do. Guess what! God knows all about you—even better than you know yourself! It doesn't work the other way, though. Nobody even comes close to understanding God! God said, "As the heavens are higher than the earth, so are my ways higher than your ways . . ." (Isaiah 55:9).

One of the hardest things to understand is the Trinity. "Trinity" means "three in one." God is three persons—God the Father, God the Son, and God the Holy Spirit. All three of these persons make one God—not three gods. We can't fully understand it now, but one day we will when we are face to face with God in Heaven.

Think how small God would have to be for us to know all about Him! Be glad there's more about Him than you can understand. The Bible says, "Great is the Lord, and most worthy of praise . . ." (Psalm 48:1). No one really understands all about God now, but when we get to Heaven, we'll understand Him more.

 What would you like God to explain to you about Himself?

_____

_____

_____

You can pray:

 Dear God. thank You that You understand all about me! In Jesus' name. Amen.

WHAT I BELIEVE

God Is Holy! 336

 Great is the LORD, and most worthy of praise.
Psalm 48:1

Do you know someone who never makes mistakes? Can you picture anyone who is always good? Have you ever met anyone who never tells lies? Imagine someone who cannot even think of doing or saying anything wrong. A person like this would be holy. To be holy means to be perfect, to never sin. Nobody on Earth is holy. The only one like that is God.

God, our Heavenly Father, is holy. God said, "Be holy, because I am holy" (1 Peter 1:16). He wants his children to be holy, too! How can you be holy when you know you sometimes sin? Does God really think you can be perfect? No, but He wants you to do your best to be like Him. God lives in you to give you the power to live a clean, holy life and not to sin. He will help you say "no" to sin. He will help you to obey His Word and do what is right.

Isn't it wonderful to know our Heavenly Father is a perfect example for us to follow? Our God is so great and worthy of our praise! Ask God to help you be more like Him today.

 What does it mean to be holy?

_____

_____

_____

You can pray:

 Dear God, I'm glad You are perfect. I want to be more like You every day. In Jesus' name. Amen.

337 God's Word Is True!

Great is the LORD, and most worthy of praise. **Psalm 48:1**

Many people try to find something wrong in the Bible, so they read it carefully. What happens? They end up finding out that the Bible really is true! God never makes mistakes or tells lies. He could never give us a book about Himself that is wrong in any way. God used many men to write down the ideas and stories He wanted everyone to know. Someone may say, "Even though it's God's book, these men might have made mistakes. Maybe some things got in that weren't right."

That's not true! God told the writers just what to say, though He let them tell the stories in their own way. The writers did not put anything in the Bible that was wrong. There are absolutely no mistakes in God's Word.

Some people don't agree with what the Bible says. Here's an example: God's Word says, " . . . Do not lie . . ." (Leviticus 19:11). That means telling lies is wrong. Some people say it's okay to tell a lie if you have a good reason, but they are wrong. You know that the Bible is always right. That's because it's from God, and He is never wrong!

Why is it never okay to lie?

_____

_____

_____

You can pray:

Dear God, thank You that I can believe everything in the Bible and not wonder if it's true. In Jesus' name. Amen.

God Can Do Anything!

Great is the LORD, and most worthy of praise.
Psalm 48:1

W H A T I B E L I E V E

What can God do? Anything He chooses! When He created the world, "he spoke, and it came to be . . ." (Psalm 33:9). We don't know how He could do that, but He did! The Bible also tells us that He keeps everything going "by his powerful word" (Hebrews 1:3).

The Bible says, "O Lord . . . Power and might are in your hand, and no one can withstand you" (2 Chronicles 20:6). God can do anything He chooses, and no one can stop Him! Remember, though, that God is also perfectly good. He never uses His power to hurt you.

God can give you His power to use when you need it! God's Word says He "increases the power of the weak" (Isaiah 40:29). You can't give your strength to anyone else, but God can give you strength when you need it without losing any of His own power. How do you get some of God's strength when you need it? Just ask Him for it! God will always give you the strength you ask for if what you are doing is right.

How has God given you strength to do something for Him?

_____

_____

_____

You can pray:

Dear God, thank You for giving me strength when I need it. Help me to use Your stength to help others. In Jesus' name. Amen.

God Has a Plan for Me!

Great is the LORD, and most worthy of praise. **Psalm 48:1**

Grown-ups often ask children, "What do you want to be when you grow up?" It's fun to think about that. Keep in mind that God has a plan for you. Since He is so great, God's plans for you are great, too.

Long ago, God told His people, "I know the plans I have for you . . ." (Jeremiah 29:11). Following God's plan means you always obey Him in every step of your life. You need to learn all you can about God. You can do this by reading the Bible and listening to people who can teach you about Him.

God always does what's right, so He plans for you "to do good works" (Ephesians 2:10). If you talk to God and read His Word, you'll know what He wants you to do each day. For instance, He'll want you to obey the grown-ups in charge of you and to be kind to other people. When you try to do what you know God wants, He'll help you know what to do next. Then, when you grow up to be a doctor, homemaker or store clerk— no matter what you do—you'll be following God's plan.

WHAT I BELIEVE

Write down three ways that you have followed God's plan for you today.

_____

_____

_____

You can pray:

Dear God, please show me Your plan for me as I try to obey You every day. In Jesus' name. Amen.

I Know God Loves Me!

 Great is the LORD, and most worthy of praise.
Psalm 48:1

How can you tell if someone loves you? That person says nice things to you. God says nice things to you in the Bible. He said, " . . . I have loved you with an everlasting love ..." (Jeremiah 31:3).

The person who loves you listens when you talk to him or her. God listens when you talk to Him, and He gives answers! "Call to me and I will answer you and tell you . . . things you do not know" (Jeremiah 33:3).

The person who loves you gives you things he or she knows you like. God has given us "everything for our enjoyment" (1 Timothy 6:17). Thank Him today for something good He's given you!

The person who loves you helps you when you need it. God said, " . . . call upon me in the day of trouble; I will deliver [help] you . . ." (Psalm 50:15).

The person who loves you keeps his or her promises. So does God. He is "faithful to all his promises" (Psalm 145:13). He always does what the Bible promises He will do.

Besides all these things, "This is how God showed his love among us: he sent his one and only Son into the world that we might live through him" (1 John 4:9). No one else who loves you has ever done that much for you!

In what special way has God shown you that He loves you?

_____

_____

_____

You can pray:

Dear God, thank You for all the ways You show me that You love me. In Jesus' name. Amen.

I Can Show God's Love to Others!

Great is the LORD, and most worthy of praise. **Psalm 48:1**

WHAT I BELIEVE

Showing God's love to others sounds easy, but it means more than just being nice to people and not hurting them. Showing God's love means you wait for your turn without getting upset. You don't feel jealous of a friend's new clothes. You let someone else have the biggest—or last—dessert. You don't call anyone bad names to get even for something they did. When others say bad things about a person, you think of good things to say. You don't tell someone a bad thing another person said about them. You say things that help others do their best. You don't laugh at someone who is having trouble with something, like soccer. You try hard to keep your promises.

You may be thinking, "I'm like that part of the time but not all of the time." Only God loves perfectly all the time. Ask Him to help you work on one way you can show His love to other people this week. Some people are easy to love and some aren't! Ask God to help you love the ones who are hard to love. He is great at helping you do what is right, and your life will show others how loving He is.

How can you show God's love to someone in a special way today?

_____

_____

_____

You can pray:

Dear God, thank You for always loving me even when I'm hard to love! Help me to show Your love to others. In Jesus' name. Amen.

God Wants Me to Tell Others about Him!

Great is the LORD, and most worthy of praise
Psalm 48:1

W H A T   I   B E L I E V E

Imagine that someone gave you money and said, "Tell your friends to come to me, and I'll give them money, too." What would you do? You'd tell everyone how he or she could get this gift!

God has given you an even better gift! If you have received Jesus as your Savior from sin, God has given you eternal life. That means you have God's life in you now. Then, someday, you'll live with Him in Heaven. All the money in the world couldn't buy eternal life, but God gives it to anyone who receives Jesus. Somebody told you how to get this gift, and God wants you to tell somebody else.

Imagine that you told a friend how to get that gift of money. You said he could get some, too. Then, the friend just laughed at you and walked away. That would make you feel bad, but you would know you did the right thing by telling him about the money.

What if you tell someone how to receive eternal life and the person laughs at you? It's still the right thing to do. Are you going to tell someone about God's gift, or are you going to keep it a secret? Do you know how to tell someone about receiving Jesus? Pages 168-173 in this book can help you.

What would you tell someone about Jesus?

_____

_____

_____

You can pray:

Dear God, help me tell someone this week how he or she can receive the gift of eternal life. In Jesus' name. Amen.

343 God Made Me Special!

Now we are children of God . . . when he appears, we shall be like him . . . **1 John 3:2**

To "create" something, like a picture, means you try hard to make it special. You do the best work you can on it. The Bible says, "God created man— male and female he created them" (Genesis 1:27). God created the bodies of every girl and boy to be special. The Bible also says He "created my inmost being" (Psalm 139:13). That means God made you special on the inside, too. He made your body the way it looks and works. He made your mind to think the way it does.

A person who paints special pictures is called an artist. He works hard on each one. His pic-tures are called works of art. No two pictures are just alike. People give lots of money to buy them.

The Bible says you are God's "workmanship" (Ephesians 2:10). That word means "work of art." He didn't make any two people just the same on the outside or on the inside. You're worth a lot to God. He created a beautiful home for you to live in with Him someday. To remember how special you are to God, read Psalm 139 in the Bible. If you don't have a Bible, read this page again!

Write down three ways you are special to God.

_____

_____

_____

You can pray:

Dear God, thank You that there is no one just like me, and I'm special to You! In Jesus' name. Amen.

I Can Belong to God's Family!

Now we are children of God . . . when he appears, we shall be like him . . . **1 John 3:2**

You'd have to love someone a lot to wish he or she could be part of your family. God loves you that much! When you're in God's family, you can always feel close to Him. You can talk to Him any time. Best of all, someday, you'll live with Him and His other children in Heaven.

How do you join God's family? By receiving Jesus. The Bible says, "To all who received him . . . he gave the right to become children of God" (John 1:12).

To "receive Jesus" means you tell God that you've sinned and you're sorry. Tell God that you believe Jesus is His Son. You believe Jesus died to take the punishment for your sin so you wouldn't have to. Tell God that you believe Jesus came back to life and He's in Heaven right now. Then, tell God you want to be His child. If you have received Jesus, you belong to God's family!

How can people tell what family you're in? One way is that you obey the grown-ups in that home. Jesus said anyone who obeys God "is my brother and sister" (Mark 3:35). The children in God's family obey Him! Can people tell you're in God's family?

How can others tell if you're in God's family?

_____

_____

_____

You can pray:
Thank You, Heavenly Father, that I can be in Your family. In Jesus' name. Amen.

I Need to Confess My Sins to God!

. . . now we are children of God . . . when he appears, we shall be like him . . . **1 John 3:2**

Isn't it great that God gives His children the strength to say "no" to sin? You don't have to give in when Satan tempts you to do wrong. The Bible says, "The Lord is my helper" (Hebrews 13:6). What happens if you do sin? If you're God's child, the Lord Jesus will never leave you. But sin spoils your fellowship (friendship) with God. It makes Him sad because He hates sin.

The Holy Spirit convicts you about your sins. He lets you know that things are no longer right between you and God. Sinning makes you feel far away from God. Only by confessing your sins to God can you be forgiven.

To confess your sins to God means to agree with Him that you did wrong. Don't say, "I made a mistake" or "I made a bad choice." Tell Him you have sinned and that you're sorry. The Bible says when we confess our sins, God "will forgive us our sins" (1 John 1:9). When you confess your sins, your friendship with God will be made right. He will hear and answer your prayers. Thank God for His forgiveness and ask Him to help you not to sin again.

WHAT I BELIEVE

Why do you need to confess your sins to God?

_____

_____

_____

You can pray:

Dear God, thank You for always forgiving me when I confess my sins to You. In Jesus' name. Amen.

God Can Give Me Victory over Sin!

. . . now we are children of God . . . when he appears, we shall be like him. **1 John 3:2**

W H A T

I

B E L I E V E

If you are God's child, you have an enemy–Satan! Satan probably thought he had won the battle when Jesus died on the cross. That was the most important battle of all time! Jesus Christ died to take the punishment for your sins. Jesus won when God the Father brought Him back to life! His victory over Satan is your victory, too. Now you can have victory over sin as you trust God to help you.

But Satan doesn't want you to have victory over sin. He tries to keep you from obeying God. He doesn't want you to please God. Fighting Satan by yourself is hard because Satan is stronger than you are! But remember the Holy Spirit inside you is "greater than the one [Satan] that is in the world" (1 John 4:4). The Holy Spirit helps you to do what's right when Satan tries to get you to sin.

You need to ask God for help every day. Learn as much as you can from the Bible. It will help you not to sin. God's Word and prayer are your weapons against Satan. Trust God to give you victory every day.

How can God give you victory over sin?

_____

_____

_____

You can pray:

Dear God, thank You that I can have victory over sin. Help me to trust You for victory every day. In Jesus' name. Amen.

I Can Use God's Armor!

... now we are children of God ... when he appears, we shall be like him. **1 John 3:2**

Long ago, soldiers wore armor to protect themselves in battle. God gives Christians special armor in their battle against Satan. You have read about God's armor earlier in this devotional book. You can also read about it in Ephesians 6:14-18 in the Bible. Can you remember what each piece of the armor is and what it's for? (If you have trouble, go back to devotional #102 for help!)

See if you can fill in these blanks: One piece is called the belt of_____. This piece helps you to know what is true and not to be fooled by Satan's lies. Another piece is the breast-plate of_____. It protects your heart and helps you to do what's right. The shoes of the Gospel of _____ help you share God's peace with others. The shield of _____ means believing God's promises. It will protect you against Satan's attacks. The helmet of _____ protects your mind. It gives you confidence that you are God's child so you can say "no" to sin. The_____ of the Spirit is the Word of God. It will help resist Satan. Ask God to help you use His armor so you can stay close to Him and not sin.

How did you use the armor this week in your battle against Satan?

_____

_____

_____

You can pray:

Dear God, help me remember to use every piece of the armor every day. In Jesus' name. Amen.

God Can Give Me Self-Control! 348

. . . now we are children of God . . . when he appears, we shall be like him. **1 John 3:2**

WHAT I BELIEVE

Maybe you know someone who gets angry and hits people or says mean things to hurt them. Maybe you know someone who can't quit playing a game or reading a book when it's time for bed. These people are letting their feelings control what they do. They do not have self-control.

Self-control is a part of the fruit of the Spirit (Galatians 5:22-23). It's something God the Holy Spirit wants to bring out in your life. You read about it earlier in this devotional book. Self-control means that you take charge of your thoughts, feelings and actions instead of them controlling you. You handle anger without hurting anyone. You can stop playing or reading because you know you need the right amount of sleep.

God wants you to be able to control yourself. Then, He can use you to serve Him better. You will also be better able to help others. Maybe someone will ask how you learned to have self-control. You can say that it is the Holy Spirit who helps you because you are a Christian. You might then be able to tell that person about Jesus. Are you allowing God to develop self-control in your life?

How can others see self-control in your life?

_____

_____

_____

You can pray:
Dear God, thank You for the fruit of the Spirit. Help me to have self-control in all I think, feel and do. In Jesus' name. Amen.

349

I Can Do Anything with God's Help!

... now we are children of God ... when he appears, we shall be like him. **1 John 3:2**

One Bible writer says, "Lord, you have made the heavens and the earth by your great power . . . Nothing is too hard for you" (Jeremiah 32:17). Another one says, "I can do everything through him [God] who gives me strength" (Philippians 4:13).

All of us need help from time to time. Sometimes God may use another person to help you. A friend may pray for you when you're sick. Your teacher may help you with a problem at school. There are other times when only God can help you do something hard, like saying you're sorry, or being kind to someone who has hurt you. The Bible says that God created the world, and He can give you strength to do anything. God can help you do whatever you need to do.

How do you get God's help? God knows when you need help. But He wants you to ask Him and then trust that He will do it. Is there anything that would be too hard for God to do? No! God's Word says, "Nothing is too hard for you [God]" (Jeremiah 32:17). The next time you have something hard to do, remember that you can do anything with God's help!

WHAT I BELIEVE

Write one thing you need God's help for this week.

_____

_____

_____

You can pray:

Dear God, You know when I will especially need Your strength today. Help me be strong when that time comes. In Jesus' name. Amen.

y Life Can Be a Witness to Others! 350

... now we are children of God ... when he appears, we shall be like him. **1 John 3:2**

WHAT I BELIEVE

Are you different since you trusted Jesus Christ as your Savior? The Bible says, " . . . if anyone is in Christ, he is a new creation . . ." (2 Cor-inthians 5:17). When Jesus lived on the earth, His life was a witness, as well as His words. In the same way, our lives are to be a witness to others.

As you get to know God better, things in your life will start changing. You won't want to do the things you used to do that made God unhappy, like lying, fighting or complaining. Instead, you'll want to do things that please God, like being truthful, kind and patient.

Your friends may see that you're different than you used to be. Maybe they notice that you smile instead of complaining. Perhaps they see that you are patient when you have to wait and wait and wait! Your life is being a witness for God. Your friends may ask why you've changed. Then you can witness with your words. You can tell them that you've received Jesus as your Savior and He is helping you do things that please Him. Let your life be a witness for Jesus today!

How is your life a witness to others?

_____

_____

_____

You can pray:

Dear God, thank You that my life can be a witness for You. I want to help people to know You. In Jesus' name. Amen.

I Can Put Others First!

... Love your neighbor as yourself. **Matthew 22:39**

Winning is more fun than losing! Being chosen first tops being chosen last! When you get to do something first, you may feel important. Many people like to think they are more important than other people in some way, but should Christians think that way, too?

The Bible says, "... Honor one another above yourselves" (Romans 12:10). You may win first prize in a contest. That's all right. But if the choice is yours–who goes first in line, who gets the best seat, who takes the first turn in a game–give that place to someone else. Why? That's what Jesus would do.

Many Christians want to do things the way the Lord Jesus would. They try to think of what others need or would like. Other Christians only think of themselves first. Which group of Christians are you like?

Jesus said, "Love each other as I have loved you" (John 15:12). When you love other people, you should want to put them first. This isn't always easy to do. God knows how hard it is, but He's promised to help you. Trust God, the Holy Spirit, to help you to be more like Jesus as He teaches you to put others first.

When could you put someone else first this week?

_____

_____

_____

You can pray:
Dear God, it's hard to think of other people first. Help me do it because that's what Jesus would do. In Jesus' name. Amen.

God Can Help Me Love Others!

  . . . Love your neighbor as yourself. **Matthew 22:39**

How do you love your neighbor as yourself? Start by asking, "How do I show love for myself?" Here are some ways you do this: You eat when you're hungry. You rest when you're tired. You don't put harmful things, like bad drugs, in your body. Sometimes, you give yourself a treat, like ice cream!

Then ask this question: "Who is my neighbor?" Someone in the Bible asked Jesus that question, so Jesus told a story that helped him understand that his "neighbor" was anyone who needed his help (Luke 10:30-37).

Loving yourself means doing good things for yourself, and loving your neighbor means doing good things for other people. Do you know someone who needs food or clothes? Is there anyone who could use some help with schoolwork? Do you know a child that nobody wants to play with? How could you help these people?

The best way you can help other people is to tell them about the Lord Jesus so they can have their sins forgiven. Many people around you need your help. God can show you what you can do to help them. Ask Him to help you "love your neighbor as yourself." He will!

 Write the names of three people you can help this week.

_____

_____

_____

You can pray:

 Dear God, thank You for sending people to help me when I need it. Use me to help someone else in need. In Jesus' name. Amen.

353 I Can Walk in Fellowship with God!

. . . Love your neighbor as yourself. **Matthew 22:39**

Just think! The Creator of the world wants you to spend time with Him every day! That's what "walking in fellowship" with God means. How do you do it?

How did Jesus do it? Jesus often went "to lonely places and prayed" (Luke 5:16). Do you talk to God alone as often as you can?

The Lord Jesus learned Scripture. When Satan tried to get Jesus to sin, Jesus answered with verses He may have learned as a boy. Once, He said, "Away from me, Satan! For it is written: 'Worship the Lord your God, and serve him only'" (Matthew 4:10). Are you learning the Bible verses in this book? They'll help you stay close to God.

Jesus went to the synagogue (meeting place of worship) "as was his custom [habit]" (Luke 4:16). Jesus prayed and worshiped God with other people. Do you try to do that every week?

When Jesus talked about God one day, He said, "I always do what pleases him" (John 8:29). Do you always obey God?

Jesus prayed, learned Scripture, went to the synagogue and obeyed God. These things helped Him walk in fellowship with God. These are ways you can walk in fellowship with God, too!

How can you walk in fellowship with God this week?

_____

_____

_____

You can pray:

Dear God, I'm glad You want me to stay close to You! Help me to walk in fellowship with You. In Jesus' name. Amen.

I Need to Fellowship with Others in God's Family!

... Love your neighbor as yourself. **Matthew 22:39**

WHAT I BELIEVE

Families come in all shapes and sizes! Your "family" is the people you live with. Maybe you're related to all of them and maybe not.

When you receive Jesus Christ, you're part of another family–God's family (John 1:12). Other Christians are your brothers and sisters in Christ. You need your Christian family. You can pray for each other and share what you have, such as money or food. Together, you can worship and learn more about God. Members of God's family like to get together. They pray, sing songs that praise God, study the Bible and help each other with their problems.

Where do Christians get together to have fellowship? Sometimes they meet in each other's homes or in churches. Ask God to help you find other Christians that you can meet with often. Maybe there is a church in your neighborhood that teaches about the Lord Jesus. You could go there to have fellowship with other Christians.

The Bible says if we walk in fellowship with God, "we have fellowship with one another" (1 John 1:7). Being in fellowship with God is the best way to be in fellowship with your brothers and sisters in God's family.

What is your favorite thing about being part of God's family?

_____

_____

_____

You can pray:
Dear God, thank You for letting me be part of Your family! Help me to have fellowship with my brothers and sisters in Christ. In Jesus' name. Amen.

355 People Are Lost without Christ!

📖 . . . Love your neighbor as yourself. **Matthew 22:39**

Have you ever been lost? Being separated from the people you're with, even for a few minutes, is scary! There's another way a person can be "lost." People who never receive Jesus Christ as their Savior are lost in sin. Because they are sinners, they are separated from God forever.

People who are lost are not part of God's family. They don't have God's peace when things go wrong. They never feel the joy God gives to His children. They don't have the assurance that God will answer their prayers.

When lost people die, they are separated forever from God.

They will never be able to be with God in the beautiful place called Heaven that He has prepared for those who love Him. Instead, they will go to a terrible place of suffering and punishment called Hell.

People who have never trusted the Lord Jesus as their Savior may not know they are lost. That's why it's important for you, as a Christian, to tell them that Jesus Christ is the only way to Heaven. Jesus said, " . . . No one comes to the Father except through me" (John 14:6). Is there someone you can talk to about Jesus this week?

WHAT I BELIEVE

 What would you tell a lost person about Jesus?

_____

_____

_____

 You can pray:
Dear God, help me to tell someone who is lost about You. In Jesus' name. Amen.

God Will Give Me Courage to Witness! 356

. . . Love your neighbor as yourself. **Matthew 22:39**

Jesus told His followers, " . . . you will be my witnesses . . ." **(Acts 1:8).** Then He returned to Heaven. A witness tells what he has seen and knows is true. Jesus' followers could witness that Jesus had come back to life.

You may think that would have been easy for them! It wasn't! They had to witness to the same people who had the Lord Jesus killed! What if these people decided to have the followers put to death, too?

The followers witnessed anyway! That must have taken courage. Courage is the strength to do the right thing even when it's hard. Where did their courage come from?

Jesus had also said, " . . . you will receive power when the Holy Spirit comes on you . . ." **(Acts 1:8).** When the Holy Spirit came to live inside Jesus' followers, they received God's power to do wonderful things! They could love Jesus' enemies. They could boldly tell them that Jesus Christ died and rose again to take away their sins.

It still isn't easy to witness! If you're God's child, He has given you His Holy Spirit, too. Ask Him to give you courage to tell someone what the Lord Jesus Christ has done for you.

How can you have courage to tell someone about Jesus?

_____

_____

You can pray:
Dear God, thank You for the Holy Spirit who gives me courage to be a witness for You. In Jesus' name. Amen.

357 Missionaries Are God's Special Messengers!

. . . Love your neighbor as yourself. **Matthew 22:39**

A long time after the Lord Jesus returned to Heaven, the Christians were still meeting together to worship. One day, the Holy Spirit spoke to them. He said, " . . . Set apart for me Barnabas and Saul for the work to which I have called them" (Acts 13:2).

Barnabas and Saul became the first missionaries. They went to many cities and told people about Jesus Christ. They helped start churches.

The Lord Jesus wants all of His followers to tell others about Him. You can tell others about Jesus where you live, at school or wherever you are. Sometimes God chooses people to be missionaries as their life's work.

There are many different things that missionaries do. Some missionaries are pastors, evangelists or teachers. They help adults, young people or children to know about Jesus. Other missionaries may be doctors, builders, pilots, secretaries or printers. They may need special training. They may have to move to a different place. Missionaries often have to depend on other Christians to give them the money they need to live and work.

Missionaries know they are chosen to do special work for God. They are God's special messengers, taking the good news of Jesus all around the world!

WHAT I BELIEVE

Why do we need missionaries?

_____

_____

You can pray:

Dear God, thank You for missionaries who tell others about You. In Jesus' name. Amen.

God May Call Me to Be a Missionary!

. . . Love your neighbor as yourself. **Matthew 22:39**

Elizabeth heard a missionary talk about his work in another land. As she listened, God showed Elizabeth that she would do that kind of work, too, someday.

Lucas was praying one night. God brought the name of a certain country to his mind. Lucas knew that someday he would go there as a missionary.

Martina read in the Bible where Jesus said, "You did not choose me, but I chose you . . . to go and bear fruit . . ." (John 15:16). She knew then that the Lord Jesus Christ wanted her to be a missionary.

Elizabeth heard a missionary talk. Lucas prayed. Martina read the Bible. Each of these children listened when God "called" them to become missionaries.

God won't "call" you on the telephone to tell you He wants you to be a missionary! He puts the idea into your mind, and then helps you to know deep in your heart that this is what He wants you to do.

As you grow up, God allows situations in your life to prepare you for His work. Stay close to God and obey Him in the choices you make each day. One day, He may call you to be a missionary!

How would you know if God is calling you to be a missionary?

_____

_____

_____

You can pray:

Dear God, help me to listen and obey if You call me to be a missionary. In Jesus' name. Amen.

Heaven Is a Real Place!

In my Father's house are many rooms . . . I am going there to prepare a place for you. **John 14:1-2**

"Heaven isn't real–it's just something people imagine!" Have you ever heard anyone say this? The Bible tells us about Heaven.

Heaven is a real place. It is God's home. God the Father, God the Son (Jesus) and God the Holy Spirit are there. God's holy angels are there. The angels surround God's throne, singing praises to Him. Also, those who believed in Jesus Christ as their Savior and have died are in Heaven with God.

Heaven is a perfect place. God is perfectly holy and there can be no sin where He lives. Also there will be no sickness or death in Heaven. There will be no sorrow or crying in Heaven. It is a place of perfect joy and peace.

Heaven is a beautiful place. The Bible says the walls around it are made with sparkling jewels. Each gate is made of one giant pearl. Imagine a pearl big enough to be used as the gate in the city's wall! Heaven also has a street that's made of gold. The city and street are made of pure gold like glass. (Revelation 21:18-21)

It's fun to picture Heaven, but–just think!–it's better than anyone can imagine! And it's a real place!

WHAT I BELIEVE

Who are some Bible people you'd like to meet in Heaven someday?

_____

_____

_____

You can pray:
Dear God, thank You for creating a beautiful place for me to live with You forever! In Jesus' name. Amen.

Jesus Is Preparing a Place for Me in Heaven!

 In my Father's house are many rooms . . . I am going there to prepare a place for you. **John 14:1-2**

In Bible times when two people became engaged, the young man added a room or two onto his father's house for his wife and himself. When he was done, he went to the bride's home to get her. He took her back to his home. The wedding took place there. After that, they lived in the rooms he had prepared in his father's house. This situation reminds us of what Jesus has promised will happen to us someday.

Before the Lord Jesus died on the cross, He told His disciples that He was going away. His disciples were confused and sad that He was leaving them. Jesus comforted them by promising that He was going to prepare a place for them in Heaven, the Father's house.

If you know Jesus Christ as your Savior, He is preparing a place for you, too. We don't know exactly what this place will look like, but it will be a beautiful, perfect place. One day Jesus will come back to take those who believe in Him as Savior to be with Him in Heaven. How wonderful that Jesus is preparing a place for you in His Father's house!

What do you think your place in Heaven will look like?

_____

_____

_____

You can pray:

 Dear God, thank You for preparing a beautiful home for me to live with You someday. In Jesus' name. Amen.

361 I Am Earning Rewards in Heaven!

In my Father's house are many rooms . . . I am going there to prepare a place for you. **John 14:1-2**

The Bible says, " . . . the gift of God is eternal life" (**Romans 6:23**). You don't have to do any work to earn it. It isn't a prize you win in a contest. Eternal life is a gift that God gives to those who trust Jesus as their Savior.

Eternal life in Heaven with God forever is the most wonderful gift you'll ever receive, but there's more good news! Someday in Heaven you will receive rewards for what you did for God on Earth!

In Bible times, athletes who won an important game received a crown made of leaves that would last only a few days.

Paul said that these people worked hard to earn a crown that would not last: " . . . but we do it [serve God] to get a crown that will last forever" (1 Corinthians 9:25).

How do you earn rewards that you will receive in Heaven? One way is by doing your best to please God. Another way is by always following Christ. God also promises a reward to those who look forward to Jesus' return to Earth.

These rewards are described as crowns. No one knows what these crowns will look like, but you can be sure they'll be worth all your effort!

WHAT I BELIEVE

How can you earn rewards in Heaven?

_____

_____

_____

You can pray:

Dear God, thank You for the gift of eternal life. Thank You for the rewards You've promised in Heaven. In Jesus' name. Amen.

Jesus Will Come Again!

In my Father's house are many rooms . . . I am going there to prepare a place for you. **John 14:1-2**

The Lord Jesus promised His friends that He would come back again. Forty days after Jesus died and came back to life, He went up into the clouds, back to Heaven. His friends watched Him go. Then, an angel said to them, " . . . This same Jesus . . . will come back in the same way you have seen him go into heaven" (Acts 1:11).

When will Jesus come back again? The Bible doesn't tell us. However, Jesus did tell about some things that would happen so we would know when the time was near. He called these events "signs" of His coming. One of them was that "this gospel . . . will be preached in the whole world . . ." (Matthew 24:14). Since then, millions of people all over the world have heard about Jesus Christ. Many of the other signs have happened, too. It's clear that Jesus is coming soon!

What will happen when Jesus comes? "For the Lord himself will come . . . with a loud command, with the voice of the archangel and with the trumpet call of God" (1 Thessalonians 4:16). All those who have received Jesus Christ as their Savior will rise up to meet Him in the air. Will you be ready when Jesus comes?

How do you know that Jesus is coming again?

_____

_____

_____

You can pray:

Dear God, thank You that Jesus will soon come again. Help me to be ready for His coming. In Jesus' name. Amen.

Not Everyone Will Be Ready When Jesus Returns!

In my Father's house are many rooms . . . I am going there to prepare a place for you. **John 14:1-2**

If you were going to take an airplane trip, you'd need to have a ticket that permits you to go. You'd also have to be at the right gate at the airport on time so you don't miss your flight. These important things make you ready for your trip.

The Bible says that Jesus will return to Earth to take those who believe in Him back to Heaven, but not everyone is ready for His return. First, you need to trust in the Lord Jesus as your Savior. That is the only way you will be permitted into Heaven. Many people have heard that Jesus died to take the punishment for their sin, but they have refused to trust in Jesus as their Savior. They won't be ready for Jesus' return.

Others who have trusted the Lord Jesus Christ as their Savior will be permitted to go to Heaven, but they are still not ready. They're not living in a way that pleases God. One day, they will stand before Him and will be sadly disappointed to find that they have lost their rewards because they were not faithful in serving God. Have you trusted in Jesus? Will you be ready when Jesus returns?

WHAT I BELIEVE

How would you tell someone to be ready for Jesus' return?

_____

_____

_____

You can pray:

Dear God, help me tell someone this week how they can be ready to meet Jesus. In Jesus' name. Amen.

I Want to Be Ready When Jesus Returns!

In my Father's house are many rooms . . . I am going there to prepare a place for you. **John 14:1-2**

WHAT I BELIEVE

Suppose a friend told you that he would come and take you to a favorite place. What would you do to be ready for him? Maybe you would put on clean clothes. You would probably be watching for your friend, and you'd be excited about his coming.

Jesus Christ has promised to come someday and take us to Heaven. He wants us to be ready. That doesn't mean that you change your clothes and watch out the window! However, there are things you can do to prepare.

The most important way to be ready for Jesus' return is to know Him as your Savior. Only those who have trusted in Him will go to meet Him when He comes. If you do know the Lord Jesus as your Savior, make sure you are obeying Him. You need to be reading your Bible, praying, obeying His Word and telling others about Him.

The Bible says that Christians should be looking " . . . for the blessed hope–the glorious appearing of our great God and Savior, Jesus Christ" (Titus 2:13). This is one of the greatest events that will ever happen in history. We should be ready and eagerly looking forward to Jesus' return.

What are some things you can do to be ready for Jesus' return?

_____

_____

You can pray:

Dear God, help me to be ready when Jesus comes again by obeying Your Word. In Jesus' name. Amen.

365 Eternity Is Forever!

In my Father's house are many rooms . . . I am going there to prepare a place for you. **John 14:1-2**

You've made it to the last devotional in this book! You've learned a lot about God and about yourself. You've answered questions and done the activity pages. You might think that this is the end—you've learned all there is to know about God and His Word—but you'd be wrong!

Learning about God never ends because God never ends! God is eternal–He goes on forever. If you know the Lord Jesus Christ as your Savior, God has given you eternal life. When your body dies, the real you inside (the part that thinks, feels and decides) will live on in eternity–forever with God in Heaven. What will you do for eternity? You'll be praising God for all that He is and all that He does!

There is so much more for you to learn about God! Don't stop just because you've finished this devotional book. Go back and read your favorite devotionals again. Read what you've written on the pages to see if you've done the things you wrote about. Keep memorizing the Bible verses in this book. If you have a Bible, continue having your quiet time with God everyday. It will be good preparation for eternity!

What favorite thing have you learned about God from this devotional book?

_____

_____

_____

You can pray:

Dear God, thank You for teaching me about You. Help me to keep on learning more and more so I'll be ready for eternity with You. In Jesus' name. Amen.

THE MEMORY ZONE

Here are some great Bible verses about what you've learned so far. Put a check mark in the box as you memorize each one!

☐ **Isaiah 55:8-9** "'For my thoughts are not your thoughts, neither are your ways my ways,' declares the LORD."

☐ **Jeremiah 32:17** "Ah, Sovereign LORD, you have made the heavens and the earth by your great power and outstretched arm. Nothing is too hard for you."

☐ **1 John 4:7-8** "Dear friends, let us love one another, for loves comes from God. Everyone who loves has been born of God and knows God. Whoever does not love does not know God, because God is love."

☐ **Galatians 6:10** "Therefore, as we have opportunity, let us do good to all people, especially to those who belong to the family of believers."

☐ **Ephesians 2:10** "For we are God's workmanship, created in Christ Jesus to do good works, which God prepared in advance for us to do."

☐ **Romans 1:16** "I am not ashamed of the gospel, because it is the power of God for the salvation of everyone who believes . . ."

☐ **Matthew 28:19-20** "Therefore go and make disciples of all nations, baptizing them in the name of the Father and of the Son and of the Holy Spirit, and teaching them to obey everything I have commanded you. And surely I will be with you always, to the very end of the age."

☐ **Revelation 4:8** " . . . Holy, holy, holy is the Lord God Almighty, who was, and is, and is to come."

This is the end of the section of "What I Believe" devotionals.

It is time to do the last activity page for this book that came to you in the mail. Remember to add your prayer request so your mailbox friend can pray for you. When you finish the whole page, fold it on the lines so the Mailbox Club address shows. Put a small piece of tape on the bottom to keep it folded. Add a stamp and mail your activity page. Your work will be marked and sent back to you, along with a personal note.

We hope you have enjoyed these devotionals throughout the year.

Keep spending time with God each day to get to know Him better and better!

Congratulations!

You have completed the entire

*Wonder Devotional Book,
Daily Adventures with God.*

You can keep learning through

*Wonder Devotional Book 2,
Walking Daily with Jesus.*

SUBJECT INDEX

Do you ever have problems? There's good news! God's Word can help you deal with the hard things that come in your life. God cares about everything that affects you. He wants to help you with your problems. The answer may be to understand God better and to trust Him. Maybe you need to let God change your heart and work in your life.

The list on the next few pages can help you find answers for some of the problems and questions you have. It will tell you which devotionals to look at for help. You will see what God has to say about the things you are going through. Ask God to use the hard times in your life to help you grow closer to Him.